Who Are You?

Platform Studies
Nick Montfort and Ian Bogost, editors

Who Are You?

Nintendo's Game Boy Advance Platform

Alex Custodio

The MIT Press   Cambridge, Massachusetts   London, England

This book was set in Filosofia OT by New Best-set Typesetters Ltd. Printed and bound in the United States of America.

Library of Congress Cataloging-in-Publication Data

Names: Custodio, Alex, author.
Title: Who are you? : Nintendo's Game Boy Advance platform / Alex Custodio.
Description: Cambridge, Massachusetts : The MIT Press, 2020. | Series: Platform studies |
    Includes bibliographical references and index.
Identifiers: LCCN 2020002049 | ISBN 9780262044394 (hardcover)
Subjects: LCSH: Game Boy video games. | Video games—Design.
Classification: LCC GV1469.32 .C87 2020 | DDC 794.8—dc23
LC record available at https://lccn.loc.gov/2020002049

10 9 8 7 6 5 4 3 2 1

For my parents

Contents

Series Foreword

How can someone create a breakthrough game for a mobile phone or a compelling work of art for an immersive 3D environment without understanding that the mobile phone and the 3D environment are different sorts of computing platforms? The best artists, writers, programmers, and designers are well aware of how certain platforms facilitate certain types of computational expression and innovation. Likewise, computer science and engineering have long considered how underlying computing systems can be analyzed and improved. As important as scientific and engineering approaches are, and as significant as work by creative artists has been, there is also much to be learned from the sustained, intensive, humanistic study of digital media. We believe it is time for humanists to seriously consider the lowest level of computing systems and their relationship to culture and creativity.

The Platform Studies series has been established to promote the investigation of underlying computing systems and of how they enable, constrain, shape, and support the creative work that is done on them. The series investigates the foundations of digital media—the computing systems, both hardware and software, that developers and users depend upon for artistic, literary, and gaming development. Books in the series will certainly vary in their approaches, but they will all share certain features:

- a focus on a single platform or a closely related family of platforms
- technical rigor and in-depth investigation of how computing technologies work
- an awareness of and a discussion of how computing platforms exist in a context of culture and society, being developed on the basis of cultural concepts and then contributing to culture in a variety of ways—for instance, by affecting how people perceive computing.

Introduction: Who Are You?

I'm holding a Game Boy Advance (GBA). Or, at least, I'm holding an object that looks and feels uncannily like Nintendo's 2001 handheld videogame platform. Pressing any of the buttons is instinctive, each touch delivering a jolt of remembrance of patterns buried deep in muscle memory. The ergonomic curves of the chassis are a homecoming for fingers that spent many childhood years clutching the console in the back seat of my parents' Corolla. I can almost hear Mario's tinny cry in the distance as he slips between blocks and tumbles into the abyss (platformers were never my forte). Encased in a translucent orange shell, this system's chips and wires seem to be trapped in amber—a precious fossil preserved against the ravages of time.

It's this impossible, jewel-like beauty that exposes the handheld as a facsimile. Below the screen where I would expect to find the console's name is nothing but smooth black glass, in which I see my own mesmerized reflection. The absence of Nintendo's stylized "Game Boy Advance" logo is the first of many signs that the platform has been tampered with. Once the system is powered on, its modifications announce themselves in quick succession. Sound rings out clearly, thanks to a bespoke audio amplifier and speaker upgrade. AA batteries have made way for a rechargeable lithium ion battery ready to withstand a voracious appetite for play. And the repurposed display is crisp and dazzlingly bright—a balm for eyes that are no longer the indefatigable ones of a ten-year-old.

The object in question is a modified (or "modded") GBA. It's a built-to-order product crafted by Retro Modding, a Montreal-based company run by a former web developer who quit his well-paying job to run a successful international business based on reimagining old handhelds. Perhaps the Frankensteinian collection of parts that makes up this customized device has no right to call itself a GBA—a statement that the good folks at Nintendo would surely agree with. But there's no denying that it performs all the necessary functions of the 2001 handheld. In fact, it might even be fair to say that it outperforms its ancestor by harnessing the knowledge protocols and material objects of nearly two decades of technological development. The modded GBA is a too-perfect version of a past that never existed outside its users' imaginations. But it's a simulation that paradoxically feels truer to what we might consider the "original" object, now that we've developed a taste for backlit, rechargeable, portable gaming.

Why open this book with an object that, by many accounts, should be excluded from the study of a platform that Nintendo released at the turn of the millennium? This is the moment at which platform studies typically conclude. Instances where the object moves beyond its intended uses, to sit squarely in the hands of players eager to tinker with its innards, have often been relegated to afterwords and appendixes. The final pages of Dominic Arsenault's incisive platform study of the Super Nintendo Entertainment System (SNES) offer his readers the briefest taste of the SNES's "parallel lives" through remastering, homebrewing, hacking, and translating; he observes that echoes of the SNES linger in software development and gaming communities.[1] I understand these resonant afterlives to be vital to the definition of the console and worthy of considerably more attention, due to the way they arise from and speak to the platform's technology and social contexts. Once the console's market availability comes to an end, mods and emulators—variations we might be tempted to dismiss as imitative or derivative—tend to be among the few lasting methods we have for engaging with its software.

This isn't to say that the field of platform studies precludes consideration of a platform's afterlives. As Nick Montfort and Ian Bogost's series forward notes, these books don't restrict themselves to studying platforms as computational systems; they also explore the rich creative work that can be programmed on them. Although these are usually understood as officially licensed videogames, creative works can equally encompass a wide range of expressive interventions that include hardware mods, homebrew applications, and other artistic achievements.

Books in the Platform Studies series have already begun to explore these creative forms of cultural production. In *Codename Revolution: The Nintendo Wii Platform*, Steven Jones and George Thiruvathukal briefly examine the hacks and mods that come to define some of the Wii's social aspects.[2] They observe that players' intercessions remind us that platforms are, to at least some degree, designed to be appropriated by their users—sometimes in ways the developers permit, but often (and more important) in ways they do not. Similarly, when studying the Family Computer (Famicom) and its remodeled export, the Nintendo Entertainment System (NES), Nathan Altice acknowledges emulators' explicit challenge to the idea of a platform as a stable configuration of hardware and software. Instead, he defines the platform as "a holistic network of objects and texts," and studies not only the NES's peripherals and advertising materials, but also the actual environments in which players continue to engage with the object through emulation, hacking, and remixing.[3] In this way, Altice's exploration of the NES probes beyond the limits of what Nintendo's developers envisioned, in order to include the creative collaborations between human players and videogame programs.

Who Are You? Nintendo's Game Boy Advance Platform builds on these expansions of the platform studies framework to consider the GBA as an accretion of sanctioned and unsanctioned afterlives inextricably linked by material nostalgia and practices of spatial, temporal, and social circulation. Designed to live in the player's pocket, the GBA emerges at the nexus of bodies, material technologies, and preexisting intellectual property (IP). Nintendo's famous advertising campaign for the handheld, which revolved around the slogan "Who Are You?" sought to capitalize on players' long-standing emotional connections to beloved, iconic characters. Billboard, transit, television, and movie ads explicitly invited players to identify with Mario, Link, Peach, Donkey Kong, Samus (and so on, and so on) through the games they purchased and played in private and public spaces. Carrying these characters around became an outwardly empowering form of self-definition that was inextricably linked to Nintendo's corporate brand. People became "Nintendo players," "Mario fans," "gamers," and a host of other identities by adopting the console and making it part of their daily lives. This framing was crucial in structuring its users' collective response to the product. The outcome of Nintendo's rhetorical gesture circulated as social currency at bus stops and in schoolyards, offering a convenient identity to a generation of young videogame players who may not quite have known who they were yet.

When the GBA entered the Japanese market in in March 2001, and the North American and European markets not long after in June, it promised to usher in a new era of console-quality portables hitherto undreamed of. Yet even as it touted the moniker "Advance," the platform—in typical

Nintendo fashion—was decidedly backward-looking. After the release of the Game Boy in 1989, the Kyoto-based consumer electronics company dominated the handheld gaming industry, with enough of a monopoly that they had deferred the need to release a convincing successor until the turn of the millennium. In the meantime, Game Boy became a household name, with over 118 million units sold between the Game Boy, Game Boy Pocket, and Game Boy Color (GBC). So, when it arrived, the GBA harnessed the roughly decade-old power of this name, with the aim of matching (if not surpassing) what the Game Boy had managed to accomplish as both a computational and cultural object.

But the name isn't the only thing the GBA took from its forerunner; in addition to the GBA's own 32-bit processor, the handheld's chassis contains an 8-bit, 8-MHz coprocessor to enable backward compatibility. This is the very same processor that powered the 1998 GBC. Nintendo could have developed a proprietary emulator to preserve the use of their existing library of games on their new handheld, but they chose to embed their outdated hardware directly into the new system. The GBA is emblematic of Nintendo's iterative approach to hardware and software development that constantly mines their own corporate and material history. Not only does the GBA draw on the lessons Nintendo learned in the production of their home consoles, it tangibly appropriates the success of the Game Boy line to synthesize the best of both playable worlds. Take the Game Boy Advance apart and you find the guts of the GBC nestled in a *mise en abîme* of Nintendo's own making.

At the same time as it drew on the computational architecture of earlier hardware, the GBA was Nintendo's sandbox, in which they could test-drive the locative media elements that would come to define their future handhelds and home consoles, anticipating a moment of renewed sociality and community in portable play. Nintendo's is a social brand, and the company has endeavored to turn pocket gaming into a communal enterprise through a handful of peripherals designed around connectivity. Many were commercial failures, with niche uses or a narrow library of compatible games. But universal functionality wasn't the point. The goal was to retool social practices through cooperative and competitive play.

Take, for example, the Nintendo GameCube–Game Boy Advance Link Cable, which introduced interoperability between GBA games in a given series and their corresponding GameCube titles. This connectivity demanded a prohibitive amount of hardware and software in the early 2000s, but the ability to turn the GBA into a wired controller with an embedded screen resonates in the design of the 2012 Wii U's asymmetric gameplay. Similarly, the Wireless Adapter bundled with *Pokémon FireRed* and *LeafGreen* worked with fewer than twenty games, but it antedated the Nintendo 3DS's innate connective capabilities. Between its portability and its emerging affordance for networked or otherwise connective gameplay, the GBA hangs on the precipice of what Jesper Juul calls the "casual revolution"—the moment where the simplicity of videogames is rediscovered for casual audiences.[4]

By virtue of its portability, GBA play exists at the liminal intersection of private and public space. While the GBA promises console-quality gaming on par with that of the SNES, it departs from one of the core characteristics of a home console, in that it's not thought of as a stationary object connected to and placed beside a television set. Users can carry the GBA through different rooms of the home, outside the home, to friends' houses, or out into those not-quite-private spaces of the backyard and balcony. Its portability allows it to impinge upon the vacant moments of commutes, queues, and waiting around for tardy friends. Here, play is publicly visible even as it insulates the player against having to interact with other people in these public spaces. GBA play is chameleonic, complicating the ostensible binary between hardcore console play in the domestic sphere and casual mobile play in transitory spaces.

In light of these factors, we might see the GBA as fundamentally contingent. "Contingency" here can be understood in two distinct but nevertheless related ways.[5] First, GBA play is contingent on a range of considerations, including the body (or form) of the platform, the body of the player, and the temporal, spatial, and social settings where engagements take place. That is, the specific situations in and against which we play necessarily affect the way we play and the way we think about this play. If we were to run through the same level of a game on the 2001 GBA in a crowded waiting room and on the backlit, modded console in bed, the experience of that same level would change as a result of the hardware and setting, even if the software remains identical.

The second meaning of "contingency" lies in the platform's malleability and uncertainty, in the way its developers and users continuously revise what the GBA means. When Nintendo released the front-lit Game Boy Advance SP (SP) in 2003, they demonstrated that the GBA is not fixed, but rather is open to conceptual and aesthetic revisions based on user feedback and data. When hobbyists peel apart the handheld's plastic casing to install a new screen while preserving the central processing unit (CPU), memory, and other computational components, they are engaging in similar acts of revision that disturb the definition of the platform as a static hardware object. The GBA contains multitudes that no single, stable configuration can capture. Each aspect of the GBA's assemblage has something to say about its history, affordances, and constraints, as well as its potential for creative expression.[6]

Today, the GBA continues to circulate through afterlives that mutate in response to social contexts and users' needs. I follow Raiford Guins in adopting a broad definition of the afterlife condition, opening it up to a range of relevant contexts and uses that exist after the GBA's design, production, and commercial life cycle come to an end.[7] While I recognize that videogames often persist under careful curation in preservationist venues—museums, labs, and universities, to name a few—I also resist foregrounding institutions as the ultimate authority in proclaiming what is and is not a legitimate facet of the platform. Backward compatibility, digital rereleases, hardware modification, emulation, and hobbyist hacks are all vital afterlives that affect the way that we experience and understand the GBA, even—and perhaps especially—if they haven't been institutionally archived and legitimized. These afterlives linger on Nintendo's website, on the shelves of pawnshops, on modders' worktables, and on homebrew development forums, ready to catalyze transformative encounters between residual media and new players.

Today, we can think of the GBA as residual media for the way that is has been, to borrow the words of Raymond Williams, "formed in the past, but . . . still active in the cultural process . . . as an effective element of the present."[8] Residual media is distinct from obsolete media, which connotes abandoned cultural practices and objects. Instead, residuality is more akin to a kind of stubborn persistence—a refusal to be wholly replaced by new objects and practices. As residual media, the GBA continues to hold active social significance. We can trace this significance to the hobbyist circles that endlessly and incrementally modify the handheld to reflect contemporary aesthetic and functional trends, and can also find it in Nintendo's corporate development strategies. The GBA exists alongside (not hidden behind) dominant cultural objects like the Nintendo Switch. The Switch's horizontal form factor and its ability to literally turn console-quality gaming into a portable experience whenever you remove the console unit from its docking station fulfills a promise that the GBA made two decades ago.

So the GBA continues to shape the possibilities of culture and technology, even though its own period as a culturally dominant object has come to an end. Temporally, the Switch is new, in that it is Nintendo's most recently released console. Ideologically, the Switch is new relative to the GBA's standing as residual media. It's precisely our encounters with residuality that constitute our understanding of the Switch as new or emergent.[9] In other words, residuality is the foil against which newness defines itself. It is not dead or obsolete media, but rather "living dead" or "zombie media."[10] These technologies continue to circulate and evolve, constantly in negotiation with culture and society, existing in an ouroboric cycle of planned obsolescence and electronic waste (e-waste). Reuse, modding, and creative forms of cultural production point to dominant and emergent technology's cyclical and codependent relationship with residuality.

Temporal distance from the handheld's release date gives this book the advantage of being able to explore the ways that both Nintendo and the console's actual users have repurposed it. I can talk about what the platform was as a new (dominant) object, but also what it has become years later, in its residual afterlife. The GBA wasn't groundbreaking. On the market, it failed to surpass the sales of its predecessor and was handily overtaken by its successor. But nineteen years after its initial release, and despite the emergence of newer platforms, the GBA retains enough popularity that amateur tinkerers can make a living by creating built-to-order GBAs. Retro Modding's handheld is an anachronism, sure. And yet, in its little computational heart, it's just as much of a GBA as the rest of them.

The Materiality of Nostalgia

The GBA often comes under fire for its substantial library of remakes and rereleases, with critics and consumers alike lambasting the handheld as a platform of ports (when talking about videogame software, the term "port" refers to game software that has been translated for a different hardware platform than what it was originally programmed for). In recounting the story of Nintendo's development from trading card company to multinational videogame giant, Jeff Ryan spends much of his chapter on the GBA describing what he saw as a lack of innovation on Nintendo's part. He concludes the section with a scathing review of its library: "this was a portable SNES, and [Nintendo] had designed plenty of SNES games back in 1993. They'd release those hits and crank out subpar licensed dreck to tie in with new movies or cartoon shows. But write new games? No way."[11] While Nintendo's contemporary home console, the GameCube, captured developers' interest with its capacity for vibrant three-dimensional (3D) graphics, GBA development was purportedly little more than a reluctant afterthought.

Compared to previous consoles, the GBA admittedly experienced a disproportionately concerted effort by Nintendo to exploit the depths of their illustrious catalog. But I struggle with the critique of GBA software development as being little more than a small-minded slew of ported games. For one thing, it elides the corpus of new titles and series developed for the GBA, many of which went on to become important IP themselves. But more important, this critique exhibits a failure to position the GBA's software library within Nintendo's larger corporate philosophy. More than any other company in the videogame industry, Nintendo has a sizable collection of cherished franchises that they constantly return to across their platforms. And the repeated revival of these properties is one of the ways that they revive interest in their franchises and keep players enamored with classic titles. Rather than seeing the GBA's software library as representative of corporate complacency, I see it as fundamental to what makes Nintendo Nintendo.

Nintendo's brand is built on nostalgia. It's sustained by a business model based on recursive innovation that appeals to players' long-standing affection for the company's hardware and software objects. Today, the term "nostalgia" has been divorced from its earlier medical and geographic associations, coming instead to describe a yearning for a different time—one activated through the objects and experiences of the past.[12] The familiar hardware and software objects of childhood come to symbolize a slower, dreamlike time when we were just starting to develop an understanding of the world and of ourselves. For many of Nintendo's consumers, Mario, Peach, Link, Zelda, and a host of other treasured characters guided their self-discovery and produced feelings of delight, frustration, pride, comfort, and control through specific software titles on specific hardware objects. Nintendo's business strategies appeal to homesickness for this time, impinging on the hardwired memories of play, but incrementally altering them from platform to platform.

In her robust typology of nostalgia, Svetlana Boym distinguishes between two variants of nostalgia: the restorative and the reflective.[13] Restorative nostalgia, as its name suggests, attempts to reconstruct the past by ignoring or effacing imperfections and signs of historical time under the pretense of a quest for a fundamental truth. It fails to acknowledge that we're no longer the ten-year-olds who first marveled at the GBA's launch chime, or that we can't go back to the playgrounds where we hid from our teachers to spend recess with friends trading Pokémon between GBAs. Restorative nostalgia is the drive behind nationalism, mythmaking, and conspiracy theory.

On the other hand, reflective nostalgia concerns itself with individual and collective memory and captures an awareness of pastness and finitude. Its focus "is not on the recovery of what is perceived to be an absolute truth but on the meditation on history and the passage of time."[14] Reflective nostalgia places longing, rationality, and affect into conversation in order to cherish fragments of memory and narrate how the past makes space for a multitude of possibilities in the present. It calls the truth into doubt. Objects imbued with reflective nostalgia become a site of potential, a confluence of personal and collective memory, and an acknowledgment of the irreversibility of time. They make space for contradictions.

Nintendo's corporate model of engagement and reengagement with familiar franchises has always been decidedly nostalgic. Any new hardware platform they release is typically joined by new software installments in the company's most recognizable and profitable series. But because Nintendo uniquely develops their platforms in tandem with the games released for them, reflective nostalgia has characterized their hardware production as much as their software development since they first began producing consumer electronics. Nostalgia is embedded in the circuits of each of the company's handhelds and home consoles.

Nintendo's historic success in the videogame market in the 1980s and 1990s has been credited in large part to the work of Gunpei Yokoi, whose invention of the *Ultra Hand* extending arm toy rescued a flailing Nintendo Playing Card Company in 1966 after the collapse of the playing card market.[15] As Nintendo president Hiroshi Yamauchi struggled to find new ways for his family business to stay afloat (including the release of a line of instant rice and the launch of a taxi service), he opened a games division that sought to lead the company into the analog toy market.

Yokoi's *Ultra Hand* toy, a wooden arm that you could use to grab objects by pressing the handles, was an overnight success, and Yokoi was promoted from his prior maintenance job. A string of equally triumphant toys followed, and, shortly thereafter, Yokoi was made head of Nintendo's Research and Development 1 (R&D1) division, where he went on to design and develop the Game & Watch handhelds, and later the Game Boy.

Yokoi's success stemmed from an influential design philosophy that emphasized repurposing old technology for creative ends. In a 1997 interview, he described his philosophy as 枯れた技術の水平思考, which Lara Crigger translates as "lateral thinking through withered technology."[16] This approach looks to outdated technologies—that is to say, to the residual—to solve present problems with respect to design, cost, and performance. Jennifer deWinter refers to this practice as "derivative innovation."[17] This mode of design takes ideas and technologies that have already been developed and combines them in novel ways, with the intention of improving upon them. She observes that this approach is part of a larger Japanese business culture predicated on the adoption and imitation of Western technologies without compromising their own practices.[18] New innovations arise out of incremental change as old, recognizable technologies are adapted for novel uses.

The Game & Watch series of dedicated handhelds explicitly embodies Nintendo's philosophy of lateral thinking. Although the story of the Game & Watch's creation has been told many times, it bears repeating now (and again in chapter 4) because of how fundamental it is to our understanding of platforms as assemblages. The Game & Watch materialized after Yokoi, on his way home from work, witnessed a train commuter feel so bored that he resorted to whiling away the journey by playing with a pocket calculator.[19] This scene fascinated Yokoi, inspiring in him the desire to create a discrete toy designed to occupy idle moments between events in the day. To realize his vision, the toy had to be affordable, and it also needed to fit into pockets and briefcases. Partnering with Sharp Corporation, Yokoi turned to outdated liquid crystal displays (LCDs) and cost-effective, miniaturized integrated circuits. Nintendo would repurpose the segmented displays intended for mathematical symbols and use them to animate small games. These weren't videogames per se because the machines didn't generate any video signals. Instead, the segmented displays flickered on and off to produce rudimentary animations. In *Ball* (1980), the first game in the series, an animated figure juggles several balls, which arc overhead as the LCD segments light up in sequence to create the visual effect of being in motion.

Although more powerful technologies existed at the time, Yokoi maintained that the systems should use the calculator's technologies because they kept battery life long and prices low. His rationale was that consumers would prefer more affordable products over cutting-edge technology that looked better but didn't offer much more beyond aesthetics. So long as a game was fun to play, Yokoi determined, people would buy it. He thought strategically, especially because the Game & Watch's target audience included children who needed to spend whatever allowance or birthday money they received, or else convince their parents to purchase the devices for them.

The novelty of the Game & Watch came from the fact that calculator segments could become fun through their innovative adoption into a simple game system (there are only so many words you can type on a calculator before it ceases to be entertaining). The success of the Game & Watch series of software hardwired into machinery eventually gave rise to entertainment systems with removable media, and many of the technological articulations of the Game & Watch continue to echo through subsequent products.

Lateral thinking has played a role in all facets of the company's production since Yokoi's tenure.[20] Their software development is predicated upon offering new ways of engaging with recognizable IP. Taking cues from Disney, Nintendo has become a veritable transmedia empire, with Mario coming to replace Mickey Mouse as the most recognizable mascot in the United States.[21] Although the gates of their walled garden are open to third-party developers, Nintendo retains in-house control of their most recognizable IP creations, and they funnel interest in new hardware through the promise of continued adventures with these treasured companions.

The continued reliance on lateral thinking is partly to do with the way that Yokoi's influential mentorship shaped hardware and software designer Shigeru Miyamoto's own approach to development. Miyamoto, who began working at Nintendo in 1977 as an industrial artist creating toys and playing cards, ascended through the company's ranks to become one of their most celebrated innovators and representatives, thanks to his emphasis on entertaining gameplay. Videogame aficionados have him to thank for *Super Mario Bros.*, *Donkey Kong*, and *The Legend of Zelda*, among other storied franchises that have come to define Nintendo's brand for over three decades. Enjoying the rare privilege of working at the helm of the development of both the hardware system and the software programmed for it, Miyamoto made a name for himself by leveraging the hardware's affordances to create coherent gameplay experiences that foregrounded the excitement and glee of play.

Miyamoto is highly attentive to the material and cultural contexts in which Nintendo's games circulate. In an interview that Shigesato Itoi conducted with Miyamoto as part of Nintendo's *Iwata Asks* interview series, Miyamoto explicitly outlines his approach to design: "I recently suggest putting ideas that were no good into a drawer with the reason why they were no good affixed to them . . . If you have a bunch of ideas like that in store, the time will come when, in some way, you can take off that label. Like, 'Oh, the rules are different now, so it's okay,' or 'It doesn't work in the day, but it'll work at night.'"[22] Ideas may not be right in a given temporal, social, cultural, political, or economic context, but that doesn't mean they're not worth repurposing. Sometimes, especially in Nintendo's case, it's just a matter of waiting for the necessary technology to become more affordable.

Nintendo consistently mines their idea drawers for innovative solutions to technical and creative problems. We can see this through the recursive nature of the company's patent history, where each document is bolstered by diagrams of their earlier inventions. But it's also tangible in their hardware's backward compatibility. While Nintendo has recently begun exploring ways of rereleasing games in digital formats for proprietary emulators, the GBA and its near contemporaries preserve access to software libraries through affordable material means. The GBA contains the GBC's processor, the Nintendo DS contains that of the GBA, and the Wii is hardwired for backward compatibility with the GameCube, preserving its computational architecture, as well as its controller ports and memory card slots. Lateral thinking is embedded into the material hardware itself. By prioritizing existing and affordable components, Nintendo incrementally produces technologies that are at once familiar and poised for future development. This recursive design practice enables reflective nostalgia to drive Nintendo's business model of technological continuity, backward compatibility, remakes, and digital rereleases. Even the name "Game Boy Advance" gestures toward brand continuity; the Game Boy is concealed within its redesigned chassis, but the device is also new, improved, and advanced.

Links between Past and Present

Miyamoto's approach to creating new gameplay experiences with recognizable IP creations condenses software development cycles, but it also builds brand loyalty to the beloved characters who have become the company's most profitable cultural currency. To illustrate how Nintendo manufactures nostalgia narratively and materially, we can look at the *Legend of Zelda* series, a cornerstone franchise that boasts a cultural cachet second only to Mario's. By Miyamoto's own admission, a strong connection to childhood is among the elements that guided his initial approach to the series; the natural environments and spiritual magic of *The Legend of Zelda* arose out of his wistful memories of exploring the caves and countryside of Sonobe, Japan, as a boy.[23] Continuity within the software series and with the hardware on which it runs gestures toward a similar attempt to re-create the magic of childhood for Nintendo's consumers—albeit one grounded in the exploration of virtual worlds, not natural, material ones. Originally released for the Famicom in 1986, *The Legend of Zelda* experienced a rerelease in cartridge format in 1994. In 1993, the Game Boy's *The Legend of Zelda: Link's Awakening* began as a port of the inaugural title and was itself later rereleased on the GBC in 1998; more recently, it was remade for the Switch in 2019. Since the series' inception, it's seen more ports, remakes, and rereleases than new installments.

Nintendo developed *The Legend of Zelda* concurrently with *Super Mario Bros.* for the Famicom's two different media forms (disc and game cartridge, respectively), and the two often serve as foils for each other. While *Super Mario Bros.* is linear, time-constrained, and rigidly sequenced, *Zelda* is open and expansive, offering, if not freedom, then at least some illusion of it as the player decides where to go and what to do next. Mario was meant to be the protagonist of both games until the development team determined (probably with good reason) that the plumber was ill suited to a medieval fantasy world of swords and sorcery. Instead, the *Zelda* games follow Link, a courageous young boy festooned in green who bears a connection to the powerful relic known as the Triforce. His goal is typically to save Princess Zelda (though it's worth noting that she often saves him too) and restore serenity to the mythical kingdom of Hyrule.

Link has been a metaphor from his inception. Recalling how the protagonist got his name, Shigeru Miyamoto says:

> It's not a very well-known anecdote, but when we started to conceive of *The Legend of Zelda*, we imagined the Triforce fragments would be made of electronic chips! The game was intended to take place in both the past and the future. Because the hero would be the link between the two, we called him "Link." . . . In the end, Link never went to the future, and it remained a heroic fantasy game.[24]

Link may not have traveled between the past and the future in the first *Zelda* game, but movement across time has since become a series staple. And although Triforce fragments aren't made of electronic chips, Nintendo's hardware is. Link's movements through chronological time and across platforms are fruitful for tracing the link (as it were) between Nintendo's coterminous hardware and software development.

Game designer and director Eiji Aonuma observes in an *Iwata Asks* interview that "to Miyamoto-san, all the games in the Legend of Zelda series are connected," a connection as much about hardware as it is about the series' intricate, diverging narratives.[25] Just as the various temporal settings of *The Legend of Zelda: The Ocarina of Time,* for the Nintendo 64 (N64), offer Link different abilities—Young Link can fit through small passages, which Adult Link exchanges for access to more powerful weapons—different systems afford Link (and his developers) alternative expressive adventures that are subject to their own trade-offs. In that same interview, *Ocarina of Time*'s developers discuss some features originally intended for their N64 title, including dynamic one-on-one battles on horseback and instances of Link dramatically lifting his sword above his head. Both actions were then impossible to execute, given the N64's graphical and computational constraints. But mounted combat was integral to *The Legend* of *Zelda: Twilight Princess*'s aesthetic and narrative development; Nintendo initially set out to develop a successor to *The Legend of Zelda: The Wind Waker* until the development team determined that the horseback riding focus of the game required a darker, more realistic aesthetic (Aonuma and his team spent months improving the realism of the horseback riding, which dominated the 2004 teaser trailer). Link piercing the sky with a blade later harnessed the affordances of the Wii MotionPlus technology—an attachment for the Wii Remote (Wiimote) that enhanced its ability to register players' movements—to become a key mechanic of *The Legend of Zelda: Skyward Sword*. President Satoru Iwata's closing observation, "After 13 years, you've fulfilled another wish," speaks to how Nintendo digs through their idea drawer to stitch narrative concepts and hardware affordances together, embedding nostalgia into circuits and plastic.

Like Mario's, Link's conception is entangled with the limitations of the platform for which he was first programmed, and every subsequent incarnation has equally been shaped by the affordances and constraints of the hardware and software for which he's intended. The red hat and bushy moustache that have come to characterize Mario (or Jumpman, as he would have been called at the time) were direct responses to the 1980 *Mario Bros.*'s arcade cabinet's graphical restrictions: contrasting colors enabled Jumpman to stand out against a variety of backgrounds; the cap circumvented the need to animate hair; and the moustache obfuscated facial expressions, simplifying animation.

Link was born out of similar computational constraints. Miyamoto wanted to create a recognizable character who used a sword and a shield—both of which had to be visible to the player—but the NES's graphics hardware restricted sprites to only three colors.[26] To ensure that players could spot what Link was holding, designer Takashi Tezuka illustrated the weapons in such a way that they became almost comically large, introducing a new challenge of how to distinguish the character from his armaments. Enter the quintessential long hat and big ears. Link's early resemblance to Peter Pan didn't go unnoticed (Miyamoto loved Disney); he donned a lime green tunic in an appropriative homage (derivative innovation was at work even in sprite design). The vibrant hue coupled with brown accents and Link's olive skin set the hero apart from the forests that adorned the Hylian landscape.

In his earliest incarnations, Link moves in four directions, as restricted by a set of software and hardware protocols. He does so by way of Gunpei Yokoi's cross-shaped input device known as the "Direction-pad" (D-pad) or "Plus controller" for its similarity to the mathematical symbol. Yokoi had developed the D-pad for the *Donkey Kong* Game &

Watch after their earlier two-handed or diagonal button configurations no longer proved sufficient. While juggling balls didn't require a large number of inputs—*Ball* only uses two buttons, "◀Left" and "Right▶," to control each of the juggler's hands—reproducing a handheld version of Nintendo's popular arcade game required more sophisticated controls. Jumpman needed to move along both axes while leaping over obstacles, so Yokoi designed an interface that played intuitively and maximized the handheld's available space. With one thumb, Jumpman could be sent to climb ladders and speed along crossbeams, while the other had him caper over pits and barrels. Each of the plus sign's arms mapped logically to one of the four cardinal directions, and unlike arcade joysticks, the flat, compact pad wasn't prone to breaking. So successful was the invention that Nintendo has repurposed the D-pad for every handheld and console controller from the release of the Famicom until the Switch's Joy-Con returned to the four-separate-buttons design of earlier Game & Watch devices. The D-pad is a key component of the GBA—a vestige of residual technologies and illustrative of the importance of lateral thinking.

When the N64 introduced 3D gameplay, it demanded a substantial controller revision to account for the explorative possibilities that its graphics engine now supported. The migration to a more immersive environment, with third-person perspectives and a full range of navigable directions, coincided with the introduction of a control stick designed to detect 360 independent directions rather than the 4 (or 8, with dual-button support) of the D-pad. While it called itself an "analog stick" and was functionally equivalent to one, the N64's control stick used a pair of optical encoding discs to determine its relative position, in a process similar to that which occurred in ball mice. Its sensitivity settings enabled characters to walk or run (depending on how far you pushed the stick), offering new ways of traversing virtual landscapes that more closely approximate the way we move through the world.

Thanks to the control stick, Link enjoyed a greater range of movement as he explored the newly opened valleys of Hyrule.[27] Nevertheless, Nintendo was unwilling to abandon the D-pad altogether. It's preserved on the leftmost edge of the N64 controller, attached to an often-extraneous third arm used for a narrow selection of (primarily) two-dimensional (2D) games. In many ways, the leftmost side of the controller is an artifact of earlier hardware development—a way to safeguard nostalgia for previous systems through a curated release of backward-looking ports.

It's difficult to overstate the significant effect that the shift from 2D to 3D had on both Nintendo's software and hardware design practices. While those of us raised on 3D games have naturalized the ability to navigate such virtual landscapes, a third dimension radically transformed players' perceptions of game worlds at the time. For nearly a decade, everyone knew that Mario was supposed to head to the right. Whatever happened between Mario's starting point and the flagpole at the end of the level wouldn't change the fundamental conceit of the game: just keep moving to the right and try not to die. So when Mario's pointy polygons burst out of a pipe in front of Princess Peach's 3D castle in *Super Mario 64*, the N64's spectacular launch title, the learning curve was pretty steep.

The 3D engine demanded that developers rethink the series' formula to make the most of the new perspective. One of the challenges that *Super Mario 64* faced was figuring out how to instruct players on targeting objects along three axes rather than two. It was imperative that the developers got it right. If *Super Mario 64* failed to teach players how to move through 3D worlds, they might write off the console entirely as too difficult. The game's camera went through hundreds of iterations before the team settled on a system using the C-buttons that felt organic for players who needed to conceive of Mario's concrete position relative to the objects in his path. So significant was this camera that the second character that you see upon launching a new game (after Princess Peach, who invites you to the castle for cake) is not Mario, but Lakitu, a bespectacled, cloud-surfing Koopa (and a former fiend in the NES's *Super Mario Bros.* game) who flies around the castle grounds while dangling a camera on a fishing line. Reporting on the scene, Lakitu assures you that "as seasoned cameramen, we'll be shooting from the recommended angle, but you can change the camera angle by pressing the C-buttons." For the first time in videogame history, you were in charge of your own perspective within the game world, with Lakitu following behind (in a thoughtful attention to detail, Lakitu appears behind Mario when he looks in a mirror).

Because *Ocarina of Time* used three of the four C-buttons for Link's inventory, it couldn't maintain *Super Mario 64*'s robust camera system. And *Super Mario 64*'s camera wasn't perfect either; there would be times when you tried to read a sign and ended up running around it in circles as the camera adjusted itself behind you. With *Ocarina of Time*'s high-stakes, fast-paced battles, the development team knew this system would be too frustrating for players. Instead, they created a new device: Z-targeting. Pressing the Z-trigger shifts the camera behind Link and locks crosshairs on his enemies, allowing him to engage his opponent without losing track of both their positions.[28] Because Z-targeting locks onto one enemy at a time, it also tells the other opponents to wait so they don't swarm Link all at once and overwhelm him. Z-targeting taught players how to move within an unfamiliar, 3D environment until they gradually learned to trust their own perspective in a changing videogame topography. Since then, Z-targeting has been carried forward as an instructional tool, through which familiar software invites players to learn about the mechanics of the new hardware by relying on the *Zelda* series' established vocabulary. Z-targeting is a metaphor. By recycling material components and software protocols, Nintendo gives players something to hold onto when they encounter the next system.

For a half-decade, Link darted between two and three dimensions as he resurfaced on handhelds and home consoles. This interdimensional flickering was as much about hardware constraints as it was about a nostalgic return to the game that started it all. Flagship's interconnected 2001 titles, *The Legend of Zelda: The Oracle of Seasons* and *The Legend of Zelda: The Oracle of Ages*—praised for their vibrant, colorful 2D designs that showed off the abilities of the GBC's display—initially came about because Capcom's Flagship proposed to remake *The Legend of Zelda* for Nintendo's latest portable.[29]

Time and again, *Zelda* games highlight the advantages and limitations of Nintendo's hardware, even as they consistently look back to the series' first installment. *The Legend of Zelda: A Link to the Past* for the SNES confesses the franchise's interest in its own history right in the title. When ported to the GBA and bundled as *The Legend of Zelda: A Link to the Past and Four Swords*, the game harnessed the interoperability between handhelds to offer a multiplayer experience grounded in tangible hardware connections. *The Legend of Zelda: Four Swords Adventures* similarly uses the GameCube's connective potential through episodic, cooperative gameplay mechanics that bring a delightfully social element to Link's usually solitary wanderings (chapter 4).

DS installments use the tactility inherent in the platform by requiring players to draw on maps using the touch screen, holler at nonplayable characters using the built-in microphone, and even use the handheld's folding hinge design to stamp a mirror image of a sacred crest displayed on the top screen to Link's in-game map on the bottom screen. In each case, the games use the hero to teach players (and, just as important, other software developers) about the unique affordances of the latest handheld, console, or peripheral.

Because *Zelda* games are often released at the beginning and end of a platform's market life cycle, they also showcase developers' growing fluency with the hardware's peculiarities. *The Legend of Zelda: Majora's Mask*, the haunting sequel to *Ocarina of Time*, updates the game engine and employs the 4-megabyte (MB) N64 expansion pack to double the usable random-access memory (RAM) for improved graphics resolution, dynamic lighting, intricate texture mapping, and complex effects like motion blur. Similarly, when the GBA's *The Legend of Zelda: The Minish Cap* emerged in 2004, it boasted vibrant graphics reminiscent of the cartoonish, cel-shaded illustrations of the GameCube's *The Wind Waker*. *The Minish Cap* mediated between the features that players expected in 2D games and the special actions and details that they had since grown fond of in 3D, blurring the distinction between handheld and console, 2D and 3D, innovation and nostalgia. While hardware limitations may not be as immediately visible today as they were when Link was a tricolored 8-bit sprite, we would be remiss to think that software isn't constantly responding to the affordances and constraints of the computational system for which it's programmed.

The lack of a linear timeline between *Zelda* games is consequently a useful touchstone for thinking about how Nintendo conceives of the relationships among its generations of consoles. It's difficult to think of another long-running series where the relationship of prequel and sequel is so tangled. Although Miyamoto has slowly and reluctantly begun to impose a timeline in response to fans' demand for one, the series itself refuses to sustain a linear trajectory. Paths protract into alternative universes and parallel worlds, connected though gameplay mechanics and physical hardware more than through narrative continuity. Nintendo's hardware development equally refuses linear narratives of progress; each console engages in conversation with the company's corporate and technological history. The only consistency is the continued return to residual media and to the nostalgia they've successfully manufactured through their stories and controllers.

Because *Zelda* games are so narratively similar, they have the advantage of continuously generating nostalgia in Nintendo's consumers. While nostalgia motivates my generation to buy the newest installment (and the console on which to play it), the games themselves are often lauded as being among the finest for the system, capturing the collective imaginations of the next generation of players. It's a testament to the series' importance as a linchpin of nostalgia that almost every main title has been ported or remade for subsequent hardware platforms, most of them more than once. These acts of repetition with differentiation encapsulate Nintendo's relationship to reflective nostalgia. Nintendo never tries to flawlessly restore past experiences. The games have never purported to reproduce the one that came five, ten, or even twenty years ago. Instead, graphics are improved, glitches are resolved, and soundtracks are remastered. Each remake carries the spirit of the hardware for which it was designed, while taking advantage of more powerful processors and larger, sharper, and brighter screens.

Nintendo is aware that the nostalgic experiences for which they're known are fundamentally constructed. On the website for their NES Classic Controller (used to play Virtual Console games on the Wii or Wii U), they invite users to "Play NES games the way they're meant to be played—with a full-size 'original' controller."[30] Their cheeky use of scare quotes around "original" reveals an awareness that the Classic Controller is not restoring an authentic experience, but rather evoking memories of how these games used to be played. Aesthetically, the NES Classic Controller is designed to mirror its 1985 predecessor, but its ability to interface with the Wiimote and connect to a plug-and-play, emulation-based NES reveals its temporal and conceptual distance from its past. The NES Classic Edition console similarly engages in a process of simulacra. One of its "fun features" is the ability to choose among three display modes: 4:3, which "gives you the original NES game look, with a slight horizontal stretch"; Perfect Pixel mode, where "each pixel is a perfect square, so you see the games exactly as designed" (*designed*, not *played* being the operative distinction here); and (my personal favorite, for how delightfully artificial it is) a cathode-ray tube (CRT) filter, which "looks like an old TV, scan lines and all."

While the 1985 NES output an analog signal to CRT television sets, the NES Classic Edition console, almost always connected to a flat-screen television, outputs a digital signal via High-Definition Multimedia Interface (HDMI). The ability to switch among three display modes—each touted as being able to capture some element of an original experience—ultimately highlights the fact that the original experience is aesthetically, affectively, and materially irretrievable. The 4:3 mode ostensibly promises an original look, but that's immediately undercut by being stretched for a different display. Perfect Pixel mode reveals the sharp, square-edged pixels of digital emulation, rather than the blurriness of actual CRT images. And the CRT filter mode's addition of scan lines to an LCD is itself a fetishized, nostalgic anachronism. Scan lines are the product of a CRT's electron gun; they have no place on an LCD outside of players' desire to look back to the time of their childhood. What the NES Classic Edition does is reveal how, even if the nostalgic experience is fundamentally irretrievable, it can be *approximated* through familiar narratives and the muscle memory attached to a controller configuration. Our minds may create aestheticized memories of the stories, but our bodies remember the adventures.

Because Nintendo predicates their design philosophy upon reworking and rereleasing existing hardware, embedding pieces of old consoles into new ones, revisiting control schemes, and folding in backward compatibility, they render the notion of a platform fungible from the outset. This is what I mean by "the materiality of nostalgia." Any platform study of the GBC would have to reckon with the GBA as a vital piece of the platform puzzle for the way that it continues to use its 8-bit processor. This platform study of the GBA similarly considers the material objects and aesthetic protocols that carry the platform decades forward. At the end of the day, experiences with a given platform are always contingent, always contextual, and often—when Nintendo is involved—longing for a halcyon past that may never have existed.

Who Are You?

In 2002, Nintendo of America launched a $50 million international marketing campaign to promote the GBA and the GameCube, revolving around the slogan "Who Are You?" The campaign's print ads and television commercials explicitly connected personal identity to Nintendo's branding strategies through this repeated phrase, often scrawled out in graffiti-style lettering. The company hailed or addressed users by asking them to see their sense of self as being indebted to and contingent upon their embodied identification with Nintendo's software and hardware.[31] In essence, you were what you played. By engaging with Nintendo's products, players had the opportunity not only to explore who they were through the games they played and the characters they were drawn to, but also to outwardly display their identities as Nintendo fans to others.

Nintendo's characters were central to the campaign. One poster had a woman looking over a cityscape, her right arm concealed beneath what looks like a paper cutout of Samus's gauntlet, which had been taped over her skin. A Brazilian print ad showed a man skydiving, his head replaced with Mario's face beside the words "*quem é você?*" (the tagline in Portuguese). A series of television commercials depicted a confused therapist asking a client, "Who are you?" as the client aped the actions of characters in games like *Four Swords Adventures* and *Metal Gear Solid: The Twin Snakes*.

These ads are part of a long history of videogame companies attempting to impinge on our sense of self to inspire long-lasting, extremely personal relationships to a corporate brand. Within games, we're often referred to as the "you" that must save the world from a sinister force, immersing us in unique mechanics and narrative landscapes by way of self-projection. In the *Zelda* universe, for example, most games offer the option to change Link's name to ours so that we can insert ourselves into the world in Link's stead (producer Eiji Aonuma has even noted that his intentions back during the development of *Ocarina of Time* were for Link to appear gender neutral, to facilitate universal efforts to relate to Link).[32] At the developer's call, we can become Link, Mario, and other recognizable characters.

Given their concern with identity, the "Who Are You?" campaign's ads reveal not just who we are, but also who *Nintendo* thinks we are. We can identify a disconnect between the actual and intended audiences through whom Nintendo choses to depict. One of the most famous television commercials attached to the campaign was released in Japan to promote the launch of the SP. The ad shows a group of schoolchildren watching the clock as their teacher scribbles on the blackboard. The second the clock strikes twelve, the children are out of their seats, parkouring through the streets, sliding down sewer grates (the pipes of a *Super Mario Bros.* game), and sprinting along the roof of an underground train. They converge in droves before the doors of the videogame store where the owner affixes an "Available Now" sign to the door. When the man turns to face the children, he finds that their heads have been replaced by those of Mario, Luigi, Peach, Yoshi, Donkey Kong, and Samus. When the screen goes black, the words "Who are you?" appear in white, inviting viewers to project themselves into this universe by adopting the newest handheld just as all those children have done. But it's worth paying attention to the fact that the crowd primarily consists of little Marios. Only three Peaches and two Samuses are immediately visible in a scene composed largely of red caps.[33]

This commercial and other similar ads in the campaign remind us that the GBA launched at a time when Nintendo games were primarily marketed to young boys. Indeed, the device's very name—Game *Boy* Advance—etched in glittering silver letters beneath its screen, admits to its ideal users. Even though it's no longer the case that Nintendo's targeted or actual audience consists primarily of boys, a history of male-oriented marketing has haunted the GBA.[34] Since the mid- to late twentieth century, videogames have enacted and mediated models of masculinity.

The deliberately gendered audience of videogames is part of a broader interest in constructing technological consumerism. Lisa Jacobson argues that promoters of a "boy market" construct boys' consumption as "technologically conversant" to make sure that their consumer practices aren't placed in the same category as girls' consumption, which is seen as frivolous materialism. "In the technologically-centered world of boy play," she writes, "consumerism became the means to display mechanical flair, inventiveness, and mastery of technical change—all measures of masculine success."[35] Boys' desire to own media technologies has been framed as a way for them to define themselves as masculine. So when

Nintendo depicted an audience mostly made up of young boys, they held up a mirror to this larger history of gendered marketing. People who weren't boys had to look beyond these advertisements (and beyond the console's name) to find a way to see themselves as the "you" that Nintendo asked about.[36]

Other ads in the campaign left Nintendo's characters behind altogether. In addition to foregrounding the way characters come to shape and reflect players' identities, the "Who Are You?" campaign put forward a similar claim for Nintendo's hardware objects. The idea that "you are what you play" isn't software-specific for a company where hardware and software development is inextricable. While it was hard for the stationary GameCube to come to be seen as a vital part of players' sense of self (though competitive GameCube fighting game players might say that their customized controllers certainly perform this function), the portable GBA SP was designed with self-expression in mind.

As a clamshell redesign of the GBA, the SP conveyed Nintendo's interest in appealing to a broader demographic than their typically youth-oriented audience. Its elegant exterior—available in a range of colors to suit all personalities—looked less like a videogame platform and more like a personal digital assistant (PDA), or even a makeup compact. Only when the device is flipped open do the frontlit screen and buttons, respectively located on the top and bottom halves of the handheld, become visible to the player. At once sleek and cute, the handheld proposed to serve as a marker for identity—one that the player could construct based on the color they chose for the shell, in addition to the software they opted to play. By adopting the SP, players fastened themselves to distinctive, identifiable, and interactive media technologies. Where the player went, Link and Mario followed, safely tucked away in a pocket.

A subset of the "Who Are You?" campaign anthropomorphized the SP, turning it into a character itself—one that acted as a consumptive mirror for the player.[37] These commercials depicted the pocket-sized, flip-screen SP engaging in activities that ranged from the mundane to the extreme: the Onyx SP chose a song from a jukebox; the Platinum SP admired itself in a mirror and applied perfume before heading to a dance floor; the Cobalt Blue SP went skydiving. Across these commercials, the handheld "walked" by pivoting its weight between the bottom-left and -right corners, "bent down" along its clamshell hinge, and "shook its head" by turning its entire form side to side. Despite its hard edges, lack of limbs, and overall dissimilarity to anything resembling a human being, the SP's actions are all nevertheless immediately recognizable in the eyes of its players, who might find themselves reflected in the handheld's interests.

These ads explicitly take up a history of humanizing consumer objects as a way to appeal to users' sense of self. Early home telephones, for example, were given an anthropomorphic appearance with rounded contours—its own ears—to reassure its new users that there were real human voices on the other end of the line.[38] Humanizing the SP turns it into something relatable, something that can be absorbed into the player's sense of self and subsequently used to broadcast their identity to others. As a portable device, the SP is designed to follow us around the private domestic sphere and out into the social public. It becomes an extension of our natural tendency to project ourselves into the world. It's through the framing of the handheld as an object of identity that Nintendo conjures up the material feeling of nostalgia. The SP is an "evocative object"—a thing that evokes memories and feelings from our past while inspiring in us a sense of being "at one" with the technology.[39] The GBA encourages players to perform their identities in a public setting, not only through the SP's communicative form factor but also through the rhetorical gesture of the "Who Are You?" campaign.

This campaign reminds us that, however personal portable games might seem to be, our consumption of Nintendo-licensed software on the SP is meant to be conspicuous (i.e., it's meant to be broadcast to others) to reflect back on ourselves. This is not a feature unique to the SP. Rather, the SP points to the way that overt media consumption, whether that media is digital or material, is one of the ways by which we communicate our taste, power, and prestige.

We can see the same phenomenon in books. Lined up on bookshelves, books are public displays of consumption that, as Lisa Nakamura observes, "produces and publicises a reading self."[40] When you browse a friend's bookshelf at a party, you're not snooping—as you'd be in any other room in the house—but rather participating in the friend's construction of herself as a reader. Bookshelves are "meant to be shown off as a marker of personal taste and, indeed, personality" through what they communicate to others, regardless of which books have actually been read cover to cover, or at all.[41] The GBA's software library performs the same function in communicating the kind of Nintendo player and consumer you are. The way you decorate your SP—first by choosing the shell color, then by accessorizing it with stickers and colored wrist straps—becomes a marker of personality (one silver SP even gets a "tattooed" decal in one of the commercials).

With the "Who Are You?" campaign in mind, it's no surprise that thousands of users and modders have taken to customizing the GBA as a way of demonstrating their technical mastery and aesthetic preferences.

Over the last three years, Retro Modding has built over 1,000 custom GBAs for people around the world—framed by the promise of creating "the Game Boy Advance of your dreams"—to say nothing of the sheer volume of shells, screens, buttons, and tools they've sold individually for tinkerers so they can do it themselves. Retro Modding and other hobbyists, engineers, and manufacturers in the modding community have created custom circuit boards, rechargeable batteries, ultraviolet (UV) printed shells, and hundreds of other components designed not only to improve the functionality of their builds, but also to allow users to bring something of themselves to the object. Modified consoles then make their way to YouTube channels, Reddit threads, and Instagram posts where they're shared with an audience primed to understand how these transformed objects reflect on their makers and users. Over fifteen years ago, Nintendo asked players to tell the company who they were. Today, players are continuing to answer that question, even if Nintendo might not quite appreciate their methods.

Methodology

In September 2017, Jan Henrik posted a tweet of an electrocardiogram-measuring machine containing deconstructed components belonging to the GBA SP.[42] The instrument, manufactured by the German company Medical Imaging Electronics, appropriated the SP's 240- x 160-pixel LCD (replete with intact plastic casing and logo) for its imaging apparatus. Shocking as this discovery was for Henrik, it's not altogether surprising that the GBA would find itself nested in other technological devices. In a 2006 design proposal, a team of researchers in Taiwan documented the successful use of the GBA as an embedded system in signal-measuring equipment. They cited the GBA's low cost, "high degree of accuracy," and "fine graphics processing capability" as improvements on the industry standards of the time, which included cumbersome computers and PDAs that created serious transmission delays.[43]

The use of Nintendo handhelds for portable medical diagnostic devices in particular has a history that extends back to a patent filed by Mitchel M. Rohde in 1997.[44] This document proposed the use of a Game Boy in medical devices as a safe, efficient, and cost-effective alternative to using bulky computers that crashed often, potentially causing life-threatening medical situations. Saving lives was certainly not Nintendo's intended goal when they developed and manufactured their handhelds, but consumers have nevertheless repurposed the platforms for uses entirely external to what Nintendo's vision of the platform entailed.

Although these are extreme examples of technological repurposing, they address a specific need within a given cultural and economic context, a need that portable videogame platforms were uniquely positioned to fill. Before single-chip computers became readily available and affordable, the Game Boy was used for everything from programming the Singer Izek sewing machine to gamifying the practice of testing blood glucose with the highly accurate GlucoBoy integrated system. These cases challenge easy preconceptions about what Nintendo's handheld platforms are and what they're designed to do.

As a field, platform studies arises out of a dearth of scholarly attention to the foundational code and hardware layers that permit more immediately visible creative and expressive practices. Historically, many scholars have focused on what Nick Montfort and Matthew Kirschenbaum have called "screen essentialism," the study of symbolic content and graphical user interface (GUI) to the exclusion of a media object's inner workings.[45] Platform studies exist within a larger movement that calls for material specificity in media studies, regardless of whether the object belongs in game studies, film studies, or any other media-related field. Consider how the literary critic N. Katherine Hayles is sensitive to how electronic text "is generated through multiple layers of code processed by an intelligent machine *before* a human reader decodes the information."[46] She calls for a medium-specific analysis to electronic hypertexts that attends to formal specificity, the signifying process of language and code, and the connections between computational platforms. She's careful to clarify that the purpose of media specificity is not to tout the superiority of a given medium, but rather to articulate its particular affordances with which writers and readers can engage in both serious and playful ways. Hayles's disclaimer is an unfortunate necessity—a reaction against accusations of technological determinism that tend to occur whenever scholars open the "black box" of technology.[47]

Technological determinism is not the fault of platform studies. Bogost and Montfort have debunked the misconception that platform studies see technology as arising and developing outside of cultural, social, and human factors.[48] On the contrary, they note that people and technology exist in negotiation with one another; technology might influence people's creative work, but people develop it in response to particular cultural, social, historical, economic, and material contexts. Privileging one side over the other results in an incomplete account of a given object. Even when the focus is on a computational hardware or software platform, Montfort and Bogost's five layers of digital media are always situated in context.[49]

In following the platform studies methodology, this book considers what Montfort and Bogost understand to be the most neglected of these levels—that is, the hardware—to situate the GBA in culture, society, and history. The GBA's release is indebted to a confluence of social, cultural, and economic factors, from Nintendo's reliance on recursive hardware development to the gendered milieu of videogames at the turn of the century that allowed the handheld to take the name it did. But this book also makes a slight departure from the typical platform studies model, in that it spends a considerable amount of time looking at the afterlives that exist in conversation with the 2001 object. The GBA does not exist solely as a product. It is also a complex, continuing *process*.

This book therefore aims to broaden the notion of the GBA as a platform to make space for the objects that challenge its easy definition. In so doing, my approach shares elements with Siegfried Zielinski's idea of variantology, a concept he proposes as a way of working against the hegemonic linearity that constructs artificial narratives of progress.[50] Zielinski's aim is to find a nonlinear layering of variations, which allows us to consider how an object is actually used, rather than simply seeing it as a necessary step on the journey toward ever-better platforms. Such a method doesn't just account for mods and hacks. It also addresses Nintendo's own practices. Indeed, there are arguably greater variations within the GBA line of handhelds (e.g., the 2001 model, the SP, and the Game Boy Micro) than there are among hobbyist interventions.

Zielinski's variantology is a branch of media archaeology, an amorphous set of methods and theories for studying media that challenges the veneration of newness. In a recent article in *Games and Culture*, Thomas Apperley and Jussi Parikka explore how media archaeology can enrich platform studies' possibilities by encouraging it to extend beyond hardware and software.[51] Although media archaeology's definition depends largely on the media archaeologist, Parikka notes that it is generally "interested in excavating the past in order to understand the present and the future."[52] Media archaeology understands that new media is often recursive in its development and dependent upon its broader infrastructure. Through physical and conceptual archives, it (like platform studies) sees culture as "sedimented and layered."[53] If the GBA has to be any particular thing, it would be a fractal—iterative, recursive, and infinite.

Within the constraints of this book, I've tried to provide an account of the GBA that is both comprehensive and precise, but I am cognizant that the study I provide is by no means exhaustive. The avenues of inquiry I have elected to address or omit speak as much to the GBA as a material and cultural object as they do to my own experience as both a scholar and a lifelong consumer of Nintendo products. If platforms are produced and circulated within a specific context, it follows that any study of the platform is also influenced by social and cultural factors. In constructing this book, I have—despite my best intentions—crafted my own GBA assemblage.

Overview of the Book

Who Are You? traces the various articulations that bring us from the dim-screened 2001 GBA to the sophisticated console mods of the late 2010s. Tempting though it may be to theorize a singular GBA that could represent the handheld's life as a corporate and cultural product, doing so threatens to ignore its actual and ongoing uses. Despite the emergence of platforms that exceed all the GBA's technical specifications, the device has persisted through various material and discursive afterlives. Nearly two decades after its release, the GBA has not only declined to disappear, but it has also generated communities that continue to hack, modify, emulate, make, break, remake, redesign, trade, use, love, and play with the platform—often in ways that Nintendo neither intended nor predicted.

While this book can't capture the GBA's entire global reach and range of uses over the last two decades, each chapter is organized around a key material or contextual component of the GBA network that, taken holistically, illuminates the way the platform operates as a computational system and a cultural artifact. These components include specific hardware objects, peripherals, and software iterations, as well as the practices of circulation, consumption, and transformation from which they issued. In terms of software, I've selected games that exemplify the platform's unique features or push against its material constraints. I tend to favor Nintendo's own games, especially those in the *Zelda* series, in part to illustrate the interwoven nature of the company's hardware and software development, but also because these games are useful for disclosing salient aspects of the platform. Whether the games are good or successful isn't important (although I'm fortunate in that most of them are engaging in their own right). What matters is that they're compelling objects of study due to the way they highlight the system's affordances or contribute to the nostalgic, almost cultish following that Nintendo generates in their consumers.

To that end, chapter 1, "Console-Quality Gaming, Anywhere," examines the 2001 GBA itself, tracing its design and computational architecture back in time through Nintendo's handheld and home console history. Physically and computationally, the device presents itself as a hybrid platform that mediates between the Game Boy and the SNES, gesturing to the ways that Nintendo fundamentally embeds nostalgia into their hardware. By examining the GBA's computational capacity, graphics and audio processing abilities, and ingrained technical protection measures (TPMs), I explore the affordances and constraints that the platform imposes on its users and developers. Throughout the chapter, I rely on two case studies: *Fire Emblem* and *Super Mario Advance*. The former is a series of narrative-heavy, tactical role-playing games (RPGs) well suited for considering the platform's graphical limitations; the latter is a series of bundled ports of NES and SNES titles that consolidate the Game Boy's portability with the SNES's processing power. Together, these case studies introduce the 2001 platform and, for better or worse, evince its reliance on existing technology and IP.

Chapter 2, "Expanding the Platform," uses the preceding technical analysis to argue that the GBA is more than the sum of the computational elements contained within the 2001 chassis. Instead, the platform exists within a complex network of backward- and forward-looking hardware and software objects. Nintendo's own advertising campaigns and financial reports bundle the GBA with the SP and the much less successful Game Boy Micro, inextricably linking the three, both temporally and economically. And the backward-compatible Nintendo DS, as well as the 3DS's Ambassador Program, continue Nintendo's legacy of interoperability and revival. Harnessing the affordance of the platform studies framework and drawing on Gilles Deleuze and Félix Guattari's assemblage theory, this chapter offers a technical analysis of the SP, Micro, DS, and 3DS Ambassador Program to argue that each of these devices gestures toward a lacuna in the 2001 GBA's aesthetics, performance, or accessibility. The range in technical specifications, cost, battery life, and retail availability speaks to the various embodied constraints that each new articulation addresses, as well as to the contexts from which they emerge.

Chapter 3, "Written in Plastic," studies the embodied experiences of physically and affectively engaging with the GBA. All videogames are embodied, operating through a symbiotic relationship of input and output between the body of the player and the body of the platform. During development, companies draw on cultural, technological, and industrial standards to conceive of idealized bodies that represent their platform's users, but these imagined users differ from the *actual* users, whose hands, eyes, ears, and minds inform their experiences of the platform's advantages and limitations. Eliding bodies—as studies of videogames often do—makes it difficult to account for the way that technology always exists in context. So this chapter is attentive to the relationship between hardware and hands, software and synapses, bodies and identities. Throughout this exploration, I zoom in on specific ways that the GBA invites us to think through the body with the aid of peripherals like the Game Boy Player (GBP) add-on for the GameCube and dynamic software titles that explicitly acknowledge how the body is always at play.

Chapter 4, "Let Me Show You My Pokemans," considers the GBA's temporal, social, and spatial circulation due to its portability. Beginning with a media archaeological excavation, I locate the GBA's position in a longer history of personal media devices. Although common-sense approaches to technology often bemoan portable videogames as the end of public culture and the beginning of a rapid descent into solipsism, the GBA participates in a form of "mobile privatization" that reaches all the way back to the adoption of the book.[54] At the same time as it serves to extend the private space, the GBA establishes patterns and precedents for new networked forms of play, aided by peripherals that invite social interaction. This chapter's second section spends time discussing these peripherals, as well as the consummate example of the GBA's social aspects: the *Pokémon* franchise. The chapter concludes with a survey of portable gaming as a contingent practice that blurs the lines between mobile and console, public and private, and boredom and play through an ethnographic approach to the spatial settings in which users interact with the handheld.

Chapter 5, "Platformizing Nostalgia," uses the GBA as a launchpad for viewing Nintendo's recent corporate decisions through the lens of platformization. Although videogames have been platform-dependent since their inception, the emergence of algorithmic logic and networked infrastructure has led to a transformation of the larger market architecture that shapes cultural production. This transformation is what various theoretical approaches, including business and software studies, refer to as "platformization." The consolidation of networked interactions into a single channel or platform by a corporate owner has significant implications with respect to the distribution of cultural and economic capital, and pointedly restricts users' agency as cultural producers. Although platformization is a relatively new concept, it's crucial for understanding the changing political economy of cultural industries. In considering the nostalgia that Nintendo manufactures through and for the GBA, I look at the role that sanctioned and unsanctioned emulation plays in preserving, circulating, and altering the platform's assemblage. Although Nintendo has historically been inclined toward litigiousness, the platformization of cultural production may push fan-generated content out of the murky legal area in which it has long been suspended.

Chapter 6, "Residual Afterlives," explores such fan-generated content by looking at the GBA's afterlives through homebrewing, hacking, and hardware modding. To this day, the GBA boasts lively hobbyist communities that continue to probe the platform's possibilities and overcome its limitations—often at the periphery of the legal system. Starting with an overview of homebrew game development, this chapter covers the punitive regulatory environment that amateur developers have managed to circumvent in order to create their own games or to hack official titles, observing how these labors are commodified by the very company that ferociously prosecutes them. I then take up an examination of the built-to-order GBA with which my introduction begins to explore the gendered underpinnings of the pursuit toward technical mastery. In the end, I argue that, despite their obvious differences, homebrewers, hackers, and modders participate in Nintendo's own design process of "lateral thinking through withered technology" by continuing to program for and reshape residual media for ongoing use.[55]

In its conclusion, "After Afterlives," the book examines the eventual fate to which all technology is consigned: e-waste. Planned obsolescence and the rapid pace of technological innovation mean that e-waste is becoming an ever-growing global problem. Salvaging consumer electronics reveals the usually invisible infrastructure of platform development—that is, the labor that users have the privilege not to think about. I examine how modder Joe Heaton's repurposing of defunct DS Lite handhelds into "Neon Advance" GBAs prolongs the platform's life cycle and resists technological obsolescence. Moments of failure and acts of repair make it impossible to ignore the platform's material residues or the labor that undergirds its development. They remind us that the platform doesn't magically appear on the shelves on an electronics store—that it still has a whole life after it breaks.

The Game Boy Advance (GBA) emerged in 2001 as the successor to Nintendo's twelve-year-old Game Boy line. In the late 1980s, the Kyoto-based entertainment company sought to harness the promising momentum of the Famicom to embed themselves into their players' pockets. Thanks to the profitability of interchangeable cartridges and the portability of their Game & Watch series, the Game Boy came to dominate the handheld gaming industry, selling an astounding 118.69 million units worldwide. Only one system has managed to outperform it since—the very handheld that would eclipse the GBA and sunset the entire Game Boy line: the Nintendo DS.[1]

Overshadowed on both sides, the GBA is neither Nintendo's most powerful handheld nor its most innovative. Rather, according to Peter Main, executive vice president of sales and marketing for Nintendo of America at the time of the handheld's release, the GBA "dramatically expands and carries on the legacy of Game Boy."[2] Thus, legacy is at the handheld's heart. Its creators took backward compatibility so seriously that it contains residues of the Game Boy's own hardware within its chassis, even while it commandeers the cultural capital of what was by then a household name. Yet its horizontal form factor also insists on a divergence from the Game Boy, both aesthetically and computationally. Its button arrangement and ergonomic bevel take their cues from the Nintendo Entertainment System (NES) and Super Nintendo Entertainment System (SNES) controllers, implying advancements in processing power and graphics rendering. What the GBA does best is vaunt itself as a hybrid of Nintendo hardware.

This hybridity articulates itself through an early slogan: "Console-Quality Gaming—Anywhere." Whispered at the end of television advertisements, this phrase positioned the GBA as a bridge between Nintendo's hugely successful handheld division and its waning home console counterpart. Unsurprisingly, this tagline has attracted scorn by some fans, who condemn the GBA as being *"just* a Super Nintendo" on community boards.[3] Such an attitude signals how lateral thinking is often perceived derisively by consumers yearning for a kind of innovation that Nintendo never promised. Instead, Nintendo's hardware—and the software developed for it—openly articulates its continuity with the past.

What's in a Name? The Game Boy Legacy

Prior to the release of the Game Boy in 1989, most handheld gaming platforms ran a game apiece. Milton Bradley's Microvision was an illustrious exception. The first handheld to use interchangeable cartridges, the Microvision had no onboard central processing unit (CPU), just controls, a liquid crystal display (LCD) panel, and a battery compartment. Processors instead came with each of the twelve games released between 1979 and 1982. Early cartridges used the Intel 8021, a low-cost alternative to the Intel 8048 designed for high-volume applications requiring limited storage. However, Intel had licensed Signetics to second-source the 8021, and Signetics imposed a limit on the amount of processors Milton Bradley could buy. Since each Microvision cartridge required its own CPU, Milton Bradley turned to the Texas Instruments TMS1100 processor, which they could not only acquire in the volume they needed, but which also offered lower power consumption. Alongside the processor, each cartridge came with 1 KB (Intel 8021) or 2 KB (TMS1100) of read-only memory (ROM) and 32 nibbles (16 bytes) of random-access memory (RAM). These slender specifications, coupled with a monochromatic 16-x-16-pixel display, restricted graphics to abstractions and thwarted genre variety.

Despite its shortcomings, the Microvision was instrumental to Nintendo's entrance into the fledgling portable videogame market. As mentioned in the introduction to this book, Gunpei Yokoi's design philosophy was and remains influential on both Nintendo's hardware and software divisions. But an equally important figure in the company's handheld history is Satoru Okada, who joined Nintendo in 1969 and eventually became general manager of Research & Engineering (R&E), the hardware spinoff of the company's Research and Development 1 (R&D1) division, formed after Yokoi departed to start his own company. Before his retirement in

2012, Okada had a hand in every Nintendo portable, beginning with the Game & Watch.

Okada loved the Microvision and would while away the hours playing its *Breakout* clone. But his familiarity with its hardwired limitations is what convinced him not to use the device as the model for the Game & Watch. The Microvision was too bulky for true portability, its graphics were crude, and the novelty of interchangeable cartridges was undercut by how similar each game was to the next. Okada and Yokoi figured, "Why not just have one game per machine, but with good graphics as least?"[4] So the Game & Watch appropriated the calculator screen and shelved the idea of swappable cartridges in favor of segmented displays and a battery life long enough to get a commuter from Tokyo to Kyoto—a six-hour journey at the time. Milton Bradley's name would come up again years later, when Nintendo tasked R&D1 with developing a portable platform to match the Famicom's success.

By his own admission, Okada was stubborn when he was young—and positively bullish when he had to defend his ideas to his superiors. In a 2017 interview, he reflects:

> The Game Boy you know today actually had nothing to do with the one Yokoi had in mind. He saw the Game Boy as a direct follow-on from the Game & Watch, which meant a cheap toy, without any real business model and no long-term ambition. To give you a clear comparison, Yokoi wanted a Game Boy that would have looked like the Microvision and would not have lasted more than one or two seasons.[5]

Okada was more ambitious. He wanted to achieve for handhelds what the Famicom had done for home consoles: introduce a lasting machine with a proper development kit that could sustain a wide range of quality software titles. After a series of heated arguments, Okada wrested responsibility from Yokoi, who purportedly gave in with a resigned, "Okay, do what you want!"[6] Okada succeeded in realizing his vision for a handheld gaming platform that married Nintendo's successful NES with their Game & Watch series. But that didn't mean eschewing Yokoi's approach to product design. None of the system's individual components was novel; the resulting product simply harnessed all their affordances in creative ways.

Far from being sleek, the Game Boy was housed in a blocky, plastic case ready to withstand encounters with the clumsy hands of children (figure 1.1). To emphasize corporate continuity, its shell recalled the light gray of the NES palette. Sharp, Nintendo's former hardware partner on the Game & Watch, returned as a collaborator (after the incisive President Hiroshi

Figure 1.1 Nintendo's 1989 Game Boy. Photo by Evan Amos, Wikimedia Commons.

Yamauchi had forbidden their partnership on the Famicom to avoid dividing the manufacturer's attention between their existing handhelds and the new entertainment system).[7] Sharp designed both the LCD from which the Game Boy receives its internal code (called DMG, for "dot-matrix game") and the CPU, the Sharp LR35902 processor, which they derived from a combination of the Intel 8080 chip and its software-compatible extension, the Zilog Z80—another instance of hardware hybridity drawing on withered technology.[8] A brand new processor would have been costly to manufacture and challenging to program for. So the LR35902 cherry-picked the more desirable aspects of both processors' architecture to handle the Game Boy's demands without need for extraneous instruction.

With a mere 8 KB of RAM and video random-access memory (VRAM) at its disposal and a 2-bit color palette consisting of four shades of olive-tinted gray—not to mention the lack of backlight, which would haunt Nintendo's handhelds for over a decade—the device's limitations were extensive.[9] Developers couldn't rely on impressive visuals to captivate their audience. Instead, much as with the Game & Watch, the experience revolved around engaging and addictive gameplay.

Much of the Game Boy's North American popularity can be credited to its software library, where one game stands out in particular: Nintendo's port of Soviet computer engineer Alexey Pajitnov's *Tetris*. In 1988, Nintendo of America president Minoru Arakawa was concerned with rebuilding the North American videogame industry after the crash that devastated Nintendo's overseas competitors. When he saw *Tetris* at an arcade industry trade show, he knew that it was their golden goose.[10] The conceit of the game is simple: players manipulate geometric shapes composed of four square blocks in various configurations as they fall from the top of a vertical shaft; once they make a horizontal line without any gaps, those blocks disappear and the ones above them descend into that space. The game ends when a stack of bricks reaches the top of the matrix. *Tetris* is portable, intuitive, and—importantly—not accompanied by lengthy textual passages that would be hard to reproduce on a small screen.

Spurning the recognizable and immersive worlds of Mario and Zelda for *Tetris* was therefore a savvy move. The abstracted gameplay was ideally suited to the low-resolution system. Fun regardless of the age or type of player, *Tetris* also had the convenient advantage of refuting critics' accusations that Nintendo's games were violent and devoid of educational value. Contemporary studies claimed that *Tetris* increased spatial awareness and improved driving skills. It gave the Game Boy everything it needed: broad appeal, an audience of all ages, and an opportunity to highlight the new platform's portability. Players could play *Tetris* on the couch, but it they could also enjoy the game in short bursts in transit. In North America and Europe, *Tetris* came bundled with the handheld, and David Sheff observes that "'*Tetris* sold millions of Game Boys," not the other way around.[11]

President Yamauchi boldly proclaimed that the Game Boy would sell 25 million units within its first three years; critics were skeptical.[12] But within weeks of reaching North American shores, the entire 1-million unit shipment was sold out, and sales barely slowed thereafter.[13] Technologically superior competitors emerged on the market, but the Game Boy continued to rake in the profits. This is the legacy the GBA looks back on.

The Lost Handheld of Atlantis

In 1996, rumors began to circulate about a supposed successor to the Game Boy.[14] Aptly codenamed Project Atlantis, the handheld never materialized, but reports told tall tales of a 32-bit handheld with a 160-MHz processor, a color LCD screen, and an astronomical 30 hours of battery life. In terms of processing power, this new handheld would have been roughly on par with the N64, with an energy efficiency that remains only theoretical today. At the 2009 Game Developers Conference (GDC), the Nintendo DSi's lead developer, Masato Kuwahara, showed an image of Project Atlantis's early prototypes, exposing it as a giant among handhelds. Standing at around 8 inches (20.3 centimeters) tall and 4 inches (10.2 centimeters) wide, it would have been larger than even the XL line of Nintendo 3DS. Contrary to popular belief, Project Atlantis was never the GBA's codename. The GBA was referred to internally as the admittedly much less exciting "AGB"— standing for "Advanced Game Boy." Atlantis was just a fantasy.

Everything about Project Atlantis was antithetical to Nintendo's central design philosophy. Shoring up the Game Boy's success was its use of outdated technologies to ensure that it sold at a fraction of the cost of its competitors. Even then, Okada cut back on many of its projected specifications to meet President Yamauchi's ceiling sale price of $100.[15] At launch, a Game Boy retailed for $89.95, while the Atari Lynx and Sega Game Gear sold for $179.99 and $149.99, respectively. And as a corollary to its modest computing system and lack of color display, the Game Boy boasted comparatively superior battery efficiency. Four AA batteries provided over 12 hours of gameplay, whereas the Lynx and Game Gear needed six AAs to get a mere 3 to 5 hours on their color screens. These exacting power requirements kept operating costs high and undercut the portability of Atari and Sega's handhelds. Nintendo understood that power wasn't all that mattered. Portability also meant not having to lug around a box of batteries. So Project Atlantis was everything the Game Boy wasn't. As the project was too large to be an effective portable, too power-hungry to sustain long stretches of gameplay, and too expensive to manufacture, its production was curtailed before it began.

There's another reason for Project Atlantis's quiet disappearance. The Game Boy experienced an unexpected second wind seven years into its life cycle, thanks to the advent of a strange little game inspired by Satoshi Tajiri's childhood fondness for insect collecting in rural Japan: *Pokémon*.[16] The cuteness of *Pokémon* complemented the cuteness of the Game Boy Pocket, a compact redesign released in 1996 that maintained the Game Boy's computational specifications. Both *Pokémon* and the Game Boy Pocket emerged as an appealing convergence of the portable, the personal, and the miniaturized. The game soon became a viral success, drawing developers back to a handheld whose popularity had begun to wane. Instead of pursuing a powerful successor to the Game Boy, Nintendo could stretch out their 8-bit generation.

Soon after *Pokémon* reached North American shores, the Game Boy Color (GBC) arrived, bringing a 16-bit color palette capable of showing 56 simultaneous colors. With four times the working RAM, twice the VRAM, and a clock frequency increased to 8 MHz, the GBC enabled more complex game engines and sophisticated mechanics. But even Okada admits this was little more than a stopgap to placate consumers until the Game Boy could advance.[17]

The Panda Prototype

A curious pattern materialized as I researched the GBA from my home in Montreal, Quebec—a province located in a bilingual country, but with French as its official language. English reviews of the GBA typically fore-grounded its technical articulations and software library; French reviews emphasized the product's industrial design. Were cultural attitudes toward technology the culprit? I wondered. Did the French—or at least French-speaking Canadians—have a greater interest in aesthetics than in performance?

It turned out that the discrepancy originates in the GBA's perceived national ties. On the English side, with the support of translated inter-views from Nintendo's hardware developers, the GBA is a Nintendo design brought into existence at the company's headquarters in Kyoto.[18] But French sources tell a different story. They credit the handheld's indus-trial design to Gwenael Nicolas, a designer born in France who won a trip to Japan in 1991 for his design of an airplane seat and decided to stay. Seven years later, he formed the multidisciplinary, Tokyo-based design studio, Curiosity, with producer Reiko Miyamoto.[19] The French Wikipe-dia page for the GBA (which seems to be the source of the increasingly fervent insistences that Nicolas delivered a foundering Nintendo from their inability to produce an evocative aesthetic) goes as far as to say that Nicolas proposed dozens of prototypes to Nintendo engineers, including a flower-shaped console and the so-called panda prototype that eventually was retained for the device's final form.[20] Clearly then, narratives sur-rounding the handheld's conception are steeped in marketing strategies on one side and national pride (in a "six degrees of separation" kind of way) on the other.

The GBA's two-year development process originated at Nintendo with the choice of CPU.[21] Because graphical output is contingent on processing power, settling on the computer's specifications indirectly determined a range of display resolutions, which imposed limitations on the size of the LCD. Nintendo already had intentions of creating a console-quality experience, thanks to the more powerful CPU, so they chose a wide-screen LCD with an aspect ratio that more closely resembled a television screen. Settling on a CPU, resolution, and screen size was as much a technical question as an economic one. Exceeding certain thresholds delivers diminishing returns, so Nintendo aimed for a balance between cost and size to keep prices competitive.

Most of the product's design took place in-house with a series of sketches and models that worked through the issue of how to fit all the components into the chassis (including a draft of a handheld with a lid like the Game & Watch devices, which was passed over due to size constraints, but it would return with the SP).[22] The trouble with the horizontal orientation that followed the lines of the screen was deciding what to do about the batteries. Relegating them to one side would unbalance the handheld, but putting them under the printed circuit board (PCB) made the system too bulky. Designers Kenichi Sugino and Masahiko Ota grappled with the battery problem for a while until they finally arrived at a solution: ask the PCB's engineers to cut out a space for the battery.[23] It worked wonderfully.

So the in-house hardware design team had already determined the handheld's basic shape before, in a move uncharacteristic of the insular Nintendo, they pried open the gate to their walled garden and invited firms to submit design ideas. Enter Nicolas. Nicolas was a stranger to the world of videogames and critical of Japan's emphasis on technological specifications, believing the electronics industry saw design as an extension of engineering rather than as a tactile experience. With the ability to play longer, more explorative games, the GBA needed something that players could hold comfortably. "My main contribution to the existing design," Nicolas says, "was a hint of softness."[24]

The horizontally oriented chassis has the classic Direction-pad (D-pad), Start, and Select buttons to the left of the screen and the A and B buttons to the right (figure 1.2). The Start and Select buttons are manufactured as a single piece of silicone with two conductive pads at the bottom, while the D-pad and A and B buttons are made of plastic and fit over their own conductive silicone pads to interface with the PCB. In response to software developers' requests for additional inputs, Nintendo added left and right shoulder triggers, enabling new features, additional menus, and more involved mechanics. In backward compatibility mode, the shoulder triggers stretch the 1.11:1 aspect ratio of Game Boy and GBC games to fit the GBA's 3:2, distorting the image but making full use of the screen. Above the A and B buttons is a small light-emitting diode (LED) labeled POWER that glows green when the handheld is on and turns red when the battery

Figure 1.2 The 2001 GBA.

is running low. Four diagonal indentations for the speaker take up the bottom-left corner of the plastic landscape.

The power switch at the bottom left, as well as the stereo headphone jack and analog volume dial at the bottom right, are consistent with those of the Game Boy. At the top of the handheld is a small port labeled EXT, which supports a range of connective peripherals (discussed in more detail in chapter 4). Small grooves in the plastic on either side of the port between the L and R triggers serve as grips to safeguard these peripherals' position during play. Behind the extension port is the 32-pin cartridge slot, which has the same length and width as that of the Game Boy and GBC, but half its depth. The more diminutive GBA cartridges—themselves a crucial component of the GBA platform—sit flush with the top of the handheld, while older Game Paks and those with additional hardware protrude over the edge without impeding players' ability to hold the device. With no game inserted, the slot exposes the cartridge edge connector, allowing a peek at the handheld's inner workings (the backward-compatible DS would later arrive with a removable plastic insert for the GBA slot to protect the connectors when no GBA game was in place). On the back of the device, an unobtrusive, removable door hides the batteries, as well as a cutout framing the mainboard revision number. Early boards beginning with 0 (e.g., 03 3–1) have a 40-pin screen connector, while those beginning with 1 (e.g., 10 1–2) have a 32-pin connector to match the SP—a distinction of great importance for hobbyists seeking to replace their screen with a backlit one. Also on the back of the handheld are three stickers: the barcode and serial number; the model number, manufacturing location (China), and Federal Communications Commission (FCC) disclaimer; and a warning to read the system manual before use.

In addition to the handheld's gentler shape, Nicolas proposed a color scheme: a white body with gray, green, or blue accents for the D-pad, the A, B, Start, and Select buttons, and curved lines leading to and including the L and R buttons. He wanted the aesthetic simplicity of the device to let games speak for themselves. Subtle accents would instruct players on how to hold the object without overpowering the software the way that the GBC, with its stark black buttons, did. Nintendo was initially resistant to this idea.[25] At Space World and in a subscriber bonus edition of *Nintendo Power*, they unveiled the handheld with a silver body accompanied by orange and electric blue accents.[26] But the white body with purple-tinted gray accents nevertheless made it back as one of six launch colors under the label "arctic." The launch lineup also included black, orange, fuchsia, glacier (a semitranslucent, low-saturation blue), and indigo, which became the default in advertisements by virtue of its pairing with the preferred indigo Nintendo GameCube.

By accident or by design (or likely a bit of both), the topography of the GBA pronounces its similarities to the SNES. Nicolas might have been able to distinguish the GBA from its blocky contemporaries like the Neo Geo Pocket, but Nintendo's own industrial design history remained inescapable. The curved lines that add a hint of softness are also found in the SNES controller's dog-bone shape, which equally purported to deliver an ergonomic form that naturally encouraged players to handle the two new additions to the interface properly. Incidentally, the "arctic" color scheme isn't too far from the SNES's light-gray-and-purple palette.

The handheld's packaging foregrounds the console, which is angled slightly so that it appears to pop out from the white background. Just as with the boxes for the Game Boy and the GBC, the leftmost side is taken up by the Game Boy name in large purple lettering above a strip printed to look like brushed silver. However, now the word "Advance" stretches out along the bottom of the image. The GBA's selling points are broadcast by three phrases that float over the image of the console: "32 bit" to signal its improvement in processing power over its handheld predecessors; "wide color screen" to allude to its ability to run ports of home console games; and "plays all games" to remind us that the GBA can tap into a decade-old library of games.[27]

Technical Articulations

The GBA is a send-off to Nintendo's dedicated videogame platforms. Here, "dedicated" refers to hardware's range of intended functions. Although there is a variety of peripherals to push the GBA beyond its uses, it was designed to play videogames. Turned on, it boots directly into the contents of the inserted cartridge rather than a home menu interface.

Today, dedicated platforms are increasingly rare. When mobile phones first emerged, they were dedicated to making phone calls. Now, the capacity for calling is an addendum to the ability to send text messages, play games, read the news, check the weather, and even pay for goods. Similarly, Nintendo's platforms are no longer functionally restricted to gaming. Ever since the emergence of the DS, players have been greeted with an interface of menu options through which they can access the internet, check calendars, and even set an alarm (a nice nod to Game & Watch). The GBA is also one of the few platforms that Nintendo produced that has no regional lockout.

The GBA was portable for its time, weighing approximately 5 ounces (140 grams), or 7 ounces (200 grams) with two AA batteries. Its shell is made of acrylonitrile butadiene styrene (ABS), the same thermoplastic polymer as the Game Boy and GBC, and it measures 5.7 x 3.2 x 1 inches (14.45 x 8.2 x 2.45 centimeters), while the thin-film transistor liquid crystal display (TFT LCD) spans 2.9 inches (7.4 centimeters) diagonally. At 15 hours of gameplay, the GBA's battery life is decent, though with the SP, a rechargeable lithium ion battery would soon replace the two AAs.

The GBA's primary CPU is a 32-bit ARM7TDMI clocked at 16.78 MHz, a member of the ARM family of microprocessors that emphasize high performance with low power consumption.[28] Its architecture is based on the principles of a Reduced Instruction Set Computer (RISC), which is one of two primary approaches to Instruction Set Architecture (ISA). In broad terms, ISA is the set of basic instructions that allow a human programmer to communicate with a processor. RISC instructions and decode mechanisms are more streamlined than those of the Complex Instruction Set Computer (CISC) used in the Game Boy. Given that each instruction type requires dedicated circuitry and transistors, a RISC system can be smaller and more cost-effective than a system with a larger set of computational instructions. The shift from CISC to RISC was well suited to Nintendo's handhelds, which had little need for all the address modes of CISC architecture.

RISC ISA privileges more efficient software—that is, compiled languages and code. It needs more RAM but executes one instruction per clock cycle, allowing clock rates to increase.[29] In addition to predictable processing, another advantage to moving to ARM's RISC processor is the ability to write more of the code in C instead of the more hardware-specific assembly language.[30] Faster processing also facilitates more sprites per screen and smarter, more responsive enemies.[31]

The GBA's ARM core can run in and switch between two modes: the default 32-bit "ARM mode" and a 16-bit subset known as "THUMB mode."[32] With 256 KB of 16-bit-wide external RAM, THUMB code offers faster processing with approximately half the performance by using half-word instructions.[33] The CPU also contains 32 KB of 32-bit-wide internal working RAM. Being embedded in the CPU makes this the fastest memory section, so time-critical ARM instructions often run from this memory area.[34] Game cartridges, without which the platform is incomplete, consist of a maximum of 32 MB of 16-bit mask ROM or flash memory for code and a maximum of 64 KB of 8-bit RAM, which can take the form of static random-access memory (SRAM), flash memory, or electrically erasable programmable read-only memory (EEPROM), all of which serve the common purpose of saving game data.[35]

Striking a balance between console-quality processing power and handheld pricing was essential. Adding pins to the CPU could increase the system's capabilities, but the components needed to remain competitively priced. Moreover, even though more advanced technologies circulated in mobile phones and personal digital assistants (PDAs), components needed to be produced in quantities that met Nintendo's manufacturing demands. Components produced in the hundreds of thousands wouldn't suffice when the handhelds were selling on the order of millions. Nintendo's choice of CPU, therefore, coincides with what could be manufactured at the volume they needed for a price they could afford.[36]

Originally, Nintendo's team wanted the GBA to have a 1-chip design for technological and economic reasons. Early prototypes were based around a single integrated circuit (IC). But when software developers in Japan and overseas tested it, they noted that there wasn't enough memory to account for the upgraded graphics. After that, it took over a year—half the development cycle—to decide on the CPU, during which time Ryuji Umezu (Digital Hardware Planning) and Takanobu Nakashima (System Programming) tweaked the circuit board to account for the demands of various internal parties, each with a vested interest in the product's technical specifications.[37] Settling on a design with two ICs and more memory slowed the production schedule and caused the price to rise above initial estimates. But these trade-offs were necessary to ensure the software's success.

As previously noted, backward compatibility with the Game Boy and GBC was one of the GBA's most salient features. Okada has explained that the decision to maintain interoperability was a given, calling it "one of the duties of developers."[38] The GBA's patent explicitly articulates the company's rationale:

> Because users may have already invested time and money into existing game systems, it is also very desirable to maintain compatibility with existing game cartridges. Thus, users upgrading to the new and more powerful game systems can continue to use game cartridges that have been purchased with prior generations of game systems. In addition, these users can play new games that take advantage of the improved capabilities of the game system.[39]

Okada understood the economic advantages of brand loyalty, so the GBA appeals to consumers' desire to feel like Nintendo is investing in them. Down the line, Nintendo's handhelds cease to accept Game Boy cartridges. But, in 2001, owners of Game Boy software could see Nintendo as a company that valued their time and money.

Materially, the ability to play earlier software is enabled by the GBA's inclusion of the LR35902.[40] Here is Yokoi's "lateral thinking through withered technology" put into practice.[41] By repurposing the 8-bit microprocessor, the Game Boy literally and metaphorically lives on in the GBA.

The absorption of a second processor also means that the handheld requires the ability to discern the cartridge type. Included in the GBA's basic input/output system (BIOS) is code used to identify the Game Pak by reading bit 15 of REG_WAITCNT 4000204h.[42] But this software detection code is dormant, never operational, likely because of voltage discrepancies between the GBA and its predecessors. Instead, Nintendo opted to use a material detection mechanism. On the lower-right corner of the cartridge slot, near the pin connector, is a soft, springy switch. Because GBA cartridges are notched on both sides of the pins, inserting the cartridge doesn't affect the switch; it remains in the neutral position that it stays in when no card is in the system. But Game Boy and GBC cartridges don't have these notches, so they depress the switch when inserted into the slot. When the system is turned on, it supplies the GBA's default 3.3 volts if the notched GBA cartridge didn't depress the switch, and the earlier systems' 5 volts if it did.[43] It's at that point that the CPU core activates to read the identification code stored in the memory of the cartridge. If the register value matches a GBA game, it boots the multiplex bus interface to access the cartridge's ROM and start the game. If the register value belongs to the Game Boy or GBC, it galvanizes the switching circuit, which halts the GBA CPU and activates the GBC core, which accesses the ROM through the general-purpose bus interface and starts the game.[44]

Although users can visually identify cartridges based on size, color, and shape, the system performs this check through cooperation between material switches and computational operations. Human users may feel as though they understand the recognition process through their ability to differentiate between the aesthetic and symbolic content of the various Game Paks, but internally, the system is wrangling voltage and data in a multistep process invisible to the human user. Even the catalytic act of pushing the switch is obfuscated by the plastic cartridge container that blocks the user's eyes from seeing the step occur.[45]

This discrepancy between what we see and what the machine understands is what media archaeologist Wolfgang Ernst gestures to when he sees technology itself as an archaeologist of computational processes.[46] His brand of media archaeology calls for "an epistemologically alternative approach to the supremacy of media-historical narratives," one that resists the human desire to narrativize.[47] Such an operation, he argues, can be accomplished only through machines. Not only does Ernst not require a human subject, he also suggests that the human desire to narrativize data limits our ability to perform a media-archaeological analysis altogether; by suspending subject-centered hermeneutics, Ernst considers computers' own analytic operations, such as data processing, signal transmission, and digital recording. The machine is both agent and archive, storing, processing, and retrieving data beyond human comprehension. Human perception filters understanding through cultural knowledge. What the GBA's patent exposes is that the process of identifying Game Boy games from GBA cartridges operates at one remove from the human users' sense of it. We see the difference clearly in terms of size, but the machine recognizes it through mechanisms concealed beneath the plastic.

In addition to the aesthetic continuity between cartridge and console facilitated by the GBA Game Pak's smaller size, this design has the secondary function of protecting the cartridge from being overcharged through insertion into the Game Boy. (Because the GBA cartridges are designed for an information-processing device driven by 3.3 volts rather than 5 volts, inserting it into the Game Boy could corrupt its memory.)[48] The shape of the cartridge, therefore, is not simply aesthetic, but rather a corollary to standards for Nintendo's electronic devices. They're designed not to be pushed into earlier handhelds.

When Nintendo manufactured the Game Boy Micro and the DS—the third face of the GBA and its successor, respectively—their engineers removed the detection switch. Consequently, neither system can play Game Boy or GBC games. But echoes of the 8-bit Game Boy remain through the GBA's legacy sound capabilities. This is worth repeating: even handhelds that don't support compatibility with the Game Boy carry support (material or emulated) for its chippy audio channels. The fact that the aural residues of hardware from the late 1980s persist well into the DS line attests to the company's reliance on lateral thinking.

In terms of audio, the GBA's sound controller is mostly consistent with that of its predecessors. It boasts six sound channels: four that were inherited from the Game Boy and two new Pulse Width Modulators (PWMs) that act as digital-to-analog converters (DACs) labeled Direct Sound A and B (not to be confused with Microsoft's DirectSound software). Channels 1 and 2 are square wave generators, commonly used for melody and chords.[49] Channel 3 is a programmable sample player often appropriated for bass lines (and the only one to experience a substantial revision from the Game Boy, in that its wave RAM is not banked for distortion-free reloading).[50] Channel 4 is a white noise generator usually used for percussion.[51] Powerful though the GBA's ARM microprocessor might be, it's not fast enough to perform real-time MP3 playback while also processing game mechanics and graphics, so samples need to be compressed. The resulting noise from the bit loss is somewhat mitigated by capacitors, the mono speaker, and human hearing, thereby masking the fact that the system doesn't use a proper DAC for all but the most well-attuned ears.[52] The BIOS also introduces functions to convert musical instrument digital interface (MIDI) to GBA data.[53]

As Karen Collins observes in *Game Sound*, Nintendo's press release for the console neglected to divulge much information on its audio upgrades.[54] Their reticence to vaunt the GBA's sound quality may be due to its failure to live up to the SNES's audio subsystem, the S-SMP designed and produced by Sony. Boasting its own self-contained coprocessor and 64 KB of SRAM, the subsystem offloaded pressure from the SNES's CPU to produce impressive 8-channel stereo soundscapes using lengthy audio samples. Composers enjoyed the rare ability to create orchestral-style soundtracks that are still well received by fans and critics alike.[55] But Sony, on the verge of developing the PlayStation Portable (PSP), hardly wanted to enhance their competition's audio capabilities. Nintendo had to develop their own markedly inferior system, one more proximate to the five-channel NES than the more robust SNES.

The GBA was at a disadvantage even before we consider the lackluster output through a single mono speaker, which hardly compares to what televisions can produce. While the scratchy static can be mitigated if the user opts to listen through headphones, the fact that audio is mixed by software results in a variable sound quality that depends largely on how much of the CPU's processing power was allotted to audio rather than to graphics and game mechanics.

GBA Graphics and *Fire Emblem*

Although the GBA's audio fails to live up to the promise of console-quality gaming, its graphics capabilities are far more sophisticated. The 240-x-160-pixel LCD has a refresh rate of 59.73 Hz, which means the entire GBA screen is updated with new data approximately every sixtieth of a second (even if the visual content of the frame remains identical).[56] It's capable of displaying 15-bit RGB colors (5 bits for red, 5 for green, and 5 for blue), with color support for 2 palettes consisting of 256 colors in character mode and 32,768 simultaneous colors in bitmap mode.[57] When the handheld was first announced, its initial specs promised 60,000 simultaneous colors, but this amount was halved late in the development process to optimize performance. While the team was apprehensive about changing announced numbers, they deemed it more important to maintain quality than bind themselves to marketing promises. In backward compatibility mode, Game Boy games use one of twelve built-in color palettes, each including seven to ten colors selectable from the system start-up screen through predetermined button combinations. The gray-scale palette (Left + B) most closely approximates the original Game Boy aesthetic.[58]

Early in the project's development, members of the hardware team considered creating a portable that used polygons like the N64, but they were constrained by a ceiling price of 10,000 yen ($89) from Yamauchi. This upper limit prevented them from including all the memory that three-dimensional (3D) graphics required—not to mention that 3D games would have compromised the platform's substantial battery life. The GBA has about a tenth of the memory and processing power of the N64. That isn't to say that *all* games developed for the GBA were restricted to two dimensions (2D); some squeezed out every bit of the handheld's memory and processing power to simulate 3D by using enough frames to make movement look realistic. But most games stuck to lively 2D landscapes invigorated by a robust color palette and impressive layering effects.

Of course, there are reasons other than hardware limitations to stick with 2D, namely, the demand 3D graphics make on programmers. Game Boy and SNES programmers were stronger in 2D by virtue of decades of experience. They could navigate GBA programming more easily than its unfamiliar GameCube counterpart. Also, 3D software development requires larger teams and more specialized knowledge. Consider how the GBA's *Fire Emblem: The Sacred Stones* credits 81 people on staff between development and North American localization (quite a high number for a GBA game) compared to the GameCube's *Fire Emblem: Path of Radiance*'s 164 the following year. If you have only half the staff, 2D games are demonstrably cheaper to produce.

I take the *Fire Emblem* series of fantasy tactical role-playing games (RPGs) as a useful case study for thinking about the affordances and constraints of GBA graphics. Made by the second-party developers Intelligent Systems, the games experienced something of a golden age during the GBA's life cycle. From 2002–2005, Intelligent Systems released a game each year: three on the GBA and the last on the GameCube. As a result of this compressed development cycle, the series is ideally positioned to highlight the GBA's salient graphics limitations through comparisons among installments.

First developed and published for the Famicom, the series now numbers sixteen main installments and three spin-offs, including a trading card game and a profitable international mobile app centered around character collection. The main games in the series combine the strategic elements of tactical simulation gameplay with all the intricate narrative and character development of an RPG. Although the *Fire Emblem* games largely take place across unrelated, feudal settings, their stories are universally concerned with ideological conflicts over territory, often with ancient spells, mythical dragons, and quarreling gods thrown into the mix. Turn-based, chaptered battles play out on gridded maps as the player—often taking on the role of tactician within the story—directs each of the heroes against an enemy army controlled by artificial intelligence (AI) in an elaborate form of chess. Each unit has a class that affects how far it can move and which weapons it can use, and all these factors are deeply indebted to the tropes and iconography of medieval fantasy RPGs. The games' challenge lies not in quick reflexes—players can take as much time as they need to decide each maneuver because no decision is time-critical—but rather in skillful deployment of soldiers and effective use of resources. The goal of each map is to defeat the enemy army or commander, while ensuring that the playable characters survive the AI's turn. The most notable (and notorious) feature of the first dozen *Fire Emblem* games is its permanent death (or "permadeath") mechanic, whereby characters slain in battle no longer appear in narrative sequences, adding a tangible cost to warfare. The series is widely touted as being a virtuosic example of its genre.

The early 2000s marked an important time in the series' development, not only due to the sheer number of games released at the time, but also because it occasioned the series' localization for a global audience after *Fire Emblem* protagonists Marth and Roy made their debut outside Japan in the popular fighting game *Super Smash Bros. Melee*. Although the 2002 *Fire Emblem: Fūin no Tsurugi (The Binding Blade)* remained formally exclusive to Japan (but as we'll see in chapter 6, many fans around the world have played it, thanks to the efforts of hackers who have extracted the game image from the cartridge and translated its text), all subsequent releases save for a 2010 remake were localized for international audiences. Localization began with the 2003 *Fire Emblem: Rekka no Ken (The Blazing Sword)*—known as *Fire Emblem* outside Japan and henceforth referred to as *FE7* to avoid confusion—and the 2004 *Fire Emblem: The Sacred Stones* and 2005 *Fire Emblem: Path of Radiance* followed in kind. Placed side by side with the GameCube title, the GBA *Fire Emblem* games' graphics point to the computational concessions necessary for the body of the platform to achieve portability, highlighting the operative chains embedded in the platform's hardware.

GBA graphics fall into two broad categories: backgrounds and objects. Backgrounds, in turn, can be subdivided into two types: bitmap and character. Because these background modes affect the way that a screen is rendered, bitmap and character modes can't be active simultaneously. A bitmap is a width-by-height matrix of colors built up in VRAM, which means that, in bitmap modes (video modes 3–5), there's a one-to-one relationship between memory content and each pixel that displays on the screen. Modes 3 and 5 have access to the full 32,768 colors, while mode 4 can display only 256 at a time—a compromise in color reproduction in exchange for a second buffer for more seamless animations and a greater ability to manipulate palettes. Although bitmap modes offer greater freedom for creative illustrations, most games use them sparingly, and only for static images, in part because they don't support hardware scrolling (short of making a bitmap some thousands of pixels wide) and because building an entire screen pixel by pixel exceeds what the system can accomplish in a single frame. Even with immaculate code and primitive backgrounds, rendering all graphics through software is a sluggish process. It can be done, of course, but the ray-casted first-person shooter *Doom* stands more as an exception that proves the rule, rather than an indication of the popularity of bitmap modes.

Instead, most games use the GBA's character modes 0 through 2. These are programmed remarkably close to the hardware, which takes care of rendering the raster, color-keying to make some pixels transparent, and affine transformation effects like rotation and scaling. Character mode composes backgrounds by way of 8-x-8-pixel bitmap matrices known as "tiles," which support a single palette of 256 colors or 16 subpalettes of 16 colors, and are stored in the 96 KB of built-in VRAM. A tile-map, also stored in VRAM, instructs the hardware on how to build an image from these preassigned matrices. There can be up to four background layers labeled BG0–BG3 (all four in mode 0, three in mode 1, and two in mode 2) that can be superimposed to generate illusory transparency effects and realistic lighting.[59] The size of these maps is set by the control registers and can range from 128 x 128 to 1024 x 1024 pixels. Because tiles are always 8 x 8 pixels, map sizes range from 16 x 16 to 128 x 128 tiles, respectively. Mathematically inclined readers will have realized that the minimum map size doesn't fill the GBA's 240-x-160-pixel screen and the maximum size far exceeds it. This is to enable layering effects and hardware scrolling. A smaller map might be used for a user interface with a life bar and mission objectives at the top of the screen, while a larger map allows a game level to extend beyond the bounds of the screen. When a player moves to a scrolling edge, the screen "moves over" the map, revealing the tiles written beyond what players can see at a given moment. There are two key benefits of tile-maps: size and speed. So long as graphics are aligned to the tile boundaries (rather than requiring incrementally altered tiles to fit together seamlessly), the tile-set will be fairly small and therefore will eat up much fewer of the precious kilobytes of VRAM than a corresponding bitmap (figure 1.3). And because graphics and scrolling are both implemented in hardware, the rendering occurs much more quickly. If we look at a bounded 240-x-160-pixel screen, character mode only requires updating a 30 x 20 grid of preexisting tiles instead of scrambling to place 38,400 pixels into a single frame.

Complementing the backgrounds are objects, more commonly known as "sprites," that are small, mobile, tile-based graphics that range in size from 8 x 8 to 64 x 64 pixels. Characters and enemies are the most common types of sprites, but other examples include cursors and status objects like health bars. Up to 128 sprites in 16 or 256 colors can be rendered each frame and can move independent of each other. Through the affine transformation matrix, sprites (and some backgrounds) can be rotated, scaled, and sheared.[60] Like tile-based backgrounds, sprites are drawn by the GBA's hardware.

To illustrate these technical specifications, let us look at a scene from *FE7* (figure 1.4). Like the other two GBA installments, *FE7*'s battles play out on square grids that make the system's graphics composition immediately visible. The screen reveals a 15-x-10-square grid of playable spaces—that

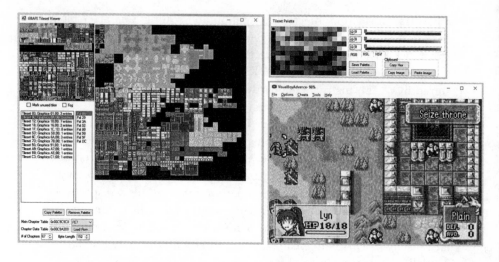

Figure 1.3 The contents of one of *FE7*'s twelve tile-sets (left) displayed through the tile-set and palette editor GBAFE Tileset Viewer. This combination of tile-set and color palette 0B (top right) is used in chapter 2 of *FE7* (bottom right). Emulated on Visual Boy Advance.

is, of positions that can be occupied by an allied or enemy unit—each composed of four 8-x-8-pixel graphics tiles, many of which repeat throughout the map. These tiles make up BG3. Layered above those tiles are the menus and semitransparent window backgrounds on BG1. Written objectives, numerical data, and miniature character portraits are in turn above those on BG0 (BG2 is empty). Enemy and allied units, as well as the cursor, are all sprites in the object layer, and they move independent of the background. Here, the sprites are above BG3, but below the content of BG1 and BG0. This means that the user interface (UI) elements will cover enemy actors but, by virtue of the windows' transparency, still allow the player to make out the shape of the sprites below. The ability to interpose sprites between background layers offered developers new ways to experiment with depth and perspective. Finally, the games use bitmaps sparingly for static, illustrated dialogue scenes that can afford to refresh more slowly.

While the GBA exceeds the processing abilities of the SNES, it's worth acknowledging that the home console was already more than a decade old at the handheld's release. In terms of clock time, the GBA is much more proximate to the GameCube, which entered the market merely five months after the GBA with an IBM PowerPC Gekko CPU at 486 MHz.[61] The GameCube's more robust processor and refined rendering capabilities enabled

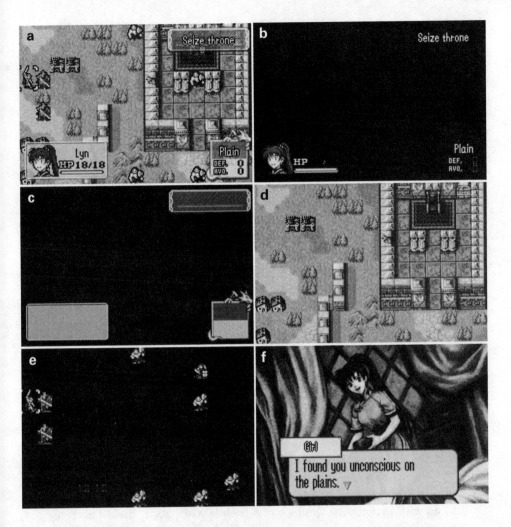

Figure 1.4 *FE7* builds its screen using three background layers and one sprite layer. Panel (a) shows the composite image, panel (b) shows BG0, panel (c) shows BG1, panel (d) shows BG3, and panel (e) displays the object layer. Panel (f) is a still frame composed in bitmap mode that is used in a dialogue scene. Emulated on Visual Boy Advance.

the 3D battlefields and full-motion video cutscenes of *Fire Emblem: Path of Radiance* that had been unthinkable on the GBA.

With only six months between the Japanese release of *Sacred Stones* on the GBA and *Path of Radiance* on the GameCube, the limitations of the former system are placed in stark relief along the lines of map design, character portraits, and voice acting. For instance, in all games in the series, characters have portraits that appear in menus and during conversations between chapters. *Path of Radiance* preserves most of the detail in these portraits when the character icon is displayed on the level map, thanks to the greater image resolution. In titles for the GBA, however, the intricacy of each portrait exceeds what can be reproduced on such a small scale within a map. The developers therefore had to design secondary, simplified portraits for use within the constraints of a level (like those from *FE7* displayed in the top left of figure 1.4). These innocuous pixelated faces point to the broader concessions necessary for the body of the platform to achieve portability at the time.

None of this is to say the GBA's graphics are objectively inferior to those of the GameCube. In fact, players have and continue to aestheticize GBA *Fire Emblem*'s graphics style in homebrew games, cross-stitch crafts, and pixel art. These practices arise not only out of media that lend themselves to rasterlike designs (e.g., aida cloth is a woven fabric that produces a gridlike canvas on which to cross-stitch), but also out of a nostalgic attachment to the hardware for which the series first entered North America. The popularity of GBA-style sprite art in fan circles attests to a lingering attraction to the system's aesthetics despite the emergence of consoles that support more realistic designs.[62]

The primary aspect of the handheld's visuals that was widely regarded as inferior had nothing to do with computational capacity and everything to do with materiality: the lack of a backlight. In 2001, backlit screens weren't as ubiquitous as they are today, but other electronics companies had already released backlit portables and proved that the technology wasn't out of reach, such as Atari with their Lynx and Sega with their Game Gear. While some consumers grudgingly forgave the lack of illumination, most would have happily traded battery efficiency for the ability to play games without a direct light source.

Nintendo anticipated backlash from their decision not to include a backlight. Promotional materials tried to frame the dim screen positively, spinning it as appealing to their consumers' desire for an affordable product. A GBA-themed issue of *Nintendo Power* justified the decision by saying: "A backlit LCD screen would be more expensive, drain your batteries much faster, and have a much smaller viewing angle."[63] The logic of cost and efficiency make sense, but the third point is an acrobatic stretch. Sure, players can tilt and otherwise move the GBA without compromising image quality. But there's no smaller viewing angle than not being able to play at all once the sun has set if there's no lamp at hand. The lack of a backlight gave rise to a cottage industry of unofficial lighting systems and catalyzed both the GBA's hardware remodels (see chapter 2) and the protocols of the hardware modding community (see chapter 6).

All Our IPs Are Belong to Us

Nintendo has a history of protecting their intellectual property (IP), trademarks, and patents through refined technical protection measures (TPMs). For decades, the company has embedded their policy decisions in their hardware and software to produce a punitive regulatory environment that discourages unlicensed development and use. The GBA is not exempt; Nintendo used discursive, legal, and explicitly technological tactics to control engagement with the platform.

The GBA is a closed system. In simple terms, this means that Nintendo doesn't publicly provide instructions on how to develop software for the platform. The result is that all access to the system—developing, marketing, selling, playing, repairing, and so on—is designed to be funneled through the company. While the open architecture of the personal computer (PC) allows individuals to program for the system, Nintendo limits who can create software for their platforms, often under the pretext of quality control. By sharing their system information only with select third parties, Nintendo prevents unlicensed developers from making games for profit. And because every game requires Nintendo's seal of approval, they can impose strict regulations on the use of their system and demand steep licensing fees to boot. The result is what Kline, Dyer-Witheford, and de Peuter refer to as "the enclosure of cultures of play by the imperatives of the mediatized marketplace."[64] We would be foolish to forget the way that closed systems are bound up with considerations of brand integrity, IP, and commercial profits.

One of the ways that Nintendo explicitly restricts access to GBA software development is through a two-part check-in system involving both the handheld and the game cartridge. The GBA's BIOS contains an image of Nintendo's logo. As a precondition for booting, the system searches for an equivalent image in the header section of the game's ROM.[65] In computing, the header is a standard, descriptive data section, as opposed to the executable code that runs the game. The first 192 bytes of standard GBA cartridges compose the header, 36 of which are dedicated to informational details: ROM entry points, game titles, developer names, software versions, and so on. A compressed bitmap of the Nintendo logo takes up the remaining 156 bytes. Given the descriptive nature of header data, a Nintendo logo is more or less extraneous; for far fewer bytes, text could provide the same information. What the image does is restrict development and prevent unlicensed copying. If the bytes in the header align with the bytes of the image stored in the BIOS, the Nintendo logo appears on the screen alongside the launch chime. But if the logo is absent, replaced, or otherwise modified, the machine flags the ROM as inauthentic and locks the system.[66]

This TPM is digital in nature, but it finds its precursor in the NES's material Checking Integrated Circuit (CIC), a custom lockout chip found in each console and Game Pak. The CIC impeded unauthorized access to software through what Nathan Altice refers to as a "special handshake algorithm," in which the console chip acted as a lock and the Game Pak chip the key. Unless both worked together, the NES entered an endless loop of system resets as it searched for missing input.[67] Players might not have even know why their game failed because the console gave no error message or explanation for the cycle of resets and failures. But developers certainly felt the sting of Nintendo's digital rights management (DRM) techniques.

The catastrophic U.S. videogame crash of 1983 had made Nintendo cautious. They had witnessed firsthand what a permissive attitude toward licensing had done to their competitors and were adamant that they'd avoid the same fate. Determined to maintain a viselike grip over their IP and the conditions of their platforms, Nintendo introduced legal impediments and hardware hurdles to prevent external parties from saturating the market with low-quality software. In light of the CIC, third parties had to sign unyielding license agreements to which they had to adhere that included exclusivity clauses preventing their games from being released on other systems. Nintendo insisted on a hefty proportion of the royalties, as well as a cash advance to guarantee production. They'd be the sole manufacturers, and they wouldn't produce anything less than 10,000 cartridges. Nintendo profited regardless of whether the game sold; developers suffered alone when they didn't.[68]

By the time the GBA entered the market, Nintendo had loosened their licensing agreements (after Atari sued them in 1988 for antitrust behavior).[69] But nevertheless, the GBA's TPMs are nothing if not thorough. Nintendo could have used any lock-and-key combination to restrict access to their proprietary system, but they chose their logo. This decision was savvy because it conflated patent, trademark, and copyright infringement for a refined system with few legal loopholes. Unless developers were willing to infringe on Nintendo's trademark by including it in their ROM header, they still need the company's blessing. ¹

Sega had attempted a similar technique in 1988 for the Genesis, but they lacked Nintendo's forethought in using trademarked content. Instead, they encoded their name in the header—a simple string of four characters. Unfortunately for Sega, four letters aren't legally subject to copyright in the same way that a trademarked logo is, a detail that came to haunt them when they filed suit against the American videogame developer and publisher Accolade on charges of trademark and copyright infringement in 1991.⁷⁰ Accolade had successfully reverse engineered the Genesis software to publish unlicensed games for the console, bypassing Sega's strict licensing agreement. When players launched Accolade's games, they saw the TradeMark Security System (TMSS) screen with a message that the game was: "Produced By or Under License from Sega Enterprises Ltd."⁷¹

Of course, Accolade's games were *not* produced by or under license from Sega, who consequently sued on two accounts. The first was trademark infringement and unfair competition; the second was copyright infringement. The United States District Court for the Northern District of California ruled in Sega's favor, but Accolade appealed to the Ninth Circuit, arguing that disassembly was a matter of fair use. Convinced, the Ninth Circuit reversed the previous court's ruling: "We hold that when there is no other method of access to the computer that is known or readily available to rival cartridge manufacturers, the use of the initialization code by a rival does not violate the Act even though that use triggers a misleading trademark display."⁷² Such a verdict has had widespread and lasting consequences: *Sega v. Accolade* was a landmark case that established that copyright can't protect some functional properties of a platform's code. According to the verdict, fair use protects reverse engineering when there's no other way to access code.

Nintendo's method seeks to avoid being subject to the same verdict. Using their logo rather than their name changes the rules. Creating any digital copy of a GBA game—even as an archival backup of purchased software—necessitates the reproduction of Nintendo's logo. And reproducing a logo without permission carries significantly more legal weight than reproducing four letters. Equally, developing unlicensed software for the GBA requires the false and prohibited use of Nintendo's logo, which complicates attempts at a fair use defense. It's possible that the spirit behind Accolade's response would still allow an independent developer to argue their side in court successfully. But it's unlikely that a hobbyist or small firm could stand in the face of the company's expensive team of litigators. Given the prohibitive economics of the legal system, negotiations are often over before they have a chance to begin.

Ports and Platformers

As previously noted, critics often condemn the GBA for its library of ports, even with the practice of porting being central to Nintendo's corporate philosophy. Ported games, not unlike those based on existing IP, emphasize brand continuity, even while the gameplay experience itself is altered to adapt to new hardware affordances. Over the course of the GBA's market life cycle, Nintendo ported some of the most influential NES and SNES games, including *A Link to the Past*, *Final Fantasy IV*, *V*, and *VI*, and four bundles of *Super Mario* installments under the *Advance* banner.

Porting these formative titles was a clever move on Nintendo's part. By the time they released the GBA, the Game Boy was already twelve years old and the Super Famicom was eleven. Now a younger generation of players who might be discovering videogames for the first time through the GBA could experience the titles that had so enticed their parents or older siblings. And for those parents or older siblings, Nintendo had a nostalgia factor. Ports are one of the key methods through which the company sustains an investment in their foundational narratives across generations.

Even when Nintendo ported games, the process involved more than putting a new cartridge around old software. At 16.8 MHz, the GBA's CPU exceeded the 3.57 MHz of the SNES's processor, but discrepancies in graphical and audio processing didn't make porting easy. The picture processing unit (PPU) of the SNES has an internal display resolution of 256 x 224 pixels. Recall that the GBA's resolution is 240 x 160 pixels. Ports therefore have to excise two tiles in width and eight in height from what could be displayed on a given screen and then adjust the camera accordingly. The GBA's lack of X and Y buttons also limits game complexity and constrains controls. And then there is the audio. The absence of Sony's more refined sound chip, paired with the GBA's cheap mono speaker, means that the celebrated soundtracks of the SNES are inferior at best when ported directly to the GBA. Developers had to learn how to work within the constraints of the new system rather than attempt to reproduce the robust sound of a home console. Once they did, they were able to create unique soundscapes more suited to the new device.

Despite their limitations, ports made a critical intervention into portable gameplay and on-the-go games like *Tetris* that defined and popularized the 1989 Game Boy. Although software developers did release bundles of arcade games, the GBA's strengths were to be found elsewhere.

Facilitated by the ergonomic, contoured chassis, the GBA introduced a library of longer games with impressive aesthetics and intricate storylines. It promised console-quality gaming, and it delivered by porting robust, narrative-driven adventure games. SNES titles—such as the storied *Final Fantasy* RPG series by Square Enix (then Square)—were among those that played well on the handheld. And despite some vocal outbursts on the part of consumers seeking novelty, most of these ports didn't disappoint fans.

Mario Advances

It's a testament to Mario's astronomical cultural significance and foundational role in Nintendo's business practices that the GBA's foremost launch title could be a game fourteen years in the making. *Super Mario Advance* isn't just a port—it's a port of a port of an obscure promotional Famicom Disk System (FDS) videogame for Fuji Television's 1987 Yume Kōjō (Dream Factory) expo, which itself began as a failed prototype for a *Super Mario Bros.* sequel. How's that for derivative innovation?

Super Mario Bros. was a prodigious success on the Famicom and the NES. Endeavoring to leverage the title's appeal to help popularize the FDS—an external disc drive peripheral that plugs into the Famicom and supports rewritable discs for larger games—Nintendo developed an FDS-exclusive sequel: *Super Mario Bros. 2*.[73] From a graphical perspective, the game is nearly identical to its predecessor. Mechanically, though, it's another beast entirely. Rather than direct their efforts toward improving the visuals and adding new worlds, the development team elected to augment its difficulty via torturous new features. To say that the game is harder is a laughable understatement. Familiar levels become frustrating obstacle courses requiring astounding dexterity and lightning-fast reflexes; blocks randomly dispense poisonous mushrooms the moment players most need a power-up; overleaping the flagpole betrays Mario by sending him back to stages that had previously been completed. Nintendo of America determined that the game was beyond the skill level of Western players, and the overseas release of such a punishing revision would jeopardize the company's emerging but still fragile popularity. Nintendo would have to find an alternative sequel.[74]

Fortunately, the company had something up their sleeve. In the mid-1980s, Nintendo partner, Systems Research and Development (SRD), had created a vertical-scrolling prototype for a two-player, cooperative *Super Mario Bros.*, where players were meant to throw each other around to reach otherwise inaccessible areas.[75] But Shigeru Miyamoto and Kensuke Tanabe didn't love the demo's execution; Famicom's hardware limitations hamstrung the potential for entertaining gameplay, and the single-player mode ironically felt flat. The project was shelved for a couple of years.

When Fuji Television later approached Nintendo to create a promotional game for the Yume Kōjō 87 event to advertise the network's fall lineup of shows and upcoming media releases, Tanabe saw the opportunity to return to the abandoned prototype. The FDS was the missing piece of hardware that now allowed him to realize his earlier vision. With the Yume Kōjō mascots as the game's new protagonists, *Yume Kōjō: Doki Doki Panikku* (*Dream Factory: Heart-Pounding Panic*) reemerged from the idea drawer, where it went on to become one of the FDS's biggest hits.

In a way, the lack of a North American equivalent to the FDS was a blessing. Scrambling for an alternative to the viciously difficult *Super Mario Bros. 2*, Miyamoto and Tanabe revamped *Doki Doki*'s licensing changes to make the game feel more like a Mario title again. Fuji Television's characters would have had little cultural significance in North America anyway, and Mario characters mapped nicely onto the game's four playable characters; Yume Kōjō's family of mascots, Imajin, Mama, Lina, and Papa, became Mario, Luigi, Princess Toadstool (or Princess Peach), and Toad, each boasting distinctive abilities. The skills and animations that each of these characters inherited from Yume Kōjō's mascots have since shaped their development in main series and spin-off Mario titles. Princess Peach's ability to float long distances in *Super Smash Bros. Melee*, for example, directly results from Lina's ability to hover. *Doki Doki*'s initial conceit of picking up other players and throwing them around translated to plucking vegetables out of the ground and lobbing them at the Bob-ombs, Pokeys, Birdos, and Shy Guys that inhabited the scrolling backdrop.[76] The hybrid title had little in common with its predecessor, but at least a substitute *Super Mario Bros. 2* was ready for North America.

Eventually, this strange, not-quite-Mario game made it back to Japan as *Super Mario USA*, where it enjoyed critical and commercial success. It later found itself bundled with the *Super Mario All-Stars* collection of remasters for the Super Famicom and SNES, where the landscape took on a more vibrant tenor thanks to the console's superior graphics capabilities.[77] When Satoru Iwata joined Nintendo in 2000 as the head of corporate planning, he noticed that there were no Mario games on the GBA development list—a most-unexpected occurrence for a company that had spent the last fifteen years building a legacy around the little plumber. Iwata suggested to Miyamoto that they add a Mario game to their launch lineup, and so began the *Super Mario Advance* series of ports, the first of which combined *Super Mario Bros. 2* with the 1983 arcade classic *Mario Bros.*[78]

Throughout its journey, Nintendo's development team adapted *Super Mario Bros. 2* to suit each platform they designed for. The game experienced various revisions and numerous Mario-ifications as the team sought to make the former Yume Kōjō title feel more familiar to Mario fans. Although *Super Mario Advance* uses the *All-Stars* remaster as its base, the development team built most of the program from scratch, recoding it for the ARM architecture and adjusting for the GBA's screen size.[79] Because of the difference in display resolution, the development team had to alter the game's presentation and convert the entire landscape to the new specifications (figure 1.5). A sizable portion of the sprites were also redrawn when their presentation wasn't, according to art director Hiroyuki Kimura, "good enough" for the GBA version.[80]

In addition to having to account for the reduced resolution, the development team had to attend to the limitations of the screen itself. Given how reflective the GBA's LCD is, they had to exercise great care in their color selection. Early in the coding process, Kimura stated, "We're still in the midst of studying [the LCD], but we're trying to find colors that take advantage of the characteristics of the LCDs as we go along."[81] The colors that worked best on the GBA differ from those suited to the earlier GBC, which themselves differ from those that the SNES outputs to a television set. Hardware changes alter the expression of creative works, and it takes software developers some time to acclimate to these alterations. For this launch title, there wasn't yet a robust record of the screen's performance to fall back on. Kimura reflects that they repeatedly verified how the colors would look, moving back and forth between software and hardware to produce a palette that suited the game's aesthetics and the device's limitations.[82] In the end, the GBA version addresses the handheld's lack of a backlight by adopting brighter, softer colors than those of the SNES remaster.

Changes to the *All-Stars* version aren't all about constraints though. One of the GBA's most exciting features is its ability to apply geometric transformations to sprites and backgrounds in real time. The SNES's famous graphics Mode 7 had allowed a single background layer with up to 256 colors to be rotated, scaled, and sheared. But these matrix transformations applied solely to backgrounds, not sprites.[83] If developers wanted to play with perspective, they had to include renderings of every sprite at predetermined sizes. Scaling was then accomplished by pulling increasingly large or small sprites as the character moved closer to or farther away from the camera, and the result was far from seamless; as sprites crossed the programmed threshold, they'd suddenly find themselves jarringly replaced with their resized version.[84] The alternative to Mode 7 was to include an additional expansion chip in the game cartridge; Argonaut's

Figure 1.5 A comparison of the *All-Stars* version of *Super Mario Bros. 2* on the SNES (a) and *Super Mario Advance* on the GBA (b). The former is displayed at the SNES's internal resolution of 256 x 224 pixels (8:7) and the latter at the GBA's resolution of 240 x 160 pixels (3:2). Due to differences in graphics hardware and display technologies, *Super Mario Advance* removes eight tiles from the top and two from the side (indicated by the box). The designers also drastically lightened the color palette to account for the lack of a backlight. Emulated on RetroArch (SNES) and Visual Boy Advance (GBA).

Super FX-2 coprocessor made sprite transformation a possibility, although it came late in the system's life cycle. But the GBA could perform affine transformations (e.g., scaling, rotating, and shearing) without additional hardware by using a 2D matrix, opening up possibilities for new, dynamic animations.[85]

Super Mario Advance flamboyantly shows off these new affordances: enemies rotate when thrown; bombs pulsate before exploding; hearts twist and throb their way to the health meter; and some enemies are positively enormous. The game exults in its ability to manipulate the sprite layer. While the SNES could display sprites of only two sizes at once, the GBA has no such limitations. *Super Mario Advance* loads sprites by the dozens. Bouncing baddies, planted vegetables, POW blocks, and flying carpets abound. Although transitions are far from seamless as the player climbs clouds, mountains, and vines to ascend beyond the range of a typical side-scroller, developers offer players plenty to look at while the game catches up. The developers aimed to dazzle with the range and sheer number of effects they could include.

The more contentious change to the game was the addition of voice samples, again highlighting how portable platforms depend upon a series of trade-offs and compromises. Unlike the SNES, the GBA doesn't have a dedicated audio coprocessor. Its CPU is responsible for sounds and background music on top of everything else. The audio's quality depends on how much processing power the developers have allocated to sound, as opposed to other aspects of a game. That isn't to say that the GBA has *no* advantages over the SNES's dedicated audio subsystem. Being walled off from the main processor has its own set of issues—namely, difficulties loading new samples during gameplay due to limited RAM; games have to preallocate memory for voice samples or different instruments. The GBA doesn't share this problem. Consequently, it can play more sound effects at a given moment.

Super Mario Advance was primed to take advantage of this feature. Mario, Luigi, Peach, and Toad found their voices in the world of gigantic turnips. And, once they did, they didn't stop talking. Mario's shouts of "Yippie" and "Ya-hoo," which had proved so endearing in *Super Mario 64*, turned into an incessant chorus of "Here I go!" "Thank you!" "Oh no!" "Ow!" and other goofy phrases—for instance, he cries, "What a tasty treat," and "Ooh, just what I needed" whenever he gains an extra life. Some players found these voices charming; others found them nothing short of infuriating. Repetitive and potentially grating though they might be, the crisp digitized samples demonstrated what developers could do with the newest addition to Nintendo's handheld collection.

In its role as a launch title, *Super Mario Advance* did its best to contrast the GBA's new abilities with the limitations of the platforms that preceded it. It features novel collectables, additional items, and save support to bring new excitement and functionality to the title. The remake of the arcade classic *Mario Bros.*, included alongside *Super Mario Bros. 2,* also began as an experiment—this one to show off the Game Boy Advance Game Link Cable that launched with the console. Until the GBA, multiplayer modes on Nintendo's handhelds required each player to have a copy of the cartridge. But with the new hardware, up to four people could play together using a single Game Pak plugged into Player 1's device, thanks to the connective hub in the center of the cable and the GBA system's onboard RAM. Players could share the game with friends; longtime fans could temporarily return to the arcade classic; and siblings could face off against each other without having to buy the cartridge in duplicate. *Super Mario Advance* appealed to a broad range of players and stood as a representative—if not a little eager-to-please—showcase of the new hardware's abilities.

Critics condemned *Super Mario Advance* for being a lazy rehash of existing Mario titles, but at the end of the day, the players loved it. *All-Stars* came out in 1993; many of the GBA's players hadn't even been born yet. Others were nostalgic for the eccentric Mario game, with echoes of its 8-bit past. Maybe it didn't make up for the lack of an original Mario title for the GBA, but it was still immensely satisfying and enjoyable. Yokoi and Okada were right: Nintendo could get away with a lot if the gameplay was fun.

In order to fully grasp what Nintendo has announced today, it's going to be necessary to alter the way you think about entertainment. . . . You can share data—from characters and teams to abilities—between the two systems and then continue gameplay even after you leave the house. . . . The uses of this gameplay tandem is [sic] limited only by the imaginations of game developers. . . . This is the kind of interactive experience that meets the three trends that I mentioned: it's entertainment fully controlled by the user; it's so immersive it's almost an alternative life; and, finally, it's entertainment that can go unwired, unplugged from everything. Games can be designed to follow you anywhere, anytime.[1]

These are the words that Peter Main said in a press conference on August 24, 2000, to illustrate the ambitious set of imagined interactions between the Game Boy Advance (GBA) and the GameCube. When Nintendo concurrently unveiled their new handheld and home consoles at the Space World trade show, they promised to usher in a new era of connective gameplay—a transformative experience that consolidated the performance of a home console with the convenience of a portable one through a form of wired connectivity that allowed players to move game content fluidly from one device to another.

GBA-GameCube interactivity never amounted to what Nintendo affirmed would be a revolution in immersive gaming. For one thing, it required a sizable amount of hardware between the GBA, GameCube, controllers, and link cables, the costs of which added up (not to mention the necessary software for both devices). But it was really the dearth of games programmed to implement these interactive affordances that consigned this interface to mere marketing filigree. Hardware and software operate symbiotically; hardware shapes and constrains the expression of creative works, but software equally mediates users' relationship to and understanding of the hardware and its abilities. Without software to demonstrate the platform's technical affordances, even the most novel features remain invisible to most users and external developers, concealed by plastic casings and technical protection measures (TPMs). While some games availed themselves of the communicative potential of the two systems by using the GBA as a second screen (I look at one example, *The Legend of Zelda: Four Swords Adventures,* in chapter 4), the GameCube–Game Boy Advance Link Cable was mostly used to unlock additional content or to transfer items between closely related games. Seldom did they embody what Main touted as "the industry's most meaningful innovation ever announced."[2]

The interface that Main described is much closer to what Nintendo recently realized with the Switch, a platform that is at once handheld and home console (blissfully united under a single price tag). The Nintendo Switch's hardware consists of, among other components, a console unit with a multitouch capacitive sensing screen, a dock that connects to a television set via High-Definition Multimedia Interface (HDMI), and two Joy-Con controllers. Users can switch among three hardware configurations: TV mode, where the console is docked; tabletop mode, where the console is supported on a flat surface by its kickstand; and handheld mode, where the Joy-Cons are slotted into the grips on either side of the screen. By placing the console unit in the dock, or removing it and detaching and connecting the Joy-Cons, the Switch captures the sentiment of console-quality "entertainment that can go unwired, unplugged from everything."

The Switch's hybridity fulfills a promise that the GBA couldn't keep, but it also reminds us how foundational lateral thinking continues to be to Nintendo's approach to innovation. Existing hardware objects, failed design prototypes, and users' past and present responses to technologies all affect the trajectory of emerging products. Although Gunpei Yokoi left Nintendo long before its engineers began work on the hybrid system, his design philosophy resonates as much as it ever did; the withered technology of GBA-GameCube connectivity, cultivated by the Wii U through the GamePad's supplemental screen, emerges again in a remix of portability and home entertainment. Nintendo's rhetorical posturing— their marketing jargon rife with words like "powerful," "innovative," and "unprecedented"—belies what occurs at the level of design and engineering. As Main's press conference illustrates, the Switch was decades in the making. Forget linear narratives of progress—recursion and lateral thinking are the Switch's lineage.

The early 2000s bore witness to the company's most concentrated period of hardware revision, remixing, and adaptation. Spurred on by mounting competition with Sony and Microsoft at the turn of the millennium, Nintendo released incrementally altered platforms in rapid succession: the GameCube and the GBA in 2001, the GBA SP in 2003, the DS in 2004, a newly backlit SP and the Game Boy Micro in 2005, and the slimmed-down Nintendo DS Lite and their next home console, the Nintendo Wii, in 2006. No period before or since has witnessed such a condensed effort by the company to rethink and adapt their hardware for new demographics, selectively highlighting the platforms' most salient affordances while modifying form factors and introducing new interfaces.

Given this compressed development cycle and the fact that the 2001 embodiment of the GBA had fewer than 700 days to stand on its own, I argue that it's impossible to study the GBA in isolation from its closely related objects. Each of the GBA's revisions is fundamental to the context in which we think about the platform. That's why this book treats the GBA not as a static object, but as an assemblage.[3] As an ontological framework, an assemblage comprises various articulations, which include concrete elements, agents, and collective subjects, as well as networks of external relations that keep them together.[4] Nintendo's design philosophy of lateral thinking extracts successful hardware and software elements to reorient them into the assemblage of the next platform. The articulations between elements are "deterritorialized" and creatively "reterritorialized" to form new assemblages or new consoles (players engage in a similar deterritorializing process to that of Nintendo across the gamut of modding practices).[5] Nintendo themselves treat the GBA as an assemblage linked by aesthetic, temporal, and economic factors; their marketing campaigns and financial reports consolidate the three faces of the GBA under a single banner.[6] Sharing the ability to play GBA games, the 2001 GBA, the SP, and the Game Boy Micro articulate a different aesthetic while concealing the same computational core within differently designed casings. And just as the GBA repurposes the Game Boy's microprocessor, the DS cannibalizes GBA hardware to further pursue a legacy of interoperability, carrying the GBA's software library forward.

If chapter 1 looked at the context from which the GBA emerged, this one looks to what it has become through Nintendo's iterative development process. This chapter offers a survey of these closely related objects that carry the GBA forward in an official, Nintendo-sanctioned environment (I'll look at unsanctioned environments later in this book, in chapters 5 and 6). Each of these objects contributes to our heavily mediated understanding of what the GBA is and what Nintendo intended for it to do as a cultural and computational object. It's impossible to talk about the GBA without reflecting on what the SP's addition of a lighting system did for the device, or what the DS's backward compatibility meant for the Game Boy brand. Successive and diverging devices highlight the affordances and constraints of the 2001 hardware. They point to the most and least successful aspects of the hardware along the lines of aesthetics, functionality, and accessibility. Taken together, this network highlights the recursive relationships among media platforms, the bodies of their users, and their cultural, economic, and material contexts.

Pocket Your Dreams: The Game Boy Advance SP

The Game Boy Advance SP began as a secret project within Nintendo's hardware development division as a way of experimenting with more sophisticated aesthetic designs. Historically, Nintendo had privileged engaging gameplay and a stable of iconic software properties above form factor and style (Yokoi's fun, calculator-inspired gameplay again comes to mind). But Kenichi Sugino, one of the lead designers on the project, wondered if the company could sell a console that wasn't just based on fun, but also looked good when carried around:

> When you talk about game consoles, most of the time it's the case that you buy a GameCube because you want to play Mario, or you buy a GBA because you want to play something else. But that's not the case with other products, right? Like, take TVs or cars as an example. Some of them are totally utilitarian, but many of them are built for style too.[7]

Although the Game Boy, and to some extent the GBA, became widely recognized aestheticized symbols, they did so largely through the narrative and material nostalgia that they inspired in their consumers, not because their designs were remarkably alluring themselves. Nintendo president Hiroshi Yamauchi once commented that "the hardware is just a box you buy only because you want to play Mario games," succinctly summarizing the company's approach to the design of their boxes.[8] Nintendo's hardware's "emotional design" (to borrow a term from design theorist Donald Norman) foregrounds the enjoyment of interacting with entertaining software rather than a visceral reaction to material components and their visual arrangements.[9] The toylike appearance of Nintendo's products is part of a long-running practice of choosing affordable manufacturing materials to keep costs low to appeal to budget-conscious consumers (or the practical, budget-conscious parents of said consumers). To extend Sugino's comparison, Nintendo's handhelds are minivans, not Ferraris.

Sugino's idea was to broaden the platform's audience by revising the look of the handheld, even as the computational components remained largely the same. To achieve the goal of producing an aesthetically appealing object, he and his team endeavored to make the system smaller than any of the Game Boy products that had come before. Miniaturization, with all its symbolic resonances, had already come to drive the design of consumer electronics. Even at Nintendo, engineers had been galvanized to slim down the Nintendo Entertainment System (NES), Super Nintendo Entertainment System (SNES), and Game Boy during the consoles' respective market life cycles. This drive toward smallness found its genesis in the mid-twentieth century. In 1965, Intel cofounder Gordon Moore announced that the exponential increase in the number of transistors that could be "crammed" into a given integrated circuit (IC) would accelerate technological innovation in computing and communications via the capacity to execute complex functions on smaller boards.[10] In addition to promising more power, greater reliability, and increased affordability, the microelectronics industry stipulated a new aesthetics of smallness. This trend led to the emergence of home computers, personal communications devices, and electronic wristwatches framed, as Mira Mills observes, "by the modern industrial ideals of efficiency, rationalization, mechanical reproduction, mobility, [and] individualism."[11] Miniaturization became entwined with notions of individual control and contemporary attitudes toward style and experienced somewhat of a zenith in the early and mid-2000s with its ever-shrinking flip phones. The year after the SP made it to market, Motorola would release the famous RAZR, the fashion-forward mobile phone of the late aughts recognizable for its metallic finish and strikingly slim form factor.

In building a videogame system for both style and function, Nintendo's development team fixed their attention on the dominant aesthetic trend at the time, making a concerted effort to capture consumers' desire for small, personalized electronics. With all the circuitry integrated (albeit without screws), the team managed to produce an initial prototype that was smaller than some mobile phones at the time. At that stage, the goal wasn't to make something sturdy, or even practical. A bit of glue was all that held the components together—hardly enough to withstand the vagaries of play. The purpose was to assess how small they could feasibly make a

Figure 2.1 A platinum GBA SP (AGB-001 model) with a frontlit screen.

semifunctional prototype while operating within the constraints of existing technologies. The iconic flip-top design, therefore, emerged as a way of producing a look of deceptive simplicity (figure 2.1). Buttons that previously broke the seamlessness of the handheld's casing were concealed by discrete design—as were most indications of the system's internal complexity. The cartridge slot, power switch, EXT port, AC adapter port, and volume dial that rimmed the edges of the almost-square base became the sole indicators that the black (or silver) box was more than it seemed.

Sugino touted the design as "something that's never been done with game machines before," conveniently positioning the SP as more innovative than it was (in typical Nintendo fashion).[12] A flip-screen machine *had* been created before—and by Nintendo themselves at that. Late Game & Watch models had adopted a dual-screen flip-top design out of necessity, to augment game complexity. Clunky though the Game & Watch may have been, its governing form factor was deterritorialized to be echoed in the lines of the SP and would come to resonate even more clearly in Nintendo's next handheld. An ancillary advantage of the clamshell lid was that it protected against dirt, scratches, and everyday abrasions, lending function to the new form.

One of the questions that Sugino had asked himself while working on the prototype was, "If people were willing to spend a little bit more money on the same GBA, what would they like?"[13] Such musing not only speaks to how cost considerations had long presided over design, but also addresses a desire to iterate on the 2001 handheld based on player feedback. Platforms are nothing without their users. As "a crystalized set of social and material relations," the GBA works for, and is worked on by, a substantial group of people, including obviously the developers, but also the actual and idealized users who interact with the object on a daily basis.[14] Two highly requested features made it into the revised handheld thanks to user feedback, time, and the concurrent proliferation of the mobile phone industry: the rechargeable lithium-ion battery pack and the illuminated screen.

Both lithium-ion battery packs and lit screens, though not as ubiquitous as they are today, existed when the GBA was in production. But developments in miniaturization rarely progress evenly across the various phases of production. This leads to disproportionate costs and volumes for discrete components that make it difficult for a company like Nintendo to release a console that responds to all their players' needs, especially given their emphasis on affordable withered technology. The leapfrogging of innovation ultimately foregrounds contingent relationships between a device's individual components and its assembly. The ability to cram a greater number of transistors onto an IC produces diminishing returns (relative to shrinking a console) if other components (like batteries) and assembly methods fail to keep up. Components and their connections must function holistically.

When Research and Development 1 (R&D1) worked on the Game Boy Pocket in the mid-1990s, rechargeable lithium-ion batteries and backlit screens were gaining in popularity.[15] The trouble was that these technologies were prohibitively expensive to manufacture. To complicate matters, Nintendo was fabricating over a million Game Boys each month. Even if they had the capital to procure enough batteries for their system, no company in the world was producing the sheer volume they required. But by the early 2000s, the growing ubiquity of the mobile phone had compounded demand for rechargeable batteries, leading to the birth of companies dedicated to the improvement and production of such technologies. Due to capacity enhancements and lowered manufacturing costs, lithium-ion batteries underwent a dramatic price reduction in a little under a decade. When high-volume production began in earnest in 1994, the bare cell price was approximately 300 yen ($2.70). By the early 2000s, however, it was down to 22.50 yen ($0.21).[16] Nintendo's patience was rewarded—they adopted the industry-standard lithium ion only once the price per unit plummeted, saving millions in the process. And thanks to the batteries' augmented efficacy, they could boast that the SP was more energy efficient than its elder sibling, able to withstand 10 hours of continuous play with the front-lighting system enabled, and 18 hours with it turned off.

This brings us to the most salient advancement in consumer electronics so far as Nintendo's users were concerned: innovations in liquid crystal display (LCD) technology. It's difficult to overstate the importance of the SP's single light-emitting diode (LED) front-lighting system in improving attitudes toward Nintendo's products.[17] In players' eyes, the 2001 GBA's greatest shortcoming was its dim screen, which had given rise to a series of unsanctioned correctives within months of the GBA's release. Nyko's Worm Light was among the first successful GBA lighting peripherals. Designed like old Game Boy lights, the maneuverable and portable lamp hooked into the GBA's expansion port and flooded the screen with light from above. Although some glare was a natural by-product, the add-on obviated the need to sit right beside a window to see the screen. Other add-ons worked similarly, with extensions that fastened onto the handheld and produced illumination running the gamut from stunningly bright beams of light to gentle, diffused glows. Each peripheral had its own drawbacks; some traded illumination for energy efficiency, while others relied on bulky external power sources to avoid siphoning hours from the GBA's own AA batteries.

Then, in 2002, Triton Labs released an alternative aftermarket solution: the Afterburner kit, a front-lighting device that overlaid the LCD from within the casing and traded 25 percent of the GBA's battery life for enhanced visibility in low-light conditions. Unlike earlier plug-and-play peripherals, Afterburner required hardware modifications, so GBA owners needed technical knowledge and soldering skills—or else they had to find someone else with the requisite expertise to perform the technological surgery. The kit itself only came with the Afterburner components, so users also had to acquire a tri-wing screwdriver on their own if they wanted to get inside the GBA's beveled box.[18]

Tools were only the second barrier to installation; the first was building up the nerve to take apart and tinker with Nintendo's proprietary hardware. Once players managed to take apart the shell and expose the handheld's inner workings, they needed a Dremel, a high-speed rotary power tool ideal for precision do-it-yourself (DIY) projects, to shave down the acrylonitrile butadiene styrene (ABS) plastic and drill a hole in the housing for the brightness dial. If users hadn't lost their nerve by this point, they then had to solder the lighting system and resistor onto the circuit board to draw power to the frontlight. All these steps had to be done while keeping the LCD screen, Afterburner system, and antiglare film free of dust, dirt, or fingerprints. Any air pockets, wrinkles, or errant hairs would become glaring blemishes above the refulgent screen the moment that the system turned on. Installing the Afterburner kit was a considerable technological challenge for those not well versed in toying with consumer electronics. But it's a testament to how lackluster the original screen was that players flocked to the solution that Triton Labs offered.

Nintendo knew about the Afterburner kit, as well as the swarm of peripherals engineered without their blessing. These interventions contributed quite explicitly to the SP's genesis. Of Afterburner, Sugino said:

> I thought they did something really impressive. . . . In a way, though, it also reminded us of exactly how many users really wanted to see some kind of light in their Game Boy Advances. It was an impetus for us to devote the time to figuring out how to finally just do it. So, in that aspect, it helped us during SP development.[19]

Research & Engineering (R&E) appropriated and innovated upon the Afterburner's front-lighting workaround to provide a salve for the strained eyes of their most stubborn players. Given how punitive Nintendo has become toward their players' TPM circumventions (discussed in more detail in chapter 5), it seems remarkable that, in the early 2000s, a member of their team would have declared the SP's indebtedness to hobbyist enterprises so openly. This rare moment of candor lifts the veil that conceals the fact that Nintendo and their consumers engage in a dialogue with tangible (or, in this case, visible) consequences, proving that while fans take from Nintendo, Nintendo equally reterritorializes innovations from their players in a seesaw of hardware alteration. In 2005, the SP experienced another revision, in the form of the brightly backlit AGS-101, which would become the model that modders came to cannibalize in order to backlight their 2001 GBA units.[20]

In the end, the SP ended up being larger than its prototype, but at 3.2 inches (8.1 centimeters) wide, 3.3 inches (8.4 centimeters) tall, and just shy of 1 inch (2.5 centimeters) deep, it made good on its promise of miniaturization. The placement of the Direction-pad (D-Pad) and A, B, Start, and Select buttons on the bottom half of the handheld mirrors that of the Game Boy Pocket (although Start and Select are round rather than oval). The speaker sits between the buttons on the lower half of the base. Near the hinge above the inputs is a small circular button styled with a little sun that turns the frontlight on and off. To account for the compact layout, the SP replaces the bumper-style L and R triggers with small, square tact switches. The handheld contains the same ARM7TDMI processor with embedded memory, as well as the 8080-derived Sharp LR35902 for backward compatibility. In terms of computational capacity, the SP is the 2001 model's fraternal twin.

As with any handheld, particularly one so small, the hardware division had to make some concessions. For one thing, the new form factor requires Game Paks to be inserted at the bottom of the device. This reorganization is fine for GBA games that sit flush with the bottom edge, but Game Boy games and titles with additional hardware protrude against users' palms as they play, and the pioneering Game Boy Camera peripheral—an entertaining spherical camera accessory that can capture 128-x-112-pixel images in the Game Boy's monochrome four-shade palette—now points in the wrong direction.

The more egregious compromise, as far as players were concerned, was the removal of the tip-ring-sleeve (TRS) headphone jack. Sugino initially wanted to preserve its presence in the redesign, but the jack's cumbersome physical hardware diverted too much cubic volume from critical computational components. According to in-house consumer research conducted at the time, only a fraction of users purportedly availed themselves of headphones when playing on the 2001 GBA, so the team designed for the majority of their audience. Economically, this was a shrewd decision: they had one fewer component to purchase and connect to the circuitry; the chassis could be smaller, and therefore cheaper to manufacture; and they could sell proprietary headphones and a stereophonic adapter that plugged into the AC charging port. But players were less amenable to viewing the compromise so kindly. Both the SP-specific headphones and the adapter impeded players from simultaneously charging the device and listening through headphones.[21] So third parties intervened again to release splitters with a power port on one side and a headphone jack on the other.

A couple of other features had been tested on the platform but never made it in, including touch technology and glasses-free three dimensional (3D) viewing. Nintendo had attempted a 3D console back in 1995 during an early wave of virtual reality fascination, but the resultant product, the Virtual Boy, had been an unmitigated disaster. The headset-based tabletop system used a parallax effect to create the illusion of 3D, requiring players to sit in uncomfortable positions in order to engage with its lackluster games. It's difficult to put into words how nauseating the red monochrome graphics were. Combined with hyperbolized health concerns, inflated costs, and a lack of entertaining software [Miyamoto was too busy working on the Nintendo 64 (N64)], the Virtual Boy met an early demise. But Satoru Iwata notes that "if it hadn't been for the failure of the Virtual Boy system, so many of our people might not have said 'As long as special glasses are necessary, 3D is impossible.'"[22] And it certainly wasn't. The R&E division managed a fully functional 3D-graphics-capable SP in 2003. Unfortunately, the LCD's screen resolution wasn't high enough to deliver sharp images for the left and right eyes separately; autostereoscopic 3D would have gutted the resolution to an effective 120 x 160 pixels. Nintendo had learned an important lesson with the Virtual Boy; there was no need to repeat its failure so soon by launching a subpar product, so the prototype went into the idea drawer for a while. In 2011, it emerged resplendent as the Nintendo 3DS once high-precision LCD technology became more affordable.[23]

By waiting for technologies to be affordable rather than producing handhelds that harnessed innovative technology, Nintendo continued to do what they did best. The SP went to market for around $100, the same price that the GBA had two years previously. The sleek form factor and range of metallic shell colors demonstrated Nintendo's attempts to cater to the aesthetic sensibilities of a more mature demographic. By addressing the most urgent complaints about the GBA's versatility (its battery life and its dim screen), the SP resuscitated Nintendo's waning brand image—just as a new challenger approached.

The Third Pillar: The Nintendo DS

The Game Boy name was never meant to go gentle into that good night. The SP enjoyed an auspicious debut in Japan and overseas. There was no reason to believe that the GBA wouldn't experience a decade-long reign as the uncontested darling of the handheld videogame industry, just as its predecessor had. Then, everything changed when Sony's president, Ken Kutaragi, unexpectedly announced the company's plans to release their own handheld system at E3. Sony dazzled the audience with the PlayStation Portable (PSP), and Nintendo was entirely caught off guard.

The PSP wouldn't come out until late 2004, but Sony promised that their powerful, backlit gaming device would be "the Walkman of the Twenty-First Century."[24] This comparison stood as a caustic reminder that

Sony was a technology manufacturer before they entered the videogame hardware market, while Nintendo was a toy company. The PSP, with its backlit, wide-screen thin-film transistor liquid crystal display (TFT LCD) and a processor powered by the latest in semiconductor technology, would make the GBA look like a dinky children's toy. Already, Sony had demonstrated their competence in the home console market; the PlayStation had wrested favor from Nintendo among mature audiences and so-called hardcore players. The PlayStation 2 (PS2) only fortified that position. Meanwhile, the awkward, low-powered GameCube entered the market after the PS2 and Microsoft's Xbox had carved out audiences for themselves, and it struggled to catch up. It's impossible to predict what would have happened to the GBA had Sony not thoroughly humiliated Nintendo at E3. The so-called console wars might have been behind the company, but the handheld wars had just begun.[25]

Under Satoru Okada's direction, Nintendo had begun working on the newest entry in the Game Boy line. Codenamed IRIS, the project took its name from *Hanafuda*, Japanese playing cards where twelve suits, each symbolized by a flower, represent the months of the year. As the fifth generation of Game Boys, the successor was named for May's floral symbol, in a nice nod to Nintendo's corporate history as a playing card manufacturer. The project was progressing apace when a tense President Iwata visited Okada. "I talked to Yamauchi-san over the phone," he said, "and he thinks your console should have two screens . . . A bit like the multi-screen Game & Watch, you see?"[26]

Yamauchi had already passed the presidential torch to Iwata, but he remained an honorary advisor on the IRIS project and retained a stake in the company. Sony's broadcast of their intention to enter the portable market caused enough alarm that Yamauchi insisted on the second screen as a way to diversify the gameplay experience—much to Okada's chagrin. He didn't understand the appeal of a dual-screen system, now that technology had rendered richer gameplay possible compared to the Game & Watch's segmented displays. "With modern screens, there was no point," he said. "We are free to choose the size of our screen, so why bother splitting it into two? Especially considering that [it's] impossible to look at both screens at the same time."[27]

Iwata didn't understand the idea either, but he dissuaded Okada from confronting Yamauchi in the way that he had once challenged Yokoi. Instead, Iwata proposed that they give the design a try. IRIS became Project Nitro, and it was released in 2004 under the moniker DS, an acronym with two meanings: Dual-Screen and Developer System. It promised to shake the very foundations of gaming.

The DS didn't just face scorn internally; it was initially received by the media with reactions ranging from skepticism to derision from the moment that Reggie Fils-Aime revealed it at E3 in 2004. Critics and competitors heralded the death of Nintendo's dominance, declaring that the aging GBA couldn't possibly compete with the PSP's superior specifications. The DS, in their eyes, was nothing more than a gimmick—just a distraction from computational inadequacy. Some compared it to the Virtual Boy and predicted that it would meet an equally ignoble fate.

Nintendo proved everyone wrong; the DS went on to surpass the Game Boy's extraordinary sales. Even Okada admitted that he was mistaken in arguing for a new GBA when Nintendo's position in the handheld videogame market seemed so precarious.[28] Nintendo had made a name for themselves through engaging gameplay on low-powered, outdated hardware. There was no way that they could challenge Sony on a purely technological level. Instead, the dual screens, touch capability, built-in microphone, and wireless connectivity reframed the gaming experience. The DS's success became a bellwether of Nintendo's participation in the casual revolution.

But history could have gone either way. Nintendo had gambled on the DS's success with previously excluded demographics (namely, women). Yamauchi is credited as having said, "In our business, if you succeed it's like you've gone to heaven, but failure is like falling to hell."[29] With the looming threat of the PSP, Nintendo stood on a precipice. Perhaps this is why Nintendo initially asserted that the DS was part of a three-pillar strategy: the GBA targeted the traditional handheld market; the GameCube targeted the home console market; and the DS forged a new market entirely, reaching out to an untapped audience of casual gamers and nongamers. According to the discourse at the time, the DS was meant to coexist with the GBA and its legacy, not outshine it.

Okada and his team took Yamauchi's comparisons to the Game & Watch devices to heart: the DS's 9.7-ounce (275-gram), 5.85-x-3.33-x-1.13-inch (14.8-x-8.46-x-2.87-centimeter), dual-screen form factor—7.7 ounces (218 grams) and 5.24 x 2.91 x 0.85 inches (13.3 x 5.56 x 2.16 centimeters) for the preferred remodel, the 2006 DS Lite—echoes the 1982 device's general shape (figure 2.2). Computationally, it's another thing entirely. The DS's main central processing unit (CPU) is an ARM946E-S Reduced Instruction Set Computer (RISC) that runs at 67 MHz with 4 MB onboard pseudo static random-access memory (PSRAM). Its graphical processing unit (GPU) comprises a 3D rendering system and two advanced two-dimensional (2D) rendering systems that derive from and extend the GBA's video controller. Graphics display across two TFT LCD screens,

Figure 2.2 The DS Lite, running *FE7* in backward compatibility mode on the top screen.

each measuring 3 inches (7.62 centimeters) diagonally at a resolution of 256 x 192 pixels and being capable of displaying 262,144 colors. The lower screen also has a resistive touch coating meant to interface with the stylus, subtly docked in an inlet on the underside of the shell (though fingertips work just as well). Accompanying the improved graphics is 16 hardware channel sound, which outputs through stereo speakers on either side of the top screen or through the headphone jack. With a processor on par with that of the N64, a more refined backlighting system, and new affordances for dynamic gameplay, the DS drew the eye and capital of developers.

The resistive touch screen offered newly embodied ways of engaging with game content using a more diverse set of operations than the traditional button-pressing of earlier handhelds. The haptic nature of the stylus-supported touch screen collapsed the distinction between receiving an image and creating one. In *The Legend of Zelda: Phantom Hourglass*, players draw glyphs on the touch screen to open doors and trace out the trajectory of Link's boomerang. The performative nature of drawing in the player's own hand alters the relationship between the player's body and the characters in the game. Unlike with button inputs, the illustrations on the touch screen don't exist until the player draws them. Of course, the game code and the handheld's hardware are designed so as to be able to parse this input and receive players' commands. But the actual shapes of the lines that players draw are their own.

Given these new tactile conditions for play—as well as Wi-Fi capabilities and the built-in microphone (found at the bottom edge on the original DS model and along the hinge in the DS Lite revision)—developers wanted to experiment with this sandbox of portable gaming. Even though the SP continued to fly off the shelves, the production of new GBA titles began to slow to a trickle as Sega, Namco, EA, Ubisoft, Square, and, more critically, Nintendo's own internal development teams migrated to the DS.

A telling indication that the three-pillar marketing strategy was little more than a tactical maneuver was the platform's backward compatibility. Just as the GBA contains the processor of the Game Boy Color (GBC), the DS contains an ARM7TDMI coprocessor clocked at 33 MHz to process sound, support the built-in IEEE 802.11 wireless network connectivity, and run GBA games innately. When a GBA cartridge is inserted into the bottom-loading cartridge slot, it instructs the ARM7TDMI to launch AGB firmware and alters the DS video layers so that only a single screen is selected. Users can choose whether the game runs off the top screen or the bottom screen from the Settings menu, but touch capabilities lose their effect anyway because the system functionally reverts to the GBA. Between the ARM processor, the 2D rendering engines, and the system's keys, the handheld's internal architecture shows its beginnings as the GBA's successor.[30]

It's not hard, therefore, to see the three-pillar strategy as a contingency plan: if the DS met the same calamitous end as the Virtual Boy, Nintendo could fall back on IRIS and continue the GBA line while pretending that the DS was never meant to be a successor, but rather a parallel platform for nongamers to fool around with. But if, as it happened, the DS was successful, it could rearticulate Nintendo's relationship to their audience and to videogames entirely. The GBA was collateral damage. Although the DS left the switching circuit behind, meaning that it could no longer play Game Boy and GBC games, this was a small price to pay for the DS's brighter backlight, wireless connectivity, touch screen interface, and expanding software catalog. There were little details that appealed as well, like the return of the headphone jack now that the handheld was larger and the introduction of a sleep feature when the handheld was closed. The latter was something that Iwata had urged engineers to include in the SP, but doing so would have meant reworking the chip; engineers projected that such revisions would add a year of development time, so sleep mode went into the idea drawer and was taken up again with the clamshell DS.[31]

At $149.99, the DS bore a steeper price tag than the SP, but many consumers were willing to spend the extra cash—even people who had never played a videogame before. At E3, Reggie Fils-Aime said, quite plainly:

> We're serious about expanding what we do. We also understand that we're not going to run our company just for hardcore gamers. There are gamers out there who aren't as knowledgeable as you. Gamers who aren't your age. Gamers who don't have your taste. . . . It's my job—it's Nintendo's job—to make sure we satisfy all the gamers and to do it better than our competition.[32]

If the GBA's "Who Are You?" campaign tended to address gamers above all others' subject identities, the DS hailed more casual audiences who had fewer experiences with videogames but found themselves drawn to the hardware's expressive possibilities. While the PSP boasted a sleek design and graphics on par with Sony's home consoles, the clunky-looking DS (before the handheld found its cleaner edges in the DS Lite) reminded people why they purchased videogame consoles in the first place. With revisions to classic titles like *Super Mario 64* and the introduction of a range of lifestyle and educational games like *Brain Age*, Nintendo exponentially expanded their audience. Everyone from hardcore gamers to children to grandmothers was playing DS.

The Forgotten Handheld: The Game Boy Micro

By the time the GBA's second redesign was released in 2005, attention to the GBA had dwindled. Between a sliding launch date and little support from developers beyond the initial promotion, the Game Boy Micro was a short-lived coda to the Game Boy Advance line. But despite its lackluster market performance (it sold only 2 million units, as opposed to the GBA's 37 million and the SP's 43 million), the Micro participates in Nintendo's conception of what the GBA is and does. It stands as Nintendo's last truly dedicated portable gaming platform. And just like with preceding hardware iterations, the Micro further highlights how handheld videogame platforms rely on a series of trade-offs and compromises in their pursuit of portability, miniaturization, and entertainment.

When Fils-Aime presented the new handheld at E3 in 2005, he held the diminutive device aloft and declared it to be "just a hair bigger and two-thirds the weight of an iPod Mini."[33] Invoking a comparison to Apple's popular music player was no accident. It's common knowledge that Iwata was an Apple fan, and the release of the Micro a year after the iPod Mini launched marked an instance of what Jones and Thiruvathukal call the "parallel evolution" between the two companies.[34] Although Nintendo's priorities revolve around creating an entertaining gameplay experience, in contrast to Apple's focus on bleeding-edge technology, both companies share a common philosophy of usability, family friendliness, and what Iwata describes as "enhancing appeal through simplicity."[35] Both companies withstood a period of difficulty in the 1990s, only to enjoy a renaissance of sorts by the early 2000s (incidentally around the time Iwata joined Nintendo as head of corporate planning and Steve Jobs returned to Apple after over a decade of estrangement). Nintendo developed their GameCube, while Apple concurrently was working on the unobtrusive Mac G4 Cube. The Wii and the Mac Mini would push the mirrored aesthetic even further when the white casing around the Wii replaced the black shell modeled at E3, alluding to the iconic white plastic of the MacBook. The Micro was yet another instance of analogous innovation between two companies that made their names through interwoven strands of hardware and software design. Despite their computational complexity, both the Micro and the iPod Mini aimed to simplify the user experience and put media right into their consumers' pockets.

The Micro took the SP's earlier interest in miniaturization to its technological extreme in what amounts to an impressive feat of engineering. At 2 x 4 x 0.7 inches (5.08 x 10.16 x 1.78 centimeters), the Micro's surface is smaller than the PSP's 4.3-inch (10.9-centimeter) screen (figure 2.3). It also weighs a mere 2.8 ounces (80 grams) compared to the PSP's 9.9 ounces (280 grams) and the DS's 9.7 ounces (275 grams), turning it into something that users could even carry on a keychain (it has a hole on the side for doing exactly that). Everything about the handheld is tiny, down to the lowercase "a" and "b" lettering on the buttons.[36] Further miniaturization was constrained only by the existing size of the GBA cartridge. Sugino would have liked to produce a thinner cartridge (like the DS Game Card) so it could fit a slimmer console, but the GBA's future was growing ever more uncertain. Manufacturing Game Paks exclusive to the Micro would have been counterintuitive—a failure to read the proverbial writing on the wall, as it were.

Figure 2.3 The Game Boy Micro, Nintendo's smallest handheld. Photo by JCD1981NL, Wikimedia Commons.

Still, Nintendo managed to cram a lot into a Lilliputian frame. The 2-inch (5.01-centimeter) screen maintains the earlier models' 240-x-160-pixel resolution for a much higher pixel density. The finer dot pitch means that that while the screen is smaller, it's also extraordinarily crisp. Its built-in backlight includes four brightness levels, the highest of which surpasses even the DS's illumination, coming closer to what the PSP produced. And whereas the front-lit SP tends to wash out colors, the Micro preserves vibrancy, with little ghosting or bleeding. Poorly suited though the Micro might be for text-heavy role-playing games (RPGs) like *Final Fantasy* or *Fire Emblem*, it nevertheless offers the sharpest display of any handheld bearing the Game Boy name.

To fit a processor, display, speakers, cartridge slot, and other electronic innards into the Micro's chassis (including the reintroduction of the headphone jack to make up for the cheap mono speaker), Nintendo made a crucial concession: the switching circuit essential to running Game Boy and GBC cartridges is absent, as it is with the DS, cutting off the long-preserved connection to the handheld's history. The other important compromise was the reworking of the extension port to fit the slimmer shell. GBA peripherals consequently can't connect to the system; users instead have to purchase Micro-only link cables and wireless adapters if they want access to its connective affordances.

All these trade-offs made it difficult for the Micro to carve out a niche for itself. Although less compact, the SP provided backward compatibility for the decade-old, deep catalog. And the DS could get away with dropping earlier generations by virtue of its new features and expanding software library. The Micro's novelty was its aesthetic. At that same E3 presentation, Fils-Aime stated that the Micro "is not new technology, but it is a brand-new look," effectively proclaiming the company's corporate philosophy.[37] Few of the Micro's components were new; they were simply articulated in a staggeringly compact form. And even this brand-new look took cues from the company's beginnings. The landscape-oriented oblong shape, the rounded corners, and the raised molding all echoed the design of the Famicom controller—right down to the button placement and the elongation of the Start and Select buttons. To emphasis their own legacy, Nintendo even released a limited-edition Micro in the Famicom's iconic red and gold.

According to Nintendo's marketing, the Micro's emphasis on a fresh design appealed to the target demographic of "the image-conscious consumer." Shrinking the system's size was one way of reaching this goal. Equally vital was the company's more sophisticated choice of materials. Any lightweight metal would have served for the handheld's frame, but Sugino chose aluminum to add to the "quality feeling of the product" (Apple would also later come to use aluminum for the MacBook Air's unibody construction).[38] Not only is the metal lightweight, sturdy, and an excellent conductor of heat—reducing the stress that the system might experience as a result of the brighter backlight—it also offers users a different tactile experience— one that feels more chic and modern than Nintendo's usual plastic shells.

To further this goal, Nintendo leaned heavily on consumers' desire to customize their electronics. Early advertisements highlighted the ability to personalize the Micro by way of interchangeable faceplates (which would return later with the New 3DS's interchangeable cover plates). While the scratch-resistant faceplates with their plastic screen covers doubled as a way to protect the handheld, their primary goal was to give consumers a sense of agency over their hardware. These were a natural extension of the SP's earlier attempts to broaden their audience through embodied identification. The promise of customization allows players to project their subjective fantasies upon the hardware object, collapsing the distinction between the Nintendo brand and the player's identity. The miniaturization of the Micro is a deliberate form of objectification—one epitomized by cuteness.[39]

While cuteness may be easier to envision when thinking about characters or babies than the unyielding aluminum of a consumer electronics device, the Micro captures the desire for ownership inherent in the cute commodity, which manifests as a growing interest in personal (and personalizable) electronics. And the tiny Micro was as cute as videogame technology could be.

Nintendo was careful to articulate at the time of its release that the Micro wasn't meant to be a successor to either of Nintendo's handhelds. Rather, it was to be "a further extension of portable play."[40] Its role as a companion to the DS is explicitly reflected in its internal name: the Micro's serial code OXY (or Oxygen) is a sibling to the DS's NTR (Nitro).[41] But bracketed by two successful handhelds, each of which offered more playable titles, the Micro struggled to find its identity and dramatically underperformed with retailers.[42]

I hardly want to credit this market failure solely to the device's software limitations because doing so elides the context in which Nintendo released it. When the Micro arrived in stores in September 2005, it came with a price tag of $99.99, at a time when SP costs had come down to $79.99 and DS costs had dropped to $129.99. Nintendo ended up competing with themselves. Their intent might have been to drown out talk of the PSP with a shiny array of new products, but they saturated the affordable portable market with too many versions of GBA-compatible hardware. The PSP launched at $249.99—far more expensive than the GameCube. Sony had their market. Meanwhile, first-time videogame players who wanted something affordable to test the waters experienced decision paralysis when contemplating the SP, DS, and Micro, stacked side by side on the shelf. For people with little technical knowledge, all three devices were virtually the same but for product packaging and industrial design.

Iwata himself cited poor resource management on Nintendo's part when reflecting on the Micro's mediocre performance; the company had focused so much energy on marketing the DS that year—convinced that the Micro would sell on name and form factor alone—that they deprived it of the promising momentum that it had enjoyed in Japan. Overseas, the product failed to catch on. Iwata went on to observe that because part of what made the Micro so attractive was the tactile experience of engaging with it, consumers who had to decide between the tiny device and the well-advertised DS without holding either in their hands gravitated to the latter. In Japan, the Micro had physically circulated at trade shows, where consumers could admire its lightness and marvel at the technical ingenuity that it took to condense the GBA into something smaller than a wallet.

In North America, it was concealed in a box not much smaller than that of the DS, where the minimalist packaging design that took its cues from Apple (the handheld against a white background, with its name written on the side) did little to provide a sense of scale. Moreover, while Japanese consumers enjoyed myriad interchangeable faceplates featuring various characters and patterns, overseas consumers were restricted to the three that came packaged with the device unless they wanted to import others from Japan or grab knockoffs at pawnshops. The Micro became a boutique collectable, and Nintendo shuttered support for the GBA. Or so it seemed.

Welcome Back: The 3DS Ambassador Program

When the 3DS launched in 2011, it carried a steep price tag of $249.90, making it the most expensive handheld the company had ever released. Early adoption was low, especially for a Nintendo platform, so less than six months after its disappointing launch, Nintendo announced that they would slash its price to $169.99. To recognize and reward consumers who purchased the system at its release price, Nintendo created the 3DS Ambassador Program. The 3DS Ambassador Program consisted of twenty preselected games that could be downloaded free of charge from the Nintendo eShop—ten for the NES and ten for the GBA. Included in the latter were some of the most beloved titles for the handheld: *The Legend of Zelda: Minish Cap, Mario Kart: Super Circuit, Metroid Fusion*, and *Mario vs. Donkey Kong*.

The 3DS departs from the other hardware objects surveyed in this chapter, in that it was not designed with the ability to play GBA cartridges in mind. But the 3DS nevertheless contains echoes of the GBA within its chassis. Unlike the titles on the Wii U's Virtual Console (discussed in chapter 5), the GBA games included as part of the 3DS Ambassador Program don't run on an emulator. Rather, they run on GBA firmware embedded in the 3DS. Following trends set by earlier handhelds, the 3DS contains two processors in its system-on-chip. Its main CPU is a dual-core ARM11 MPCore-based processor clocked at 266 MHz and manufactured at 45 nm, in which one core manages games and applications and the other is responsible for the operating system, multitasking, and background activities. But its coprocessor is, unsurprisingly, an ARM946, to enable backward compatibility with DS software. When Ambassador games run on the 3DS, they use GBA components that piggybacked their way into the 3DS through the DS hardware and firmware—a Droste effect of Nintendo's handheld technology.

There are important technical distinctions between emulation and what the 3DS Ambassador Program does. The 3DS has four firmware modes: NATIVE_FIRM, the default firmware for the 3DS's home menu and software; SAFE_MODE_FIRM, for applications like the System Updater and the System Settings; TWL_FIRM, with the DSi's native firmware enhanced from that of the DS (the successor to the DS, the DSi, was codenamed "Twilight"); and dedicated GBA firmware called AGB_FIRM. When DS software runs on the 3DS, it does so in a distinct environment by using the ARM9 processor and the TWL firmware, rather than the 3DS's defaults. Similarly, GBA titles downloaded as part of the 3DS Ambassador Program run on dedicated firmware on a clocked-down ARM9; just as with DS Game Card compatibility, the AGB_FIRM puts the game's read-only memory (ROM)—that is, the game image—and the .sav data in the appropriate locations to run the game. This is simulation, not emulation. The salient difference between running a GBA game on a 3DS rather than on a backward-compatible DS is that here the ROM images are digitally downloaded from the Nintendo eShop instead of being accessed through a material Game Pak and the physical interactions between edge connectors. Thanks to the DS's architectural inheritances from the GBA, a peculiar form of backward compatibility persists.

There are, of course, downsides to running the games on firmware rather than software. Because 3DS Ambassador Program titles play on a GBA mode inherited from the built-in DS hardware, the 3DS's innate features are suspended during play as the handheld computationally reverts to 2001. Folding the lid ceases to put games to sleep because the hardware-based sleep mode of the DS hadn't yet been implemented, wireless connectivity (SpotPass and StreetPass) is equally disabled, and pressing the Home button can't launch the 3DS menu because the GBA had no such interface to return to.

The 3DS Ambassador Program raises interesting ontological questions about the GBA platform. Is the platform a physical configuration of circuits, chips, and plastics? Is it a cartridge-based game library? A ROM software library? Something else? Aesthetically, the 3DS looks nothing like the 2001 GBA. Everything from its manufacturing materials to its industrial design proclaims it to be from a different decade, and it's packed with technological features that would have been too crude or too expensive to include in the GBA: stereoscopic 3D, a resistive touch screen, StreetPass and SpotPass tag modes, augmented reality viewed through two 3D cameras, Virtual Console support, and access to a range of apps, including an online distribution store (figure 2.4). And yet these features are suspended when the 3DS reverts to GBA mode.

Figure 2.4 The 3DS. Photo by Evan Amos, Wikimedia Commons.

3DS Ambassador Program games aren't emulated, but neither are they physical objects that can be exchanged, resold, dropped, or damaged. Players can't lend their friends their free copy of *Fire Emblem: The Sacred Stones* without lending them their entire 3DS system. Nintendo's legacy of interoperability turns platforms into abstractions. It seems that the more material objects we must grapple with, the fuzzier the distinctions between them become.

Articulating the AGB

Critical and academic discourse surrounding videogame history traditionally makes sense of it by grouping consoles into discrete generations. Initially, these categories were defined quantitatively by processor architecture (8-bit, 16-bit, 32-bit, etc.), but as these distinctions gradually became less relevant, consoles came to be grouped along qualitative factors like media formats, connectivity, and chronological time. Such sorting often privileges the home console; the fifth generation of videogame hardware known as the 32-bit, 64-bit, or 3D era predictably includes the N64, PlayStation, and Sega Saturn, but it also includes the decidedly not 3D-capable 8-bit GBC. The generational metaphor has its uses as a tool for historizing hardware, but leaning too heavily on what often amounts to discontinuous distinctions runs the risk of eliding some of the important articulations of a given platform. As we can see from this chapter, generational categorization is more porous than videogame history might like it to be: the DS emerges as the first handheld in the seventh generation, even while Nintendo presents it as a third pillar for the sixth; the Micro makes its debut as the GBA's stepsibling once the DS was already around for a year; and the 3DS is clearly of a different generation, even though it can play GBA games without emulation. Upon examination, the GBA's articulations demand to be understood as an ongoing, ever-mutating assemblage (table 2.1).

Different revisions make it difficult to talk about the GBA as a unique platform not only due to hardware considerations, but also with respect to how creative works are developed within technological constraints. Before the SP implemented a backlight, early GBA games used bright color palettes to compensate for the unlit screen, and consequently the images lacked the visual depth that players had come to expect from the SNES. These tactical color selections are particularly visible in ported games from home consoles designed to interface through a cathode-ray-tube (CRT) television; when played on the SP, DS, or Micro, colors appear washed out or overly bright. Once the SP gained popularity, developers began to design with the frontlight in mind, using slightly more nuanced palettes that appeared richer on the screen. *Fire Emblem: The Sacred Stones,* released in 2004, uses a more subdued palette for character portraits, maps, and menus than *Fire Emblem Fūin no Tsurugi* and *FE7* (published in 2002 and 2003, respectively). Placing installments from the series side by side allows us to attend to the material distinctions between screen technologies that affect the software developed for the device.

The revisions and expansions (or, in this case, "miniaturizations") that the GBA witnessed over its life span highlights how Nintendo's developers conceive of their platforms relative to emerging competition in the hardware market. The 2001 handheld's lack of a backlight allowed Nintendo to release an affordable platform, but it failed to account for its customers' primary complaint about the GBC. Competition with the PSP propelled Nintendo to turn to outdated but cost-effective screen-lighting technology to remain competitive in what Sony hoped would become a technological arms race. The 2001 handheld's button placements and the SP's flip-top form factor converge in the DS's industrial design, while, internally, the DS draws on the GBA's computational architecture. If this weren't enough to prove the inadequacy of rigid categorization, the DS and the Micro were simultaneously in development despite ostensibly belonging to different hardware eras.

Looking at the ways that GBA technology is articulated reveals the fundamental importance of lateral thinking to Nintendo's corporate philosophy. Many of the technologies that would go on to become mainstays of later platforms found their origin (sometimes clumsily) in the GBA systems. As the first portable to use the ARM processor, it introduced the energy-efficient microprocessor that would become a staple in Nintendo's handhelds. The ability to connect four GBAs via link cables and short-range wireless predates the DS's inbuilt Wi-Fi connectivity, the glasses-free 3D that came to define an entire line of handhelds was prototyped on the SP, and the GBA-GameCube connectivity is echoed in the Wii U's industrial design and the Switch's hybridity.

Even more clearly, the GBA's breadth of remakes and ports was proof-of-concept for consumers' appetite for Nintendo's back catalog. Not long after GBA games were released as part of the 3DS Ambassador Program, Nintendo trumpeted the handheld's arrival on the Wii U's Virtual Console. Although the GBA's life cycle feels ephemeral compared to that of the platforms that bracket it, it lives on—first embedded within the DS's chassis, then in 3DS firmware, and ultimately in the hands of its players, who continue to modify and appropriate its hardware and software. Tracing the handheld's articulations reveals it to be emblematic of the way that Nintendo capitalizes on a model of continuous revival and manufactured nostalgia.

At 81.51 million units sold worldwide among the three iterations, the GBA didn't quite reproduce Game Boy's market success, but it was nevertheless the fastest-selling videogame system in North America at the time of its release.[43] The number of units sold is doubly impressive, considering that the Game Boy spent a dozen years on the market before the GBA succeeded it; the latter was on the market for only four years before the DS became Nintendo's dominant line of handhelds. The GBA had price, size, and backward compatibility with the Game Boy and GBC, but the DS was poised to attract both hardcore and casual audiences. After the release of the DS, Nintendo quietly supported the GBA until the late 2000s, when they finally ceased hardware production of the 2001 model, the SP, and the Micro. By then, the DS had already experienced a sleek, lightweight

Table 2.1 Handheld Hardware Comparisons of GBA Articulations

	2001 GBA	SP
Release (JP)	March 21, 2000	February 14, 2003
Release (NA)	June 11, 2001	March 23, 2003
Discontinued	2008	2010
Cost at release	$99.99	$99.99
Dimensions	5.7 x 3.2 x 1 in	3.3 x 3.2 x 0.9 in
Weight	5 oz	5 oz
North American launch colors	Arctic, Black, Fuchsia, Glacier, Indigo, Orange	AGS-001: Cobalt, Platinum, Onyx, Flame Red AGS-101: Pearl Blue, Graphite, Pearl Pink
CPU	ARM7TDMI at 16.8 MHz LR35902 at 8.4 MHz (GBC) or 4.2 MHz (Game Boy)	ARM7TDMI at 16.8 MHz LR35902 at 8.4 MHz (GBC) or 4.2 MHz (Game Boy)
Memory	BIOS ROM: 16 KB IWRAM: 32 KB EWRAM: 256 KB VRAM: 96 KB	BIOS ROM: 16 KB IWRAM: 32 KB EWRAM 256 KB VRAM: 96 KB
Display	2.9-in TFT LCD	2.9-in TFT LCD
Resolution	240 x 160 px	240 x 160 px
Color depth	15-bit	15-bit
Lighting	None	Frontlight, with on/off switch (AGS-001) Backlight, with two brightness levels and on/off switch (AGS-101)
Audio output	Built-in mono speaker Stereo headphone jack	Built-in mono speaker
Connectivity	AGB link port	AGB link port AC adapter port
Power supply	Two 0.5 V DC (AA battery)	600 mAh lithium-ion
Battery life	15 h	10–18 h
Media	GBA Game Pak Support for Game Boy and GBC cartridges	GBA Game Pak Support for Game Boy and GBC cartridges

* Dates during which early adopters could download Ambassador titles

DS	Micro	3DS
December 2, 2004	September 13, 2005	December 16, 2011*
November 21, 2004	September 19, 2005	December 16, 2011*
2013	2008	August 12, 2011*
$149.99	$99.99	$249.99
5.85 x 3.33 x 1.13 in	2 x 4 x 0.7 in	5.3 x 2.9 x 0.83 in
9.7 oz	2.8 oz	8.3 oz
Titanium, Sky Blue, Candy Pink, Snow White, Lava Red	Silver, Black	Aqua Blue, Cosmo Black
ARM946E-S at 67 MHz ARM7TDMI at 33 MHz (for DS sound) or 16 MHz (in GBA mode)	ARM7TDMI at 16.8 MHz	Dual-core ARM11 MPCore at 266 MHz ARM946 at 134 MHz
BIOS ROM: 36 KB (16KB for GBA) Main RAM: 4,096 KB WRAM: 96 KB VRAM: 656 KB 3D memory: 248 KB Flash: 256 KB	BIOS ROM: 16 KB IWRAM: 32 KB EWRAM 256 KB VRAM: 96 KB	VRAM: 6 MB in system-on-chip FCRAM: 128 MB Flash: 1 GB
Two 2.0-in TFT LCDs. Bottom is a resistive touch screen	2-in TFT LCD	3.5-in autostereoscopic LCD (top) 3.0-in resistive touch screen (bottom)
256 x 192 px	240 x 160 px	800 (400) x 240 px (top) 320 x 240 px (bottom)
18-bit	15-bit	24-bit
Backlight, with four brightness levels	Backlight, with four brightness levels and on/off switch	Backlight, with four brightness levels
Two stereo speakers Stereo headphone jack	Built-in mono speaker Stereo headphone jack	Mono, stereo and (virtualized) surround sound through speakers Stereo headphone jack
802.11b, WEP Wi-Fi AC adapter port	Game Boy Micro link port	802.11b/g Wi-Fi, infrared, AC adapter port
850 mAh lithium-ion	460 mAh lithium-ion	1300 mAh lithium ion
6–10 h	5–10 h	3–5 h
DS Game Cards Support for GBA Game Paks (until DSi)	GBA Game Pak	3DS Game Cards Support for DS Game Cards, 3DS Virtual Console games, and downloaded 3DS Ambassador Program titles

redesign of its own in the form of the DS Lite, which became the preferred embodiment of the platform.

Although the discontinuation of the GBA saw Nintendo leave the Game Boy brand behind, "Game Boy" nevertheless retains enough cultural capital to become somewhat of a proprietary eponym. While the platform's name may have formally evaded becoming a genericized trademark, many of my generation's parents and grandparents refer to any videogame handheld as a "Game Boy," regardless of whether it was manufactured by Nintendo, much less whether it was part of the Game Boy line.

In February 2019, Catherine (Cat) DeSpira presented the untold history
of how people really played *Pac-Man* during its arcade heyday in the
1980s.[1] *Pac-Man* cabinets, she reveals, inspired a near-universal physical
response in players: within seconds of grabbing the joystick, they would
grip the side of the machine with their free hand. This reflexive action was
as fundamental to gameplay as the joystick itself, and a direct consequence
of the cabinet's material construction. *Pac-Man*'s fighting game contemporaries typically occupied both of the player's hands with a joystick and
action buttons. This configuration led to the ubiquitous adoption of the
"power stance," a posture in which players stood with their feet planted
firmly apart away from the cabinet, with their weight on the balls of their
feet and both hands on the control panel. *Pac-Man*'s physical configuration
differed in that it registered input through a single joystick. As a result of
players' tendency to center themselves in front of the screen, they would
stand close to the panel, with their dominant hand in front of their bodies
to access the controls. Unbalanced without their bracing stance, players
would rock side to side as they directed the hungry yellow circle through
the glittering maze. They'd then instinctively grab the side of the arcade
cabinet and hold on tight to avoid losing their balance as they took hairpin
curves with their entire bodies.

   In writing about how players physically interacted with the materiality of *Pac-Man*'s arcade cabinet, DeSpira makes a compelling case for not
only radically reconstructing how we think about *Pac-Man* and its players, but also the way we think about videogame preservation altogether.

Much has been written about *Pac-Man* as an object of acute fascination and as a historical scapegoat for proclamations that videogames are addictive and immoral (local ordinances had even sought to shut down videogame arcades in response to the "Pac-Mania" that had come to grip North America at the time). And yet the way that people actually played the game has never been explicitly taken up in scholarly work. Part of the reason this fundamental aspect of playing *Pac-Man* has been so underdiscussed is because most players didn't even realize it happened each time they placed their coins in a machine. But the more significant implication of this revelation is that previous works on *Pac-Man* seldom revisited the hardware.

DeSpira didn't discover this embodied pattern of play by speaking to former players or *Pac-Man* aficionados. She identified it by looking at used, unrestored physical cabinets, the left sides of which inevitably displayed this pattern of use; the yellow paint was always stripped off by the thousands or millions of fingers that gripped the sides of the cabinets tightly throughout their lifetime. The near-universal physical response to playing the game is documented not in reviews and retrospectives, but through the visible residue left on the cabinets. So common is this pattern that it can even be used to determine how cabinets were positioned in the arcade: when wear is restricted to the very edges of the paneling, the cabinet was likely wedged between others.

For DeSpira, then, restoration is a destruction of evidence of how we really play games—an effacing of the desire paths that highlight actual interactions. "Desire paths"—a term taken from architecture and urban planning to represent the most common routes between a point of origin and a destination—are the trajectories that people prefer rather than those created for them, the natural responses to repeated human use. When applied to a videogame object, desire paths map actual uses instead of those intended by the manufacturer.

As the material traces of bodies, desire paths tell us about gameplay techniques and about how players touched the object or, in the case of the Game Boy Advance (GBA), how they held it in their hands. For instance, there are two popular ways to hold the Micro: one is with the back of the console braced against the middle fingers, with the bottom corners cushioned by the player's palms; the other is with the handheld more precariously balanced on a "pinky finger shelf." The size of a player's hands, their dexterity, and the demands of a given software title lead the player's body to choose how best to hold the device, often without the player being aware of the decision-making process. Instead, these choices become visible based on the material traces left on the aluminum.

So much of videogame history is written in the plastics, paints, and lacquers of its handhelds, consoles, and cabinets. Just as games leave emotional impressions on players, players leave physical impressions on their handhelds. But the people who buy and sell videogame hardware often conceive of these impressions negatively. Search for secondhand GBAs on eBay, and you'll find most users trying to assure you that the handheld is in "mint condition" or has experienced "minimal wear." If it has "normal wear," you might even be able to haggle the seller down a few dollars. But wear is a natural result of use. A GBA in "mint condition" in 2020 is either a reproduction, a modded unit, or a handheld that endured a sad existence in a vacuum-sealed box for nearly two decades.

We can borrow the term "patina" from antiquarians to describe these material records of use. It originated as a way to talk about the oxidized layers that form on copper, bronze, and other metals, or the sheen on wooden surfaces produced by age and wear. Patina is the literal form of residual media. It's the manifestation of repeated exchanges between materials and a vital part of its history. On the GBA, the patina is the buildup of dirt, grease, and human oils, or the yellowing of the gray buttons from solar exposure.

There's an argument to be made that the patina on the GBA is a source of value added. While there's often a desire to own a pristine handheld, the GBA is retro. And Nintendo's target audience for the GBA was largely children. Combined, those two factors mean that most GBAs have not escaped the ravages of time and use. The patina makes the GBA valuable by showing that the product is worthy of said use; it's a physical testament to the handheld's allure. Taking a washcloth and some cleaner to the shell effaces the mutual relationship between player and platform.

As we play, our bodies perform an array of responsive processes. When a difficult boss appears, our heart rate might increase, and our hands might start to sweat. Our skin naturally secretes oils, and sweat-slicked palms and natural oils leave marks on the shell over time. This is a *feature* of play, not something that should be occluded in favor of immaculate plastic. The areas around the Direction-pad (D-pad) and the A button on my secondhand black GBA are shiny from thumbs—mine and my brother's—repeatedly leaving biological residue. Some of the scratches on the plastic lens are from my own nails when I accidentally scuffed it while trying to remove dust. On the back of the shell are patches of dried glue from the stickers I removed, stickers placed there by the device's previous owner. All that holds the battery door in place is a faded wad of blue sticky tack I swiped from the back of a poster in my sixth-grade classroom. I can erase these traces of use with cleaning supplies, a lens replacement, and a new battery door. But doing so would eliminate the record of my engagement with the handheld and erase part of its history.

We can see how important a GBA was to its user by the patina that accrues through time, use, and exposure. We can tell which games a player returned to most often by the wear on the gold-plated cartridge pins caused by swapping them in and out of the slot. We can glimpse the world that the handheld inhabited by the things that sneak inside the casing: by the residue of spilled soda, by the bits of lint and colored thread, and by the dust, the dead cells of the hands that held it, echoes of the player, now enveloped in plastic.

Extended Embodiment and Portable Play

Thus far in this book, I have argued that a platform's affordances and constraints operate in symbiosis with the expressive software produced for it. But there is also a mutual relationship of affordance and constraint explicitly derived from players' bodies. While the size, shape, and technical specifications of a hardware object influence the way that users engage with it, human sensorimotor activities impose their own limitations. How Nintendo conceives of the idealized bodies of its users through technological, cultural, and industrial standards is essential to what the platform becomes. It's important to note that Nintendo's idealized users differ from their *actual* users, whose bodies approach the platform in diverse ways. The design of the 2001 GBA makes many suppositions of its players: it presumes they have fluid range of motion, that they're able to reach the shoulder triggers, that they have fine motor control and rapid reflexes for twitch gaming, and that they have the endurance to hold the device for an extended period of time. These assumptions are embedded in the hardware, excluding some players and inspiring innovative workarounds for others based on the needs of their bodies.

Recently, studies of motion-controlled platforms like the Nintendo Wii or Microsoft Kinect have been fruitful in refocusing our attention on the relationships between videogames and bodily movements. But scholars' overwhelming focus on these consoles where the body is at the forefront risks occluding the way that *all* gaming occurs through the body.[2] This isn't to say that we should neglect the very real ways that the "gestural excess" of the Wii alters our understanding of videogames.[3] Quite the opposite, in fact—later in this chapter, I look at a precursor to the Wii's motion-sensing technology by taking *WarioWare: Twisted!* as a detailed case study. But before we get there, I want to look at the body's role beyond its overt interactions with mimetic interfaces, in order to study how gameplay always occurs at the nexus of body, platform, and contextual cues.

The dualism between physical body and disembodied mind is deeply embedded in Western culture.[4] It seems an obvious claim—though nevertheless one worth making—that our thoughts and experiences of the world are necessarily affected by and dependent on our bodies.[5] However, even though our physical bodies mediate our involvement in the world, we experience ourselves as more than a physical body performing a series of actions.[6] As we move through the world, our perception of ourselves come to include the tools we use and the representational objects we wear and carry around with us.[7] We describe our affinity for certain material things and styles as being "on brand." We project our identities to others through the games we play and the hardware we use (this is the extended identification that Nintendo strove for through the "Who Are You?" campaign). It's due to the flexible interweaving of neural networks, sensory organs, hands, hardware, and code that we might wince or gasp if we drop the GBA and witness the battery door skitter across the floor.[8] We're not absorbing the physical shock of being thrown to the ground, but because we extend the idea of our bodies to include the handheld as a part of our identity, we flinch as though we're about to sustain a collision of our own (I've apologized to my handheld on more than one occasion after such an event). When playing *The Legend of Zelda*, we might duck, sway, or vocalize in response to projectiles directed at Link, even if we're safely settled on the sofa, because, in guiding Link through Hyrule, we extend our sense of self to include the virtual avatar of the in-game experience.[9]

I suggest the extension of embodiment occurs to a greater degree with handhelds than it does with home consoles. When playing on a home console, we can expand the idea of our bodies to incorporate the controller as a tool to bridge the perceptual chasm between what we do with our hands (on the controller) and where we look (the television). Absorbing the controller into our sense of our bodies removes the need to look down at our fingers each time we press a button. But videogame consoles are much more than their controllers; a web of cables extends from connective ports to the console, television, and electrical outlets. In most configurations, the console is spatially separated from the player; it rests beneath the television, while the player sits some feet away on the couch. But with the GBA, we can feel the full weight of the console in our hands. As we play, our hands bracket the game world at the peripheries of the screen, literally framing in-game actions. By virtue of our ability to take the handheld wherever we go, we can more easily see it as an extension of ourselves.

The relationship between the body of the player and the body of the platform is not unidirectional. We have as much to do with how the GBA works as the inverse. Just as the GBA's technical specifications outline a set of constraints imposed on both player and software, they also respond to the various constraints that human bodies impose upon product design. To achieve portability, the GBA must be light enough to hold for an extended period to access the promised "console-quality gaming," while also containing a processor, batteries, a screen, and a game cartridge. It must be small enough for someone to carry around and play on the go. It must fit comfortably in purses and pockets to accommodate the needs of the people who use it. Unlike home consoles, the GBA is meant to circulate, which exposes the hardware to a wealth of unintended injuries, so durability is another key demand that players' bodies make of the handheld's industrial design. In sum, Nintendo always has to have the player's use in mind.

When the GBA was first released, *Electronic Gaming Monthly* put it through its paces to see how it stood up to the vagaries of play: it was dropped on cement from a height of 5 feet, burned in a campfire for half a minute, stepped on by a 218-pound news editor, doused with water for 5 seconds, and finally dropped into a toilet to endure an entire flushing cycle (a fitting trial, given that the bathroom is a common site for GBA play). By all predictions, the device should have stopped working. And for a while, it did crash within seconds of turning on. But a miraculous (and symbolically resonant) three days later, the GBA started to work perfectly again.[10] Nintendo's industrial design is predicated on anticipating the accidents and abrasions that their devices will endure at human hands. By default, embodied gaming is written in plastic.

Console-Quality Gaming on . . . Your Console?

The GBA's size, weight, and durability highlight the embodied relationships articulated by the hardware. But it's worth remembering that, as part of a system with interchangeable media cartridges, GBA software code isn't tethered to a handheld by design. Two years after the GBA's launch, Nintendo released the Game Boy Player (GBP), a peripheral that uses near-identical hardware to the GBA (meaning that it doesn't rely on emulation) to display GBA games on a television. The GBP connects through the purportedly future-proofing high-speed parallel port at the base of the GameCube to use the home console as a conduit for power, user input, and audiovisual output.[11] Game Boy, GBC, and GBA games slot into the cartridge connector in the front of the peripheral, which seamlessly integrates with the GameCube's footprint (figure 3.1). The GBP

Figure 3.1 The GBP, with a GBA game inserted, ready to attach to the GameCube via a high-speed parallel port. Photo by Evan Amos, Wikimedia Commons.

also includes the GBA's expansion port in order to enable its connective peripherals. Input can come either from the GameCube controller or the GBA itself, connected through the GameCube–Game Boy Advance Link Cable (though this drains the batteries). While the GBP itself is region free, it relies on a region-locked boot disc to launch the interface, frustrating image-conscious consumers who wanted to purchase a peripheral that matched their GameCube's color (it only came in Jet Black in North America). The boot disc menu offers six customization options, including an alarm (a nod to the timekeeping capabilities of the Game & Watch), the ability to swap cartridges safely without having to turn off the console, and the choice to change the colored frame around the game to one of twenty designs, similar to the aesthetic function of the Micro's interchangeable faceplates.

Placed side by side, the GBA and the GBP highlight salient hardware affordances and trade-offs: portability at the cost of accessibility. Consider some of the specific demands that the GBA makes on its players just concerning visibility. Users might have to continuously adjust the angle of their screen when playing in a setting where illumination is inconsistent, such as when in transit. When the sun sets, they need to use lamplight to illuminate the screen. Some players might need to wear reading glasses or remove their regular glasses. Straining to see the screen causes headaches and jaw pain, while prolonged and frequent use can even alter a player's vision enough that they need a new prescription altogether. Even when the Micro arrived, with its refulgent screen, the display itself was suddenly even smaller. Portability promises convenient access to creative works, but the handheld's physical configuration precludes groups of people from using it.[12]

The GBP shatters some of these constraints by connecting itself to a larger television, viewed from a distance and in a broader range of light environments. In this way, players can experience a game that they might not be able to otherwise.[13] Audio similarly enjoys a boost because television speakers can be cranked much louder than the GBA's single mono speaker. If we experience stories through eyes, ears, and muscles, then the GBP invites new forms of embodied engagement with the GBA's narratives.[14]

Indeed, each of these experiences is unique. Let's look for a minute at what happens when a player opts to use the GameCube controller rather than a linked GBA. To the uninitiated, there might not seem to be a difference between the two input systems. Why should there be? They're both held with two hands, the D-pad is Nintendo's patented classic Plus controller, and the A, B, Start, L, and R buttons are all present. Sure, Select is missing from the GameCube controller, but there are enough extra inputs that it's simply a matter of finding one to take on the selecting task (usually X or Y). But the reality is that the configurations differ in ways that, however slight, stymie reliance on muscle memory. The shoulder triggers go from sensitive, clicky switches on the GBA to buttons with enough travel (the total distance the button needs to be pushed down before the input is recognized) that a light brush of the fingers isn't enough to depress them. The D-pad is located on the lower half of the GameCube controller, meaning that the thumb hits it at a 45-degree angle rather than straight on, troubling the mental mapping of cardinal directions ingrained after hours of play. Using the analog stick instead of the D-pad confers a feeling of newfound freedom, but that reveals itself to be illusory when, despite the ostensible greater range of motion, GBA sprites remain confined to two-dimensional (2D) maps. Because inputs are our way of affecting the virtual world, reconfiguring controls inevitably reconfigures the sensation of play.

There are also subtler ways in which our embodied relationship to the platform shifts when we move from the handheld to the GameCube add-on. While the GBP uses GBA hardware, its internal refresh rate of 59.73 Hz differs slightly from National Television System Committee (NTSC) televisions' standard broadcast rate of 59.94 Hz. Because of the mismatch between refresh rates, a duplicate frame occurs every few seconds, causing a hiccup felt through the body as latency. "Latency" or "lag" refers to the time between a signal's input and its correlative display on the screen. It's easy to ignore in turn-based strategy or puzzle games, but it's felt acutely in time-sensitive games that call for twitch reactions, like Konami's *Ninja Five-O*, Orbital Media's *Racing Gears Advance*, and other sports and shooting games. Games with scrolling levels also suffer from picture judder, where the image occasionally stutters while scrolling. Latency isn't just a mental phenomenon. The body, primed by its usual experiences of scripted actions, is suspended in anticipation of a character's corresponding movement. Lag foils the body's natural responses and rhythms.

Latency is a product of the GBP's boot disc software, the GameCube's video output, and the television itself. In its simplest definition, video is the rapid display of sequential images. Due to the speed at which the images appear, our brains process them as one smooth motion. So differences in frame rates can be measured and monitored by attentive players with the right tools.

The GBP's boot disc can output video at 480i or 480p. These abbreviations refer to two scanning methods used to draw a picture on a television: interlaced and progressive. Interlaced scanning draws an image in alternating odd and even pixel rows (known as "scanlines") that, seen together, compose a single composite frame of video. Each scanline is drawn approximately thirty times each second to get the rate of 59.94 Hz. The phosphor luminance of cathode-ray-tube (CRT) televisions—the dominant display until plasma display panels (PDPs), and then high-definition liquid crystal displays (LCDs), came to be the home entertainment standard—bleeds around each scanline and softens the image. Combined with the rapid pace at which the CRT's electron gun fires, this blurring conceals the raster. However, due to a combination of the boot disc software and the mismatch in frame rates, the GBP produces visible flickering when displayed at 480i.[15]

Progressive scanning, on the other hand, scans each row of pixels approximately sixty times per second to produce smoother frame transitions that soften the image. With progressive scanning, there's no need for antialiasing (i.e., intentional blurring) to reduce flickering in games with many rapidly moving sprites in the object layer. But the trouble with progressive scanning on the GBP is that it only works on GameCubes manufactured prior to 2004 because only DOL-001 (named after the GameCube's codename, Dolphin) hardware models include the necessary Digital AV Out port beside the Analog AV Out. Even if you managed to find the right GameCube model, you then need a rare and exorbitantly expensive video-only component cable to replace the composite cables packaged with the console.[16] Practically speaking, the GBP almost always displays at 480i.

There's another variable at play beyond distinctions between 480i and 480p—namely, the kind of television the GameCube connects to. On the GBA, graphics achieve coherence, thanks to the small screen that allows our eyes and minds to fill in any missing details. Televisions adopt elaborate mechanisms to reproduce the images on a larger scale. In the early 2000s, analog CRTs still dominated North American living rooms, but flat-screen plasmas were gradually edging them out. By the end of the decade, brighter, slimmer, and more efficient LCDs came to supersede them both.

The significance of the transition from analog to digital display when it comes to the GBP is that, unlike CRTs, plasmas and LCDs have fixed resolutions, which has concrete ramifications with respect to how GBA matrixes are scaled. CRTs' phosphorescent screens use three different phosphors, each assigned to red, green, or blue. Together, they form a triad. Triads don't obey the rigid geometry of the pixel grid, nor do they produce the clean square pixel that we've come to fetishize as part of the retro aesthetic. A single pixel can comprise one triad or a cluster of them, depending on the size of the image and the screen, so CRTs can scale graphics without compromising integrity. Ironically, the bleeding of the triads that results from the excitement and decay of the phosphor's electrons also softens the image by blending the colors around the edges. Highlights and shadows take on rich depth, whereas LCDs reproduce these same pixels as white or black. The transition to digital output exacerbates the softening by virtue of the scalers built into PDPs and LCDs, which translate the GBA's resolution to the television's native resolution. Without these scalers, the 240-x-160-pixel image would take up only a small fraction of a 1,600-x-1,200-pixel LCD. The by-product of this scaling is a blurry, distorted image.[17]

In addition to the standard 480i and 480p output modes, the GBP includes a full-screen mode. But because there aren't enough pixels in 480i or 480p to double the resolution, the GBP can't produce perfect pixel scaling. Instead, it stretches the image just as the GBA extends Game Boy and GBC games in wide-screen mode. The result is a fuzzy video that stutters—hardly worth the additional screen space.

Another feature included in the boot disc's software that is worth mentioning is a filtering option to addresses the flicker trick used in some GBA games. Once programmers achieved fluency with the GBA's graphics modes, they managed to achieve a range of pseudotransparency effects through controlled flickering. Programmers would turn sprites on and off every sixtieth of a second to create convincing spectral illusions. The screen's smearing and ghosting became a feature, not a bug. But these clever programming tricks optimized for the GBA's LCD translate poorly to a television screen; sophisticated effects turn into a dizzying light show. The GBP software can impose a motion blur filter to soften these sprites, but it smudges the rest of the graphics in the process. The cost of offloading the GBA's display to a larger, brighter screen is an unavoidable loss in sharpness.

Despite all these material differences between the GBA's embedded LCD and a television set, the experience of latency on the GBP is always contingent on familiarity with the way that games work on the handheld. In other words, it's contextual. If a player were ever to experience a GBA title only through the GBP on a high-definition, flat-screen LCD television set, their eyes, ears, minds, and muscles would attune themselves to that performance. Moving to the GBA after that would feel strange and inauthentic—even if that's generally regarded as the "original" experience. This is why it's imperative to consider the platform as assemblage rather than a stable configuration of hardware and software. The fact that the GBA has its own screen lends the illusion that software developers have guaranteed control over how their game looks, but this is rarely the case in practice. Just as the GBA, SP, and Micro display colors differently, the translation to a home console environment with an ever-growing array of televisions frustrates universality.

Manipulation and Mapping

The fact that videogame experiences change depending on the hardware object speaks to two essential elements of the platform: materiality and mapping. Outside of extracting and tweaking software code (discussed in chapter 6), we can't directly engage with virtual worlds. Instead, we participate by way of an interface that maps a physical action (pressing the A button with a thumb) onto a virtual action (Link holds his shield in front of him).[18] This coupling provides physical and intentional affordances when navigating an in-game environment.[19]

When we've been playing videogames long enough, we might forget that we learn mapping over time.[20] If we believe that videogame controls are intuitive, it's because we've been conditioned by these configurations. There's nothing innate about what an A-button is, does, or means. In fact, its function differs depending on the game: in *Super Mario Advance*, it makes Mario jump, but in *Mario Kart: Super Circuit*, it accelerates the go-kart. Similarly, while the D-pad feels intuitive for the way that each arm of the plus sign corresponds to a cardinal direction (especially in 2D games), the actual movement of the thumb is only downward. In this way, mapped actions on the GBA are arbitrary. They take on meaning by way of experience.[21] Mapping's arbitrary nature is clearest when playing the same game using a different controller. We already saw the example of the GameCube controller with the GBP; the same disconnect occurs when using a keyboard with a GBA emulator. There, the right hand might control navigation with the arrow keys, while the left controls actions with Z (A) and X (B)—the inverse of Nintendo's typical configuration.[22]

Nintendo teaches players how to assimilate to a new controller through their industrial design. In the introduction, we saw how the D-pad is a material representation of the directional constraints of 2D games. On the GBA, buttons stand out from the body in a contrasting color. The plastic stripe on the side directs the hands to the L and R triggers, emphasizing that they're new to the handheld. On a GameCube controller, the A button is bright green and larger than those around it, stressing its primacy. On a standard white Wii Remote (Wiimote), buttons are white or clear, signaling that input comes more from isomorphic movement than button pressing. The comparative simplicity of Nintendo's controls show how they invite more casual players into their virtual worlds; Sony's substantial controller might intimidate people who have never played videogames before, or who might long for the halcyon days of the simple, one-button arcade joystick.[23]

Eventually, the interface becomes naturalized and ceases to require conscious direction. This is the point at which input becomes part of muscle memory and deliberately thinking about your hands makes it harder to play. As Melanie Swalwell notes, once it becomes kinesthetic knowledge, "it might be difficult to explain how you actually executed a move, as the knowledge is not in your head."[24] Ask players to narrate what they're doing while they play, and you'll suddenly see their gameplay become increasingly sloppy. The knowledge rests in the body.

This correlation between a player's physical input and virtual entities' actions connects players to Nintendo's characters on an instinctive level. This is the conceit of the "Who Are You?" campaign. At the same time that Nintendo emphasizes brand continuity with recognizable intellectual property (IP), each of Mario's or Link's permutations calls for altered bodily engagement, while overall control interfaces retain consistencies. Perception, proprioception, and skill development must be translated to the new platform, even if a game is ported with few alterations. The bodily skills necessary to engage with Mario or Link on the GBA are certainly similar to that of the Super Nintendo Entertainment System (SNES), but they nevertheless demand incremental relearning. And developing these hand-eye coordination and action skills through experience connects the player to Nintendo's brand identity.

Breaking Pots and Taking Names

Released in Japan and Europe in 2004 and North America in 2005, Nintendo and Capcom's *The Legend of Zelda: The Minish Cap* mediates between the mechanics of the 2D, SNES *Zelda* and the cell-shaded art style of the GameCube's *The Legend of Zelda: The Wind Waker*. The instant you launch a new file, you're prompted to enter a six-character name for the sprite you'll control. Although this hero is traditionally known as Link, you're invited to connect yourself to the character through the act of renaming. Identification becomes literalized when your physical actions begin to enact consequences in the game world.

The game's action begins when the king of Hyrule nominates Link to embark on a quest to save the petrified Princess Zelda from the wicked Vaati. To do so, Link must enlist the help of the Minish, a small race of fairylike people based on the *koro-pok-guru* in the folklore of the Ainu people of northern Japan. Only children can see the Minish, so Link affords adult players a nostalgic return to childhood not only through iconic IP, but also through the narrative itself. It takes something youthful in the player to go meet the Minish.

Not long after his quest begins, Link encounters Ezlo, an enchanted green cap. Much like the other helpers of the *Zelda* series (the most famous being Navi, the fairy navigation system developed concurrently with Z-targeting), Ezlo guides Link through his adventures. But he also transforms Link's body—first by leaping up to rest on top of Link's messy blond hair (thereby becoming a sentient version of Link's iconic hat, altering the in-game sprite in the process) and then by enabling Link to shrink to the size of a Minish. When the display is scaled for a television set, Minish Link is somewhat visible. But on the GBA's tiny screen, he looks more like a 10-pixel spec of dirt, so he gets an icon over his body to pinpoint his position. Aesthetically the Link icon is an imposition; mechanically, it's a necessity.

Before Nintendo released the game, they launched a website featuring concept art illustrating Link's ability to shrink. This was a savvy way of priming players for the new mechanic—a reminder that games are not as intuitive as we imagine them to be. Navigating the overworld as a Minish is perilous; puddles that pose no threat to full-sized Link can now drown him. The new mechanic alters conventions that players take for granted, so the website attempted to brief players in advance. Through transformation, Link and the player can enter sections of the universe where only the Minish can travel. There, he returns to his former pixel resolution, but the constituent features of the world are magnified. Small plant leaves become majestic arches; a tiny bramble becomes an impassable roadblock; a leaf becomes a platform that carries Link across a puddle like some vegetal gondola. The world is viewed from a new perspective.

Of course, this world of bitmap grids, sprites, and tiles already operates differently than our own. This is, in large part, thanks to the way games are segmented—temporally through discontinuous engagement and spatially in terms of the discrete fragments of the world glimpsed on the display at any given moment.[25] Paradigmatic of this discontinuity is the looping maze of the Lost Woods in the Royal Valley. There are two ways to navigate the maze: one by reading the signs along the way ($\uparrow \leftarrow \leftarrow \uparrow \rightarrow \uparrow$), and the other by following instructions from the gravekeeper Dampé, who remembers all but the last turn ($\leftarrow \leftarrow \leftarrow \uparrow \uparrow \uparrow \uparrow$?). Although we can write out these directions as I have just done, mapping out the Woods is impossible due to the way that the maze defies the conventions of space. Taking a wrong turn brings Link to the preceding screen, while moving downward invariably brings him to the maze's entrance. Narratively, it is said that anyone who becomes irreversibly lost in the Woods turns into a monster. For the player, this monstrosity manifests as frustration and "rage-quitting"—the tongue-in-cheek name for when defeated players storm away from the game, occasionally breaking their hardware in the process.

The Lost Woods and other dungeons remind us that not all cognitive processes take place in the mind. These processes also extend into our material environments.[26] For instance, we can reach over and jot down some solutions to puzzles or hints from nonplayable characters on a notepad as a memory aid. Because *Zelda* dungeons often take longer to complete than the average commute, these notes can help us pick up where we left off. Nintendo eventually incorporated our tendency to support cognition with tools like pen and paper into the diegetic interface of *The Legend of Zelda: Phantom Hourglass*, where the touch screen allows Link (through the player) to leave little reminders on the world map by way of the stylus. Pen and paper operate as an external environmental storage and retrieval system that isn't meaningful apart from biological memory and later becomes part of the games themselves.[27]

Like most videogames, *The Minish Cap* is goal-oriented, structured around the completion of certain tasks in a specific order. Retrieving four elemental artifacts enables the broken Picori Blade to be repaired into the Four sword, the only weapon capable of defeating Vaati (by narrative necessity). But the game also includes nonpurposive actions extraneous to the simple fairy-tale plot. There are simple pleasures found in aimlessly exploring the utopian world of forests and rivers. The player can wander for hours in search of collectables, their mind occupied with other concerns while directing Link by hand through woodlands, mountains, caves, and meadows.

Short of hacking and modifying the game, the conditions of the software code limit player agency. But our influence is equally constrained to a set of actions in the physical world. Consequently, as Torben Grodal observes, "the only necessary condition for experiencing agency is that our actions make a difference."[28] Here, agency may not be related to physically altering the world, but rather to changing the player's own mental state. The game therefore affords players a different kind of freedom, agency, and pleasure than what they might experience in the real world. Link experiences no exhaustion or pain from wandering; he can walk all day if the player wants him to.

Rhythm and Kinesthetic Responsiveness

With a few exceptions, gestural expression has no direct effect on GBA software. But studies have shown that the tendency to tilt, swerve, and duck in response to actions on the screen heightens the enjoyment of play.[29] While taking a corner in *Super Circuit*, a player might lean over to the side as if to help the character stay on the track. Or the player might reel after a projectile collides with Link in *The Minish Cap*. Researchers believe that these actions lighten the cognitive load and permit players to dedicate more attention to navigating the game. When players self-consciously try to suppress these gestures, they reduce the pleasure of play.[30]

Nintendo built an acknowledgment of players' movements into the GBA's marketing. *Nintendo Power*'s GBA promotion defends the choice of a nonbacklit thin-film transistor liquid crystal display (TFT LCD), in part based on its wide viewing angle, which allows players to see the screen even if they move the handheld.[31] So there's already an expectation on the developers' part that players will move with the device even if kinesthetic responsiveness has no direct effect on signal input. As a self-contained object, the GBA amplifies the feelings of tension, anticipation, and elation that occur through play. Users move with the software. The hardware, gripped by the fingers, moves with them. The relationship is mutual and direct.

Nintendo's last game for the GBA, the Japanese-exclusive rhythm game called *Rizumu Tengoku* (リズム天国, or *Rhythm Heaven*), exemplifies this mutual relationship.[32] Mechanically, the game asks players to press GBA buttons in time with aural cues to advance through forty-eight minigames ranging in duration from a little over a minute to slightly under four minutes. More saliently, the game asks the players to groove to the beat of the music. Its chief creator, Tsunku, described the game as a way of improving "groove-sense," a sort of embodied expression of rhythm distinct from mathematical counting.[33] *Rizumu Tengoku* arose from the desire of Tsunku, a renowned record producer, singer, and songwriter, to remedy what he perceived as a poor sense of rhythm among young Japanese videogame players.

The DS had already become the company's dominant line of handhelds in 2006 when *Rizumu Tengoku* was under development. But Kazuyoshi Osawa from Software Planning and Development (SPD) wanted to foreground the tactility of button inputs rather than the bells and whistles of the touch screen.[34] There's a simplicity that makes the game uniquely suited to the GBA's less powerful hardware. Unlike popular rhythm games that rely on coordinating input with visual cues (such as *Rock Band*), *Rizumu Tengoku* emphasizes aurality. If players have enough familiarity with the game, they can complete levels without even looking at the screen's delirious graphics. The reverse doesn't hold true. Its minigames require sound cues that push the GBA's audio capabilities to their extreme.

Before players explore the beats and pulses of the levels, they must complete a three-part rhythm test stylized after a medical exam. In the first task, they tap a button along with a 120-bpm pulse indicated by a beeping sound. In the second, the pulse remains, but now a display on the screen counts down from 7. Players need to tap the button when the countdown reaches zero, but the game eliminates the visual and aural cues until only the initial number 7 displays; players must keep time internally to press the button when the sequence reaches zero. Finally, players must continue to press the button with the initial 120-pbm pulse while a drumbeat plays in and out of sync. These tests demand active body awareness. They evaluate the player's ability to feel through the rhythms of the game while introducing its mechanics.[35] To fulfill the game's instructional aim, players can return to the rhythm test at any point to track their improvement.

To obtain a shared awareness of rhythm, the development staff took dance lessons in Tokyo. Movement is at the game's heart even though, in terms of direct input, all the player is doing is pressing buttons. Kinesthetic responses—tapping feet, bopping heads, humming along, or the excesses of swaying and dancing—are paramount not only to players' enjoyment of the game, but also their success. In her ethnographic research into Japanese *Rizumu Tengoku* players, Miki Kaneda reveals that users find the game easier to complete when they move their bodies.[36] Suppressing these motions takes deliberate effort, which draws attention away from the game. And as I write this chapter while listening to the game's soundtrack, I find it almost impossible not to groove along.

WarioWare—With a Twist!

The paradigm of embodied gaming on the GBA is a collection of 223 high-tension, fast-paced, 5-second microgames called *WarioWare: Twisted!*. *Twisted!* emerged late in the GBA's life cycle—2004 in Japan and 2005 in North America (it never made it to Europe)—and was a collaboration between Nintendo's Software Planning and Development and Intelligent Systems. Refusing to be constrained by the contents of the GBA's chassis, the developers of *Twisted!* added a gyroscopic sensor and rumble pack to the cartridge itself. The additional hardware detects the platform's rotation in space and provides force feedback to produce what reviewers have called "an insanely successful design that really shows off the potential of the Game Boy Advance platform."[37] Rather than rely on button input, most microgames require steering, tilting, turning, or otherwise moving the GBA, self-reflexively calling attention to the interactions between the body of the player and the body of the platform.

Twisted! isn't the only game to employ additional hardware. The GBC's *Kirby Tilt 'n' Tumble* similarly included an accelerometer in its transparent pink cartridge. The Japanese-only コロコロパズル ハッピィパネッチュ！ (*Koro Koro Puzzle Happy Panechu!*) was the first GBA game to use a tilt-sensor chip, a feature that *Yoshi Topsy-Turvy* later reprised. And Game Freak's *Drill Dozer* included a rumble cart to deliver force feedback. But there are important reasons to single out *Twisted!* For one thing, its motion-sensing technology is the most sophisticated of the bunch. For another, the *WarioWare* series uniquely appeals to both casual and hardcore gamers, and it also poignantly reflects on videogame production and circulation.

The series launched on the GBA in 2003 when *WarioWare, Inc.: Mega Microgame$!* introduced a gauntlet of increasingly difficult 5-second challenges. Its narrative follows the greedy Wario—a sort of Mario foil—as he tries to make quick cash developing a videogame. But Wario is lazy, and game development proves harder than anticipated. Together with his friends, Wario develops simple, addictive microgames to turn a profit—a sardonic spoof of a narrative that we often hear echoed in the discourse around videogames.

The casual nature of *WarioWare*'s microgames is well suited for the GBA's portability, speaking to the way that it positions itself as an object that mediates between console-quality gaming and casual play. Despite its satirical narrative, the series captures Nintendo's changing conception of their target audience. In a 2006 *Iwata Asks*, Iwata said:

> I feel that the *WarioWare* series represents what Nintendo always aims for; finding ways to reach new types of customers, and this type of game is paving the way for us to do so. These games have opened the door to a whole new realm where the playing field is large and you can choose how you want to play, whether you concentrate on the game for a little while or become engrossed in it for hours. This dynamic range, the idea that there is no set way to approach how you play the games, is very close to the direction that Nintendo hopes to take.[38]

Unlike so-called hardcore games, *WarioWare* possesses what Jesper Juul refers to as greater flexibility along the lines of skill, attention, and time commitment.[39] Simple microgames appeal to players along a spectrum of experience, and each microgame is accompanied by contextual clues and brief instructions. The result is an addictive experience that demands little commitment from its players.

Despite developers' low expectations for the title, *Mega Microgame$!* enjoyed considerable acclaim, so Iwata requested a GameCube version to capitalize on its growing reputation. The home console's affordance for a multiplayer environment helped shape the remake's direction. *WarioWare, Inc.: Mega Party Game$!* launched a few months later, having adapted the microgames for competitive play. A handheld sequel was subsequently planned, but producer Yoshio Sakamoto was concerned with originality: "We didn't just want to release a new collection, we wanted to add a new twist to the series. . . . For the upcoming release we were at the stage where we needed to find an original way to use all the new microgames we'd amassed."[40]

Fortunately, Kazuyoshi Osawa—a member of Nintendo SPD, as well as director and chief programmer of *Rizumu Tengoku*—fabricated a *WarioWare* prototype that employed motion-sensor technology to control the game's action. As the oft-cited anecdote goes, the team brought the prototype to Iwata, who put the GBA on a swivel chair and spun it around to complete the record player minigame on the screen (he had to spin the record like a turntable). This was a memorable experience all around. In an "Iwata Asks" interview, Sakamoto reflected that "as Iwata-san was spinning that chair round and round, he'd occasionally say: 'This is ridiculous!' with a big grin on his face!"[41] The glee at physically engaging with the hardware in new and creative ways came to determine the game's development. Twisting literally became the twist that Sakamoto was searching for, just as the DS's touch screen, the Wii's motion-sensitive controller, and the DSi's camera shaped the mechanics of *WarioWare: Touched!*, *WarioWare: Smooth Moves*, and *WarioWare: Snapped,* respectively. Each of these games emerged out of a contextual relationship between the players' bodies and technological interventions.

Nintendo has a long history of adding supplementary hardware to their platforms by way of peripherals or extensions. As developers learn to navigate the hardware's peculiarities and technologies become cheaper over time, they can move beyond the machine's initial capabilities. Consider, for example, the MotionPlus attachment for the Wii that arrived in 2010—four years after the Wiimote's release—once microelectromechanical systems (MEMS) technology became smaller and cheaper to produce.[42] The Wii MotionPlus plugs into the Wiimote's expansion port and contains a small gyroscope to correct for the shortcomings of the Wiimote's triple-axis accelerometer.[43] With this attachment, software developers could work with more precise input mapping. There's an astounding difference between *The Legend of Zelda: Twilight Princess* swordplay with the Wiimote, where a light flick of the wrist prompts Link to slash through the air, and *The Legend of Zelda: Skyward Sword* battling, where the MotionPlus registers unique strike and slash patterns depending on the angle of the swing.

Although the gyroscope in *Twisted!* wasn't a direct predecessor to that of the MotionPlus, they shared a common ancestor—handheld video camera stabilization technologies—and led to an instance of parallel evolution in Nintendo's hardware.[44] *Twisted!* uses a Ceramic Gyro piezoelectric gyroscope manufactured by NEC TOKIN to capture the GBA's rotational movement.[45] The principle behind the sensor is fairly simple. A piezoelectric ceramic oscillator rod is induced to vibrate, causing it to function like a pendulum. The resulting perpendicular Coriolis force—an inertial force that operates in rotating frames—converts to a voltage signal proportionate to the velocity of rotation through which the system can determine rotational motion. There are two key advantages to this technology: high accuracy and small size. The sensitive system allows the games to respond to both minute and exaggerated motions, lending developers great freedom in devising microgames. The game's downsized Ceramic Gyro CG-L43 measures a mere 0.31 x 0.6 x 0.2 inches (8 x 15.5 x 5 millimeters), which is small enough to be embedded into the Game Pak without making it unwieldy or unbalancing the handheld. Reflecting on Nintendo's use of their gyroscope for "an unprecedented game system," NEC TOKIN observed that their gyro sensor "has opened a new possibility in the field of games."[46] Indeed, motion control would come to define the next generation of home consoles, with the Wii and later Sony's PlayStation Move and the Microsoft Kinect.[47]

Included with the gyroscope is a responsive rumble pack to complement the motion sensitivity. The motor offers several forms of feedback, from the quality vibration of a kind included in the GameCube controllers to mechanical "clicks" as the player navigates the rotary-phone-style menu. The rumble adds texture in subtle microgame situations: a flower begins to bud, a key clicks into a lock, a sheep leaps over a fence. In addition to reinforcing audiovisual cues, the feedback "completes the interface loop which, previously, had consisted of only non-registered haptic inputs/outputs."[48] It validates the relationship between the bodies of the player and of the platform.

As a result of the additional hardware, the cartridge in *Twisted!* is closer in height to the Game Boy's. A 1-inch bevel containing the gyro sensor and rumble pack protrudes above the edge of the GBA, which sounds more cumbersome than it is in practice. Over time, the body adapts to the additional weight and size. It's also worth noting, incidentally, that the gyro-sensor contained within the game cartridge was Nintendo's greatest protection against piracy. Because the sensor is in the cartridge rather than the handheld, it often frustrates emulation. Players can't separate the code from its material container without losing a critical piece of the game.[49]

Because the gyroscope recalibrates each time the system powers on, the game works, regardless of whether it's inserted in the top-loading GBA or the bottom-loading SP, DS, and Micro. Although the instruction manual states that the game isn't compatible with the GBP, that's not entirely true. Given that the GBP runs GBA hardware, the game loads and (at least theoretically) works perfectly. The difficulty is that, to control the game, players would have to pick up and rotate the entire GameCube—cables, add-on, and all. Nintendo's disclaimer has less to do with functional incompatibility and more to do with their idea of how human and hardware bodies should come together to perform the game's requisite actions. Nintendo sees their GBA as a portable, movable platform, and the GameCube as a static fixture in the living room. The disclaimer is a reminder that the company develops their hardware with human bodies and movements in mind.

Like most *WarioWare* games, *Twisted!* is deliberately self-mocking—a playful jab at players and their preconceptions of Nintendo's software development process. The game opens with Wario throwing his GBA against a wall after failing a microgame—a display that humorously calls out the rage-quitters. Counter to Nintendo's hardware design, the virtual GBA actually breaks after the collision, so Wario takes it to Dr. Crygor's lab, where the scientist places the handheld into his Gravitator machine. In what amounts to a clever absorption of the gyroscope into the narrative, the Gravitator spits out dozens of devices shaped like buttonless GBAs. When Wario's friends arrive on the scene, they take up these objects to model the rotational motions necessary to complete the microgames.

Each batch of microgames consists of a few dozen rapid-fire challenges delivered in a randomized order and grouped around specific control mechanics or aesthetic features: Mona's games require subtle movements that use the gyrosensor's high accuracy, while Jimmy's receive input from more exaggerated motions. Rather than mapping abstract actions onto a series of button presses, the game simulates direct actions on in-game objects. One microgame has the player perform a bouncing motion with GBA to break a vase with a spring. Another has the player tilt the system like a pitcher to pour water into a glass. Mundane actions take on a playful tenor through the game's kinesthetic dimensions.

As the game progresses, its pace increases along with the tempo of the music. These twin accelerations have notable effects on the body. Lulls are minimal; there's a continuous negotiation between figuring out the microgame's demands and executing the vital action—all within a few seconds. The pulse starts to race; palms get sweaty; the body shakes with excitement. All these effects make it difficult to complete each challenge without stumbling or mishandling the device, ratcheting up the stakes.

While many videogames seek to eliminate interface altogether (the full immersion promised of virtual reality), *Twisted!* foregrounds the contingent interactions between human and hardware. The tilting, turning, and twisting actions hark back to Nintendo's early work as a toy company, recalling one of Gunpei Yokoi's inventions: the テンビリオン (*tenbirion*), known in English as the "Ten Billion Barrel." Developed in 1980, the barrel-shaped toy presented a puzzle like the Rubik's Cube, where the goal was to twist the discs that composed its cylindrical frame until the balls in each column were the same color. The movements in *Twisted!* explicitly foretold how Nintendo built its reputation on providing users with tactile interactions.[50]

True to the company's nostalgic design philosophy, *Twisted!* also includes several nods to Nintendo's hardware and software history. The NES's Robotic Operating Buddy (R.O.B.) makes an appearance in a nice acknowledgment of Nintendo's early attempts at using spinning gyroscope technology. Donkey Kong, Link, and Samus all take on roles in the game's "Spintendo Classics" collection. *Super Mario Bros.* levels are twisted in on themselves, so Mario must now make his way to the castle by way of a circular journey, demanding players unlearn the time-tested linear levels to account for the way that gravity operates differently when the game is controlled not with a D-pad, but with a gyroscope; thanks to the platform's rotation, Mario can leap unthinkable distances, which sometimes lands him in trouble when he overshoots his mark and misses a nefarious Goomba.

Another acknowledgment of Nintendo's robust corporate history can be found in the game's souvenir collection—an assortment of randomized, unique items. Included among these items' ranks is the Love Tester, a "doodad" designed to predict a couple's compatibility. To use it, two people face each other while holding the GBA between them. Over a rich magenta background, the game instructs the players to look deep into each other's eyes and press the L and R buttons together at the beep. The system then ranks the couple's compatibility on a scale from 0 to 100 and charts their projected love life over a ten-year period. Accompanying messages range from words of caution ("I see trouble. You might want to stick with being just friends. Or you might just want to run away screaming") to promises of an amoebic interpretation of romantic bliss ("You will only grow closer as time passes. Soon, you will be the same person!").

The Love Tester in *Twisted!* refuses to take itself seriously. But it also harks back to a novelty toy of the same name that Nintendo released in 1969. Designed by Yokoi, the original Love Tester purported to determine the attraction between two people who held hands while each gripped an electrode. In actuality, the Love Tester operated more along the lines of a lie detector (it was actually marketed as a Lie/Love Tester in North America), in that its sensor impinged upon the electrical currents that exist in the human body. Rather than measuring love, the contraption measured conductivity. But scientific rigor wasn't the point. Describing his invention, Yokoi stated: "The Love Tester came from me wondering if I could somehow use this to get girls to hold my hand. . . . I wound up holding hands with quite a few girls thanks to it."[51] And, speaking of lies, he also admitted that he enjoyed explaining that the device delivered more accurate results when couples kissed.[52] In both its incarnations, the Love Tester is little more than a thinly veiled excuse to get human bodies in close proximity to each other. And in that respect, even this gimmicky toy harks back to the company's history; in the 1960s, Nintendo opened a chain of "love hotels" that rented rooms by the hour—a detail conveniently left out of their carefully curated corporate history webpage.[53]

At the end of the day, both versions of the Love Tester, with their computational conceptions of love, are about connection. And isn't that what videogames are built on? From the transistors that make up an integrated circuit to the hardware affordances that guide software design, from the battery voltage illuminating the screen to the process of human input and signal output, and from the affinity between player and character to the circulation of the object through space and time, it's all about material, embodied connection. *Twisted!* doesn't aim for immersion and the dissolution of interface. It reflects on the role of the hands, eyes, ears, muscles, and mind, showing us how videogames offer sites for expansion and relation.

On April 20, 2005, an image of two cats looking at a Game Boy Advance (GBA) was posted to the Thai forum Pantip. About a year later, the YTMND user commıe appropriated this image for a demotivational poster meme, pairing it with the popular phrase "Let me show you my Pokemans" (figure 4.1). Nothing about either posting is extraordinary on its own. By the mid-2000s, demotivational posters with austere black borders and cynical taglines had become common spoofs of the cheesy motivational posters found everywhere from corporate buildings to doctors' offices, the LOLcat had long been a revered internet mascot, and even the deliberate misspelling of "Pokémon" was old news.

What most interests me is the convergence of these elements to produce a coherent image that exposes salient aspects of the GBA's portability. For one thing, the frozen interaction between the two felines occurs outdoors, a reminder that portability extends the spatial possibilities of gameplay beyond the family living room. But the meme also captures how the GBA mediates between the personal and the social, the private and the public, and the casual and the invested player. Overcoming the absence of opposable thumbs, the first cat holds out the purple GBA, eyes riveted on the screen, mouth open in elation, while its companion seems as passively interested as any nongamer friend can ever be when exposed to a lengthy (albeit enthusiastic) introduction to digital avatars. The second cat humors its friend, even while it may be only casually curious about games as a way to escape the tedium of waiting for the food bowl to be refilled. Nevertheless, the second cat is invited into the experience

Figure 4.1   The viral "Pokemans" meme, which the YTMND user comm1e created using an image from the Pantip forum.

not only spatially—that is, its body leaning into that of the first cat—but also through the poster's language: "Pokeman. Let me show you them." Together, the image and text remind us that sharing the GBA with other people (or cats) means inviting them into our personal space. There's an intimacy in this proximity that's predicated on the diminutive size of the handheld's screen—an intimacy not freely given to everyone. While the GameCube and Wii disseminate graphics content through a television screen, the self-contained GBA must be *shown* to others. There's a sense that the handheld's pocket portability privileges personal use, but here, we can see how it circulates through intimate invitations to share in an experience.

Perhaps my arguments about the GBA's social aspects are a lot to put on the shoulders of these two cats and the orthographically (and grammatically) questionable phrases surrounding them. But it seems apt to open a chapter on circulation with a meme that's both a reflection on the GBA's social context and a directive on how to use it. Historically, the study of videogame circulation has taken a backseat to analyses of screened content, but Dilip Parameshwar Gaonkar and Elizabeth Povinelli observe a broader (and necessary) turn in cultural and media studies toward a view of circulation "as the enabling matrix within which social forms, both textual and topical, emerge and are recognizable when they emerge."[1] Circulation isn't just movement, but a cultural process. What Lee and LiPuma call "cultures of circulation" aren't reducible to objects; they're contingent on discursive practices.[2] Cultures of circulation invite us to consider how players actually use the GBA.

We tend to group gameplay into two distinct categories. On the one hand, we see casual play as something that occurs on mobile devices in public (and often but not always transit) spaces. These solitary and often fragmented experiences are meant to distract from the boredom of waiting, while they themselves are rife with distractions: switching subway lines, a flight attendant handing out beverages, the doctor calling a patient's name. On the other hand, we see longer, more involved play sessions as taking place in the private (domestic) sphere. We presume that they occur on a home console in the family room or the bedroom and are understood to be more immersive or "hardcore."

As a handheld, the GBA complicates distinct categories of play. It marries the console quality (and ported software titles) of the Super Nintendo Entertainment System (SNES) with the portability of the Game & Watch and the Game Boy, and it emphasizes the important distinctions among portable and mobile gaming platforms.[3] The GBA is a portable platform functionally dedicated to videogame software. Its inputs and form factor have been designed expressly for play. Its software was purchased *in* stores. Conversely, mobile devices like smartphones and tablets are designed around telecommunication or personal productivity. Games are found *on* store sites—usually Google Play or the Apple App Store—and use touch screens intended to navigate applications that have little to do with play. On mobile devices, users can switch between making a phone call, checking their email, and playing a game, all with the swipe of a finger, whereas people who want to change GBA games must save their current progress, shut down the system, swap the cartridge, and turn the system back on. The GBA is equidistant from the mobile device and from the home console and brings with it unique forms of use.

This chapter traces three ways of approaching the GBA's circulation: temporally, socially, and spatially. The first section borrows the tools of media archaeology to excavate the links between the handheld's portability and a longer history of personal media technologies. The second explores the GBA as a social platform through three connective peripherals. And the third considers the spaces in which actual users play GBA games. Studying the GBA on its own terms reminds us that its ability to circulate within and between spaces challenges the binary distinctions that tend to be between private and public, solitude and sociability, casual and hardcore, handheld and console.

Gameplay experiences are always contingent on the "here-and-now" of the encounter.[4] As I move through the spaces the GBA inhabits, I draw on ethnographic materials from short interviews I conducted in 2019 with current and former GBA players in and around Montreal. These instances offer the opportunity to reflect on the confluence of material technologies, cultural contexts, and the actual ways we explore game worlds.[5]

More Interesting Than a Pocket Calculator

Videogame history often traces its origins to the experiments of male programmers in Cold War research centers like the Massachusetts Institute of Technology (MIT) in the 1950s and 1960s.[6] *Spacewar*, widely regarded as the first videogame, was the "illegitimate child of the marrying of computers and graphics displays," a product of the "enthusiasm of irresponsible youngsters" as they sought to exploit the affordances of new machines.[7] From there, the story traces videogames from batch processing and interactive computing to the golden age of the arcades in the late 1970s, through the boom (and crash) of videogames in the 1980s, and then from the console wars of the 1990s to the increasing ubiquity of mobile gaming and networked play.[8] While this conventional history is useful in many ways, it also neglects broader cultural and social trends around mobile media that existed before videogame technologies emerged.

The GBA has another genealogy—one linked to space and boredom and the desire to pass the time. As the story goes, Gunpei Yokoi famously conceived of the idea behind the Game & Watch after watching a bored train commuter play with a pocket calculator. In that case, the calculator operated as a distraction rather than a tool of corporate office culture—a form of fidgeting or virtual doodling meant to relieve some of the tedium of urban transit. Repurposing the calculator's segmented display to animate videogames came much later in the development of the Game & Watch. According to Satoru Okada, "what this memory from the train really created [for Yokoi] was the will to create a discreet toy for adults so they could kill time while on public transport."[9] The resulting product allowed commuters to not only kill time (game), but also to tell time (watch). In so doing, it addressed the two things that most occupy commuters: getting where they want to go on time and making sure that they're not overly bored while doing so. The Game & Watch needed to be only marginally more engaging than a pocket calculator.

Nintendo often elides this lineage (and the material underpinnings of lateral thinking) when marketing their new devices. Instead, they seek to position their latest device as wholly innovative (the Wii's internal codename was "Revolution," after all). Months before the GBA's release, Peter Main declared: "Our aggressive marketing campaign for the Game Boy Advance is designed to communicate the message that the Game Boy Advance transforms downtime into playtime."[10] But the idea of turning downtime into playtime was hardly new; Nintendo had been doing just that for decades with the Game Boy.

More generally, mobile and portable media—technological or not—have long performed a similar role as contemporary games in transitory spaces, and we would do well to look back to before the 1980s for the nascency of mobile entertainment.[11] Before Nintendo cornered the hand-held market, Sony dominated personal entertainment with the Walkman. And before the Walkman, people spent their time in transit reading books or newspapers. The candid camera, women's hand fans, and the wrist-watch equally circulated in public spaces, catalyzing new ways of see-ing and being in the world.[12] Each of these mass-produced objects was a successful medium of portable entertainment or communication. And this longer history of mobility is useful for understanding the goals and intended experiences of playing the GBA in intermediary public spaces.

Mobile Privatization

The advent of the railway fundamentally altered the way in which people experienced travel. Wolfgang Schivelbusch writes that in the late nine-teenth century, "the train was experienced as a projectile, and travel-ling on it, as being shot through the landscape—thus losing control of one's senses."[13] The speed of the railway caused a dizzying blur of blues and greens to replace the comparatively pastoral panoramas of transport by carriage. Leaves and flowers became hazy flecks—there one second and gone the next. "This loss of landscape," according to Schivelbusch, "affected all the senses." The sounds and smells of the country air were, for better or worse, replaced by those circulating within the train carriage.

To cope with the increased passivity of travel—no longer mov-ing through the world, but *being moved* by an economy of industrial transportation—members of the European upper classes turned to books. In England and France, patrons of railway bookstores were almost always members of the bourgeoisie, and reading while traveling was a decidedly class-based pastime.[14] Working-class people, who had begun to travel only with the arrival of the railway, had no explicit desire to read during their journey because the proletariat compartments were open and heavily populated; conversation was constant and unencumbered by reflections of how much more idyllic it was to travel by coach. But for the bourgeoisie, the train was awkwardly public and highly monotonous. Reading became a way to make up for the jarring loss of a more intimate connection with nature. At the same time, it was a salve for the loneliness caused by the railway's alteration of travelers' relationships to each another now that journeys took hours rather than days.[15]

While the late nineteenth century experienced the industrialization of travel and the emergence of modern mobile entertainment, it also gave rise to the increasing popularity of home entertainment, particularly for the middle classes.[16] While upper-class families had long convened in drawing rooms to occupy themselves with journaling, letter writing, embroidery, and music playing in a shared space, the invention of the phonograph, radio, and television in the twentieth century placed new primacy on the home across all social classes.[17] Raymond Williams reflects on the complexity of these two seemingly paradoxical developments, which nevertheless were intimately connected to modernity and urban living:

> On the one hand, mobility, on the other hand the more apparently self-sufficient family home. The earlier period of public technology, best exemplified by the railways and city lighting, was being replaced by a kind of technology for which no satisfactory name has yet been found: that which served an at-once mobile and home-centred way of living: a form of *mobile privatisation*.[18]

Williams defines mobile privatization as the extension of the private home to the commute, which transplants the affective experience of being at home to the object. Users' attachment (both physical and emotional) to their mobile devices confers a feeling of security as they move through the public sphere, while also serving to exclude others from the users' experiences. For him, the portable radio was emblematic of this sensation of being at home during the commute. But it isn't difficult to see how books or newspapers enabled a similar escape from the awkwardness of public travel for bourgeois Europeans a century earlier. As much as the printed word offered a way to distract from the blur of the countryside outside the train window, it also communicated to others that a reader didn't want to be disturbed by conversation, especially with strangers.

From Walkman to Game Boy

A distinct but nevertheless parallel phenomenon of personal media adoption occurred in Japan. Larissa Hjorth and Ingrid Richardson observe that in cities like Tokyo, where people spend long periods of time during lengthy commutes in cramped, crowded spaces, the use of an individuated device provides "a cocooned individual space that does not intrude upon the personal space of others."[19] Sony's Walkman is representative of this phenomenon—evidence of a "culturally specific notion of individualism within a highly collective context."[20]

Released in 1979, the Walkman introduced the rest of the world to the quintessence of Japanese technology. It's "Japanese-ness" was a product of the country's postwar economic growth, high-tech consumer electronics engineering, effective global marketing strategy, and aesthetics of smallness.[21] In the United States, a nation so invested in perceptions of its own grandeur and virility, the adoption of smallness and cuteness was deferred until the late twentieth century. "Conversely," writes Sianne Ngai, "in post–World War II Japan, an island nation newly conscious of its diminished military and economic power . . . the same aesthetic (*kawaii*) had a comparatively accelerated development and impact on the culture as a whole."[22] The cultural impact and global exportation of *kawaii* would reach its zenith when *Pokémon* became a worldwide phenomenon. But the Walkman was an early introduction to this aesthetics of smallness; small size and its corollary, portability, afforded new, sonic ways of engaging with the world.

As the first low-cost and portable stereo, the Walkman enjoyed international popularity. In China, it occasioned a cultural and historical rupture with ideas of listening as an activity that was both public and collective.[23] For Western Walkman users, the pocket-sized technology gave rise to an intimate, privatized space of aural reception that produced an impulse to treat life as if it were a movie. Through its headphones, the unobtrusive Walkman introduced a private, extradiegetic soundtrack as the user moved through public spaces.[24]

While the Walkman became a cultural phenomenon globally, it held special meaning in Japan. Characteristic of what Tetsuo Kogawa calls "electronic individualism," the Walkman paradoxically isolated users from each other at the moment when they were most connected, "totally integrated into an electronic collectivity" through the act of listening to sources that were subject to government control and the whims of their cultural industries.[25] For Kogawa, the advent of the Walkman, itself a product of social and cultural tensions, suspended Japan on a precipice between the radical democracy of electronic collectivity and the government control of the collectivist Emperor System.

Unlike the Western individualism introduced to Japan in the nineteenth century, electronic individualism connects to Japanese technonationalism. Since the 1970s, Japanese technologies have embodied what Ito, Okabe, and Matsuda call portable, personal, and pedestrian—qualities that have defined the market success of Japanese electronics as sociocultural artifacts enabling precisely the kind of electronic individualism Kogawa articulates.[26] Here, "personal" refers primarily to the desire for individual privacy in dense urban spaces; "portable" speaks to miniaturization and materiality; and "pedestrian" describes the devices' patterns of use. Patterns of use that emerged from the Walkman contributed to new technological developments in entertainment and communication, which in turn rearticulated people's relationships to technology, space, and each other. Likewise, as the most popular handheld, the Game Boy helped redefine contexts of play, slotting into empty moments and public spaces. In 1999, DoCoMo's i-mode—which Hjorth and Richardson see as a precursor to the iPhone—introduced Japan to online media and mobile play a decade before mobile internet gained popularity in most of Europe and North America.[27]

The proliferation of mobile and portable technologies led to what Kenichi Fujimoto refers to as the distinctly Japanese practice of "*nagara* mobilism," the pedestrian portion of Ito, Okabe, and Matsuda's "three Ps."[28] Analogous to Williams' notion of mobile privatization, *nagara* (or "while doing something else") mobilism refers to parallel processing and asynchronous multitasking, such as if someone were to play *Super Mario Advance* while ambling through a park. Fujimoto locates the emergence of *nagara* mobilism with high school girls' prevalent use of the pager in the 1990s, arguing that it prefigured and indeed circumscribed contemporary *ketai* (mobile phone) use. The "pager revolution" challenged the male social hegemonic order and triumphed, resulting in a shift in mobile media literacy and the feminized contexts that surround it. As Fujimoto notes, the young women behind the pager revolution brought *nagara* mobilism into the streets by the early 2000s, where older audiences of all genders now move through the world with their eyes and hands on their phone.

But even this dual-focus media use has an analog precedent, in the story of the nineteenth-century Japanese figure Ninomiya Sontoku (born Kinjiro), who famously read while he gathered firewood. Sontoku became a national role model for his ability to split his focus between mundane tasks and media. While the GBA is decidedly more playful than studying, simultaneous play and movement are a descendent of *nagara* mobilism inherited from this Japanese context. Some of the GBA users I spoke to confessed that they ceased paying as much attention to the sidewalk once they began playing SP while walking home from school; cultural practices of moving through the world were exported along with Nintendo's hardware. Centuries of cultural history and social practices surround the GBA's materialization at the turn of the century. The image of the GBA—like the Walkman and the Game Boy before it—becomes symbolic of a distinctive kind of material media culture, of a way of moving through and being in the world.

Social Peripherals

One of the reasons I've spent so much time on this archaeology of the GBA is to contextualize it into a longer material history. Videogames and mobile entertainment are often blamed for the decline of public culture. As a portable videogame platform, the GBA embodies this perceived evil twice over, coupling the ostensible solipsism of mobile devices with the addictiveness and moral vacuousness of videogames. But there's a longer history of mobile privatization at work. Those who bemoan the halcyon days of reading books on public transit might be interested to learn that nineteenth-century critics actually resented books for replacing conversation during travel.

Media archaeology productively reminds us of these continuities. Rather than heralding the erosion of polite public behavior, the GBA participates in the development of networked media, establishing webs of relation through a variety of social peripherals, each of which occasions new modalities for connective or otherwise interactive play.

"Pokemans. Let Me Show You Them" (Game Boy Advance Game Link Cable)

When I asked my interviewees about their social experiences with the GBA, they overwhelmingly recalled their enjoyment of the *Pokémon* series:

> [The SP] was very social, particularly while playing *Pokémon Yellow*—because I played it in high school for the first time and most of my friends had played it already and had much more experience with gaming in general than I did, it was almost a group effort—which Pokémon I chose for my team, which moves were better, etc. (Bailey Cohen-Krichevsky)

There was Pokémon exchange with friends that, at the time, felt revolutionary. (Geneviève Paris)

Whenever there were new *Pokémon* games out, I would race with my friend to see who could finish it first. It was always a fun competition [and it] was great, being able to trade Pokémon with my friends. (Carolyn)

The experience that Bailey describes is that of our meme cats, a spatial sharing of game content whereby more experienced players offered tactical advice over her shoulder. But the trading discussed by Geneviève and Carolyn is a material form of social sharing, one reliant on the connectivity between GBAs using the Game Boy Advance Game Link Cable (AGB-005), which continued Nintendo's tradition of Game Boy connectivity.[29]

Pokémon is indebted to early incarnations of the link cable. Creator and game designer Satoshi Tajiri famously conceived of the series after witnessing two children battle each other on connected Game Boys. Recalling his childhood love of collecting insects, Tajiri envisioned ants crawling back and forth across the link cable, which gave rise to the idea of a portable bug collection where children could use the Game Boy's connective affordances to trade their findings as virtual entomologists. Nintendo was impressed enough with Tajiri's reputation as a game designer that they entertained his pitch for what would become the *Pokémon* franchise—a romanized portmanteau of the Japanese ポケットモンスタ, or *Poketto Monsutā*—even though they didn't quite understand the concept behind it. Little did Nintendo know that these beloved critters would resuscitate waning interest in the Game Boy, become a multibillion-dollar intellectual property (IP), and reshape handheld connectivity.

Mechanically, *Pokémon* games are straightforward and designed to be accessible to children as young as four. In both paired core-series games released for the GBA, *Pokémon Ruby* and *Sapphire* (2003) and *Pokémon FireRed* and *LeafGreen* (2004), players select a male or female trainer to serve as their avatar as they explore the tile-based regions of Hoenn and Kanto, respectively. Throughout their journey, players collect, tame, and train wild Pokémon, with the goal of capturing every creature and becoming the very best Pokémon trainer (as the earworm of a theme song goes). Together with their sister installment *Pokémon Emerald*, the *Pokémon* games were the GBA's three top-selling titles.

Collecting every Pokémon requires social interaction. Before the inception of the series, Game Boy connectivity was more or less synonymous with competitive multiplayer battles. Here, however, the link cable doesn't just enable player-vs.-player contests, but also allows players to exchange Pokémon with each other—the foundational conceit of the series. As per *Ruby*'s game box, "over 200 Pokémon appear with over 100 newly discovered species—you'll have to link up and trade with a friend who has Sapphire Version to catch them all!" Because the roster differs between titles, *Ruby* trainers have no choice but to trade monsters with *Sapphire* players to collect them all.

There are cultural and political factors undergirding Tajiri's motivation to create a game predicated on communication and companionship. Anne Allison observes that, for Tajiri, millennial Japan became associated with "a loss to humanity" not because kids were too occupied with videogames, but rather because they seldom got a chance to play at all.[30] In Japan's "academic record society," pressures to study, perform, and compete edge out opportunities for children to be children. Allison observes that many 10–14-year-olds only return from school at 8 p.m., where they eat dinner alone. Intimacies with technologies address a lack of meaningful human relationships in a capitalist culture of overwork. Pokémon then become surrogate families. Consequently, and like Shigeru Miyamoto's miniature gardens, Tajiri's *Pokémon* is deeply nostalgic. Its landscape is natural, inviting exploration, gathering, and reflection. While there's more evidence of human intervention here than in the pastoral *The Legend of Zelda: The Minish Cap*, the bulk of the adventure nevertheless occurs in woods and caves, with the towns interspersing the routes serving as reminders of the game's social mission.

Until the release of the hybrid Nintendo Switch, all core-series *Pokémon* games were exclusive to the company's handhelds, enabling players to move through physical spaces while navigating virtual ones. Later installments even include pedometers—first as the Pokéwalker peripheral, and later built into the 3DS itself—that allow players to level up their monsters by physically walking (or, because cheating at videogames is as old as videogames themselves, by manually shaking the device). Niantic's *Pokémon Go* for Android and iOS takes the locative and locomotive experience even further, with augmented reality features that use mobile phone cameras to project Pokémon into the player's own environment. Pokémon spawn throughout cities and parks—as do players engaged in similar acts of Pokémon catching. Relationships to the brand are continuous whenever players walk around with their phones out and the game open.

Even without the peripatetic aspects, embodied brand identification exists in the GBA installments. One of the ways that the game sustains this continuous identification is through the mechanics of capturing Pokémon and inscribing their data into a Pokédex, an aesthetically fungible device that indexes information about the monsters accrued throughout the adventure. The Pokédex visually resembles whichever handheld the game is released for; for instance, in *Ruby* and *Sapphire*, the Pokédex is landscape oriented to mirror the GBA. In this way, *Pokémon* literally and metaphorically connects players to each other through "cuteified" software on cute hardware.

In his insightful case study of the idiosyncrasies of Nintendo DS play, Christian McCrea observes three key elements that distinguish portable videogames from their mobile counterparts: affordances (of the platform), literacies (of the game's mechanics), and loyalties (to the series). *Pokémon* play, he notes, "requires a social knowledge; it rewards co-operative trading and competitive play; it rewards a long-term commitment to the Pokémon universe, and so on."[31] As Carolyn's comment reminds us, *Pokémon* has cultivated outstanding loyalties among its fans, and these loyalties are carried through the materiality of the handheld. Beginning with the Game Boy, each generation of games in the series follows the release of Nintendo's handhelds with enhanced remakes of earlier titles coexisting between installments. Players move from generation to generation, sometimes purchasing the newest platform simply to collect pocket monsters with friends in tow, linked by the purple-and-gray connective cable.[32]

A Virtual Brush of the Shoulders (Wireless Adapter)

In 2004, Nintendo released the Game Boy Advance Wireless Adapter (AGB-015) as an alternative to the AGB-005.[33] Although the peripheral's popularity was curtailed by its lack of backward compatibility—fewer than three dozen games support its use—it's nevertheless an object worth spending some time on when considering GBA connectivity, lateral thinking, and the trajectory of the *Pokémon* series. The adapter was packaged with *FireRed* and *LeafGreen* and increases the number of players who can convene in the virtual space from four to thirty-nine.[34] Trainers can meet in the Union Room, a virtual hub of interconnectedness that allows them to trade Pokémon and test their mettle against friends, acquaintances, and strangers. While connecting two GBAs with the link cable presupposes a certain familiarity between players, the relative anonymity of the wireless Union Room broadens player networks. I say "relative" because the wireless adapter still requires that players remain within 10 feet (or 3 meters) of each other. At the height of *FireRed* and *LeafGreen*'s popularity, playgrounds, schoolyards, and public transit facilitated trades and battles among strangers, but the tendency for these spaces to be transitory made coordination difficult to manage.[35]

Although the wireless adapter saw little use outside the *Pokémon* games, the peripheral found new life in the 3DS's locative StreetPass feature. Again, we see how many GBA features echo in later Nintendo products. When turned on, StreetPass enables passive communication between 3DS systems so long as they're in sleep mode or running an application on 3DS firmware (which means not playing DS or Ambassador games in backward compatibility mode). Like the wireless adapter, systems must be in close proximity, though the range extends to 90 feet (or 27 meters).[36]

Both the wireless adapter and the 3DS's StreetPass feature change how we think of strangers in public settings, refiguring them as potential participants in a shared virtual world. But with these proximity-based wireless features, physical space still matters just as much as virtual space. This is not the connective freedom of Wi-Fi. It's profoundly locative and connected to the movements of player and hardware—as the bus leaves the stop before the data transfer is complete, players disperse without ever knowing about the missed connection.

Making Links (Nintendo GameCube–Game Boy Advance Link Cable)

The eleventh installment in the *Zelda* series, *Four Swords Adventures*, launched for the GameCube in 2004. One might wonder what business I have spending time with a game that wasn't released for this book's titular platform, but *Four Swords Adventures* serves as the paragon of Game Boy Advance–GameCube connectivity. Although the game supports solo play using the GameCube controller, it's in the cooperative, multiplatform, multiplayer mode that it shines as an example of the way Nintendo imagines their hardware and its audience.

Four Swords Adventures is a site of convergence. Its graphics resemble those of *Four Swords* for the GBA (a cooperative coda to the remastered *The Legend of Zelda: A Link to the Past*), but its stylized explosions recall the visual effects of *The Legend of Zelda: The Wind Waker*. It's a nostalgic mishmash of *Zelda* tropes. Narratively, the game takes place after the events of *The Minish Cap* and *Four Swords*, with Dark Link stirring up trouble. Forced into an altercation with his nefarious doppelganger, Link removes the Four Sword from the stone in which it's sealed and suddenly splits into four himself.

By connecting the GBA to the GameCube with the GameCube–Game Boy Advance Link Cable (DOL-011), up to four players take control of their own individual Links in a competitive and cooperative adventure. While the DOL-011 usually just enables the use of the GBA as a controller with the Game Boy Player (GBP) or unlocks additional content in cross-platform franchises like *Fire Emblem, Sonic,* and *WarioWare,* here it puts both screens in play. The console and handheld work in tandem to invite a new form of exploration through Hyrule. *Four Swords Adventures* wasn't the most successful game in the series. It sold far fewer copies than most *Zelda* titles due to its material requirements, because Nintendo was wrong to assume that players would be as amenable to purchasing four GBA units and their attending cables as they were to buying four Game-Cube controllers. But it's indisputably the most social of the *Zelda* games.

As players undertake the game's challenges, their attentions are directed back and forth between two screens. The television displays the collective public overworld, where players can follow along with their friends. But when Link enters a private space—be it a house, cave, or other dungeonlike environment—he migrates to the GBA, where he's visible to others only if they navigate their own Links to the same area or look over their friend's shoulder to see the handheld's screen. This fluidity of movement between the television and the screened controller anticipates the conceit of the Wii U by over a decade.

The visual distinctions between public and private virtual space run parallel to the game's cooperative and competitive directives. Players are bound together by the frequent appearance of levers, switches, and obstacles that require the combined strength of four Links to act upon. Progressing to the next area often demands that all Links stand together at the scrolling edge, meaning no Link can get left behind. Advancing necessitates camaraderie and coordination. At the same time, at the end of each level, players receive a score based on how many enemies they killed, how many Force Gems they collected, and how many lives they lost. They can also vote by secret GBA ballot for the player who was the most and least helpful to the campaign, introducing a competitive element at the eleventh hour that may come to shape players' approaches to subsequent levels. Through these twin elements, *Four Swords Adventures* is both collaborative—with its linguistic origins as the "treacherous cooperation" with enemies during wartimes—and cooperative.[37] There's a hint of deviousness to the idea of collaboration, a hint borne out by the coconstitutive aspects of the game. Navigating an indoor space by way of the much-more-private GBA screen, players can race to plunder treasure chests before their companions arrive or can ambush their friends, throw them into a pit, and steal the Force Gems shaken loose in the fall. Alliances are formed and broken throughout the span of a level, but reconciliation is mandatory in a game so concerned with space. The Links cannot proceed to the next level without moving as one through the portal. And colocated players must remain together on the couch to continue the game.

Studies of cooperative games tend to focus on online co-op, eliding the important distinction between local and online multiplayer gameplay. Here, location is critical. Players are linked by the cables snaking out from the GameCube, and *Four Swords Adventures* is grounded in the ethos that two—if not four—heads are better than one. Rather than pushing players toward online walkthroughs, frustrating puzzles become something for them to work through together, bouncing ideas—and occasionally bolts of energy—off each other to further their journey. In addition to the sounds emitted from the television speakers, *Four Swords Adventures* is typified by peals of laughter, ongoing banter, and exclamations of affront when one player accidentally picks up another while trying to grab a rock.

Nevertheless, competitiveness can sometimes overtake enjoyment. Mikael Jakobsson observes that the collaborative framework of colocated co-op games generates a bond of trust, but pushing against this bond turns the experience into "adversarial couch co-op," an altogether different approach that can ruin play:

> Two informants (brothers and self-declared hardcore gamers) stated that *The Legend of Zelda: Four Swords Adventures* (Nintendo 2004) is unplayable. The possibility of picking up and throwing other players off cliffs coupled with a need for all players to complete the levels was an insurmountable obstacle for them. This surprised me who only had played the game with older, more casual, academics and not encountered these issues.[38]

Competitiveness and aggressiveness aren't default approaches to *Four Swords Adventures*; adversarial couch co-op is (for Jakobsson at least) anomalous. He implies that questions of identity underlie relationships to the game. Older, casual players have no problem collaborating, while younger players who identify as "hardcore gamers" find collaboration impossible in a game where competition still exists, even if only in brief instances at the end. For most players, however, the multiplayer mode is the game's raison d'être. The interactions among people and platforms in a shared space is a form of conviviality—a delightful way to bring physical proximity back into play.

Every Game Has Its Place; Every Place, Its Game

The Switch has been lauded as a device that transforms play by circulating (or *switching*) between domestic and public play. But as these case studies of *Pokémon* and *Four Swords Adventures* have already begun to suggest, there is no one space in which the GBA circulates. The players I interviewed reported using the GBA on the bus or subway, in school hallways and lunchrooms, in living rooms and bedrooms. I've witnessed people playing their GBAs in line at La Ronde, Montreal's amusement park, where, approaching the gate, they'd save and shut down their game, tuck it into a cushiony fanny pack, and strap themselves into a roller-coaster. If there's one constant about GBA play, it's that it's contingent, fluid, and multifaceted.

Pausing, Packing, and Preparing for Play

In a study of DS players, Samuel Tobin articulates a qualitative, spatial, and temporal distinction between the acts of pausing and saving:

> When we pause rather than save[,] we also keep (save) play from veering to [sic] close to work, to seriousness, to a kind of long-term planning. We keep it casual. Play we save is then more work-like, which DS commentators associate with longer train trips. [This kind of play] would be unsatisfying and frustrating if attempted during an uncertain period of waiting on the platform for a train to arrive or during the short duration of a two-stop subway ride.[39]

For Tobin, the play saved by pausing is casual and low-stakes, typified by movement or the anticipation of movement. But there are material differences between the DS and the GBA that make these distinctions between pausing and saving less defined on the GBA. Between the DS's clamshell form factor and the sleep functionality embedded in its code, the DS can be folded shut to pause a game. Like slipping a bookmark between pages, this act of closing prevents the narrative from continuing without the player's participation. They can then slide the DS into a pocket, purse, or schoolbag, switch from one subway line to another, and extract the handheld without anything happening to Link. But apart from the SP, the GBA isn't protected against accidental button pressing, and sleep features exist in only some software titles rather than being hardwired into the device. Pausing a game still demands attentiveness to ensure that it isn't unpaused and Mario dropped in a chasm between blocks. Although the Micro can slip easily into a pocket, the movement of a leg can interact with the inputs without users' knowledge. If interruptions draw a player's attention away from the handheld for longer than a few moments, saving might be a necessity—even if play has been short-lived.

On the GBA, saving, quitting, and shutting down feel less permanent than the mirror actions on the DS. This is thanks, in large part, to its interface. When the GBA turns on, it boots directly into a game; saving and shutting down amount to just an extended pause. But with the DS, turning the system on prompts the player to acknowledge Nintendo's Health and Safety screen and then select an option from the Home menu, pressing the A button to progress to each step. While this process takes only a few seconds, it's enough to create the impression that saving isn't worth it for short durations.

Tobin's identification of a distinction between pausing and saving reveals the fact that not all games are suited for every space. A *Zelda* game, with its lengthy, puzzle-heavy dungeons and few opportunities to save play, is ill suited for a space where interruptions are abundant. Other games may be more forgiving of players' other commitments. In *Fire Emblem*, for instance, you can suspend play midbattle and return your units to their positions on the battlefield the next time you turn on your console. But spend too many days away from the handheld and you might forget the brilliant tactical plan that convinced you to place your mage in range of a contingent of hatchet-wielding brigands—one misstep and said mage could perish, permanently erased from the roster. Playing *Pokémon* in a friend's basement differs from a two-minute match in *Tetris Worlds* while waiting for the bus. If a game is based around twitch reflexes, having to change subway or bus lines or direct attention to a flight attendant can spell disaster for the avatar. And, while games with lengthy levels are well suited for play at home in the living room or in bed, we'd be foolish to assume that these spaces aren't also subject to the interruptions of work, chores, outings, and sleep.

Given the contingencies of and potential settings for play, the GBA demands some level of forethought from its players. Officially, apart from the 3DS Ambassador Program releases and the Virtual Console titles for the Wii U, GBA games exist in physical form, making portability inversely proportional to how much of your software library you choose to carry with you at a given moment. Deciding what game to insert into the device means weighing what you're in the mood to play against what you can play in public without disturbing others (tilting the GBA to play *Twisted!* isn't advisable in the close quarters of economy airplane seating), against how much time you have to progress through the game, and so on. Players therefore negotiate between locking themselves into one game and carrying their entire library with them when they leave the house. As one player explained to me:

I got a little pouch for my SP at some videogame store that I could fit four or five games in. I'd switch them out sometimes depending on where I was going and for how long. (Gaetan)

Even so, changing game cartridges in transit requires juggling two Game Paks as well as the handheld, all the while keeping your balance against the motion of the train or bus—a challenging enough feat on its own.

Playing in Public

In January 2010, the Tokyo Metro ran a public service ad campaign addressing obtrusive portable play in busy public settings. The "manner poster" shows a man so deeply absorbed in the adventures on his screen that he blocks other passengers from accessing the doors to the train. "Please do it at home," the poster says, reminding the viewer that, although portable platforms allow gameplay outside the home, there are etiquette rules to follow in public.[40]

Although the GBA might not invite the gestural excesses of the Wii, we've seen that it's nevertheless a sensory and embodied experience. Even the micromovements required to press the A button and the Direction-pad (D-pad) require coordination and elbow room. When standing on a bus or a subway car, physical acts of play must be combined with the bodily shifting required to keep your balance and avoid sprawling into the arms of a nearby commuter. These physical demands exist in concert with the impositions on a player's attention. The result is an elaborate set of techniques and protocols for public play that include such things as a posture that enables play in cramped quarters and a method for supporting the device in a way that prevents damage in case of jostling.

Like the books that first entertained commuters, the GBA occupies the gaze. Like the Walkman, it tunes out the raucous rhythms of the outside world in favor of curated gameplay sounds. The result is a heightened experience of Ito, Okabe, and Anderson's "cocooning," the bidirectional process through which media use allows individuals to shelter themselves from local and spatial interactions, while also reducing the need to be aware of other people.[41] Public transit is the primary site for cocooning, and many people double up on media use to maximize the effectiveness of their cocoon (e.g., combining the use of an mp3 player with reading a magazine). The GBA's effectiveness as a cocoon is compounded by the necessity of physically engaging with the platform through the body, a kinesthetic distraction from the swaying of a subway car or the immobility of a waiting room. It's visually, aurally, and haptically demanding.

Although public play is typified by a bifurcated attentiveness between what's occurring in the game world and what's occurring around the player, the cocooning effect occasionally results in the transgression of social norms.[42] Carolyn, who was playing the GBA in her thirties, reflects on a particularly memorable experience of negotiating play in public spaces:

> I was on the metro, listening to music with my iPod, playing GBA, and I noticed people were staring more than usual. I remember thinking, "What? You've never seen a grown woman play GBA before?" It was only later, when I went to play during my break at work that I noticed the volume was on, and I had treated those poor people on the subway to quite the soundtrack for their ride into work that day.

Here, the iPod cocooned Carolyn not only from the other commuters, but also from hearing the sounds emitted from her own handheld's speakers. Coupled with her assumption that the stares had more to do with questions of identity—a fair presumption given the stereotype of the young male gamer and the hostility that "grown" women who play videogames often encounter as a result—Carolyn didn't register that her play was sonically disruptive to the other passengers. That her fellow commuters only stared rather than said or did anything speaks as much to the familiarity of such an occurrence as to the politeness of Canadian subway riders. But staring is a deliberate reminder of wrongdoing—one that Carolyn herself recognized, but not until it was too late. If console games are characterized, as Chris Chesher suggests, by the glaze—a hybrid between the gaze of cinema and the glance of broadcast television—public portable play may be more akin to a glimpse.[43] Throughout her commute, Carolyn's eyes danced between the activity on her screen and the derisive looks of her fellow travelers, but never with enough attention to discern the true reason for their glares.

The use of the handheld's tinny speakers in public settings is an aural mirror for the physical obstruction of subway doors due to preoccupation with a screen. Although diegetic sounds might be necessary for the full enjoyment of a game, forcing others to hear them in a public setting is seldom viewed favorably. In some cases, it can even hinder people's ability to hear public announcements for the next stop on the subway or the calling of the next patient in a clinic. Someone engaging in public play always implicates other people who are sharing the same space, regardless of whether they ignore the play, passively tolerate it, or actively participate in it.

Cocooned public play sometimes even has the opposite of the desired effect—it invites attention instead of repelling it. Most commonly, this manifests as people looking over the player's shoulder to try to discern what's happening on the screen (while the dim 2001 screen certainly had its faults, it did offer an extra layer of protection against prying eyes). Other times, play becomes a conversation starter. Take the story of Bailey Cohen-Krichevsky:

> I played [the GBA] late (I picked up my GBA SP for the first time in 2010), so the nostalgia of it was a great conversation starter—people I barely knew would come over to ask me what I was playing and talk about their favorite games. Once I was using it while on a stationary bike in the college gym, and the gym supervisor came over—I thought he was going to tell me off, but he just wanted to know what I was playing, and we had a discussion about whatever game it was.

Playing while exercising is a way to avoid having to reciprocate the gaze of other patrons of the college gym, but the GBA's familiarity and the nostalgia of its software titles encouraged strangers to join Bailey and reminisce about their own experiences. In some ways, using the GBA in a public space communicates playfulness to others, as well as a shared interest in the Nintendo brand cultivated by strategic marketing. Even when play is solitary, it's recognizable to others by the handheld's shape.

Stories like Bailey's remind us of the way that Nintendo's "Who Are You?" campaign turns the GBA into a method of communicating aesthetic preferences to others. It would be more surprising to hear of someone approaching a stranger with an iPod to ask, "What are you listening to?" But "What are you playing?" is not only common, but also, in Bailey's case, taken with receptiveness and candor. Whether public GBA play deters or encourages social interactions is situationally contingent and ultimately unpredictable.

Other respondents equally observed that, despite its branding as a personal technology, the GBA changed how they interacted with others in their immediate surroundings:

> It was a great way to hang out with my brother (we got our GBA SPs at the same time), and it was also a great way for me to fill my time; as a kid, I wasn't the *most* social, so playing videogames was a good way for me to connect with other kids and find things in common ... It kind of helped me choose friends during elementary school. (Andrea Wahba)

> My brother and I would swap games around. [We] would take turns with the games we played and compare our success/failure with

certain levels or show each other our progress while playing at the same time. (Abbie "spoopy" Rappaport)

A friend of mine and I traded games during a summer trip. I borrowed *Backyard Hockey* and *Backyard Baseball*. (Nick)

Due to its popularity, the GBA was well positioned—like the Game Boy before it—to unite children on the playground through shared interests. For instance, it served to reinforce Andrea's relationship with her brother and allowed her to build new ones with her peers. The materiality of the interchangeable game cartridges also matters. Once players finish with a game or want to play something else, they can trade the cartridge with their friends or family members. Software data occupies physical space in silicon and plastic. Exchanging these tokens is profoundly social, even if actual gameplay is solitary. Both Abbie and Nick use words that connote an ongoing exchange—"swap," "borrowed"—signaling that these trades are not anonymous transactions, but rather social loans that are open and ongoing, not unlike lending a book to a friend. With decades of software titles through backward compatibility, GBA players can build close friendships through recommendations that grow ever more accurate as the exchanges continue.

Home Is Where the Batteries Are

When we speak of videogames, the home is often understood to be the realm of the console, a black (or purple, or white) box neatly tucked beneath the television set with a network of wires crawling out. However, in a 2008 article, Dean Chan observes that mobile and portable gaming most often also occurs in the home, despite assumptions to the contrary.[44] The affordances of the platform's size and weight tend to obscure the realities of play.

While the convenience of handhelds is that they're not tethered to a single setting, this is itself an illusion. Portability is constrained by power. If users of the 2001 GBA had the forethought to throw a handful of AA batteries in their pockets before leaving home, they could extend the duration of play in public spaces beyond the 15-hour average. But when built-in, rechargeable lithium ion batteries entered the scene with the SP and the Micro, the need to recharge limited how far the GBA could travel. At the highest brightness level and with the sound on, the Micro affords a mere 5 hours of play.

It's unsurprising then, that, despite what we might think, GBA play mostly occurs in the home. The important distinction between handheld and console play is that the GBA often moves within the home from couch to bed to backyard to bathroom. This is a point that often came up in my interviews:

> I definitely played mostly at home—in no room in particular (bedroom, living room, at the kitchen table, etc.). I may have occasionally played in the car on long road trips as well, but generally the GBA never left the house. (Jake)

> I had [a GBA] that I had to share with my brother, so bedroom wasn't ideal [and] I wasn't allowed to bring it out of the house at that age. (Evan Brown)

In these cases, locative play is constrained not by the specific platform, but by the interests of the players or their parents, who owned the domestic space. There are many reasons why parents don't want their children playing in public, including concerns that their children won't pay attention to their surroundings, concerns that other children will pay too much attention to the object, and worries about children losing or breaking the handheld. Evan's case is also particularly compelling for the way that it exposes that, even though the platform is branded as a personal technology, it isn't always conceived as such by its consumers. Here, we have a shared GBA. From the moment of purchase, this device is a social one.

Sharing the device is one form of domestic social play. A family GBA challenges the idea of the portable as personal technology. As we've seen with the meme cats, it's also possible to share the screen with others, inviting those in intimate proximity to show off their digital collections or to ask for advice on a challenging puzzle. It can be social through colocative, cooperative, or competitive play by virtue of the three aforementioned peripherals. And it can also be social, in that domestic play recognizes the potential disruptions occasioned by portable play; enfolding it into the home is a way of preventing the public from having to tolerate dynamic social play in a communal space.

Rizumu Tengoku (リズム天国), or *Rhythm Heaven,* again provides a useful example of this kind of playing at home, given its reliance on aural cues and its predilection for getting players to groove to the beat. Within the domestic space, the game's performative dimensions offer a social experience—one that is inappropriate when, say, waiting in line at the bank. In the home, it's a form of shared conviviality. According to testimonies from *Rizumu Tengoku* users, playing in the home strengthens family bonds.[45] Family members watch a player dance while grooving along themselves and offering commentary. Miki Kaneda observes that the game becomes part of family life, integrating social functions and broadening the platform's audience.[46] Play here occurs communally with the implicit permission of the family, who themselves are willing participants.

Things to Do in the Dark

In April 2006, a Japanese market research study conducted a public survey on videogaming that revealed the GBA remained the most popular portable platform. More saliently, it found that the bedroom was the most popular location for portable gaming. According to the data, 71.2 percent of respondents reported that they usually played in their bedrooms rather than in other spaces inside or outside the home.[47]

The bedroom is a curious space, in that it's a site of privacy within a space already conceived of as private. Since the 1970s, Japanese housing has seen an increase in "Western-style" bedrooms with fixed walls and doors, a trend that corresponds with a growing interest in personal privacy.[48] It's within this highly personal, private space that the GBA sees the most use among Japanese players.

For children, the privacy of the bedroom facilitates the development of a sense of self. Moira Bovill and Sonia Livingstone observe that, for young people, the bedroom is at once a space in which they can explore and experiment with their identity and an environment in which they can cultivate a sense of taste based on media consumption.[49] This is especially true of girls, who can retreat from the gaze of others to explore videogames for themselves.[50]

Table 4.1 Most Popular Spaces for Portable Play in Japan

Location	Percentage*
Bedroom	71.2
Home (other rooms)	39.7
Work or school	12.2
In transit (bus, train, car)	33.4
Waiting for transit (bus stop, train station)	9.1
In parks or shops	91.

Data from Yasumoto-Nicolson, "Gaming in Japan."
*Participants were invited to select multiple answers. This is why the sum of the percentages exceeds 100.

But for adults—particularly cohabiting adults in relationships—the bedroom is understood to serve two purposes: sleep and sex. The formal treatment of the master bedroom in real estate only reifies these perceptions. This means that playing on the GBA in bed is often the product of a negotiation between activities understood as part of the culture of the bedroom, a tension that Nintendo identified when marketing the GBA SP.

It's impossible to address GBA play in the bedroom without discussing the gendered print campaign that the Leo Burnett agency ran for Nintendo in 2003. The campaign's goal was primarily to rebrand the compact SP as a device no longer just for boys, but also "for men" (perhaps Nintendo wished that they had taken a page out of Sony's book and called the Game Boy the Gameman back in 1989). As part of the campaign, they ran a two-page magazine spread in *Maxim, Dazed and Confused, Mad Magazine*, and many other publications that foregrounded these negotiations. On the left page, a (presumably) naked couple lies beneath satin sheets. The woman, either asleep or bored, rests against the man's side, while the SP in his hands illuminates his chest and occupies his attention. On the ink-black background of the facing page, the sleek SP glows above the words, "The second-best thing to do in the dark." The hierarchy of bedroom activities is thus having sex, playing SP, and then sleeping.

This ad participates in a history of campaigns predicated on Nintendo's perception of their audience's masculinity and the innuendos they use to highlight the attractiveness of their handhelds. The 2003 ad is in fact a more tasteful version of one by the same agency that ran in 1997 to promote the Game Boy Pocket. This one featured a woman in lingerie tied by the wrists to a headboard in what looks like a slovenly teenager's basement bedroom. She wears a terrified expression (one that Nintendo's account director at Leo Burnett maintained was meant to convey frustration, but which read as distinctly fearful). In the lower-right corner of the page, a man's hands occupy themselves with the Game Boy Pocket beside the words "Seriously distracting."[51]

Both ads use women as props to suggest how appealing these handhelds were to men, leaving women and girls to question what Nintendo presumed about their own relationships to the platform. In a 2008 study, Gareth Schott and Siobhan Thomas observed women's responses to the SP, first after inviting them to play a few minutes of *Zelda* and then after showing them the Leo Burnett campaign. They observe that "the handheld device, Game Boy Advance SP, was perceived by a female sample as a gender-neutral design that offered good tactile and aesthetic qualities as well as an intuitive interface. It was the gender-specific advertisement strategy employed by Nintendo that served to undermine their potential endorsement of the product (even retrospectively)."[52] In their conclusion, they posit that, had Nintendo openly supported women's use of the platform instead of reducing them to sex objects, the company could have enjoyed a much more viable consumer market of women long before they deliberately tried to broaden their user base with the DS.

What the Leo Burnett ad campaign did most successfully was highlight the way the introduction of a backlight produces a spatial opening of the GBA's potential uses. Previously restricted to well-lit environments, playing GBA became something to do in the dark of one's bedroom. It became one of the last activities before falling asleep, a way to reorient the mind from the concerns of the day.

In our conversation, respondent G-stant reflects on the location of GBA play: "Definitely the bedroom, before bed. Had to always complete at least one checkpoint before turning it off to sleep." The portable device allows players to settle in a relaxed position to ease themselves into sleep. Whey players begin to doze, they can shut off their SP console and store it on their night table or leave it folded on the bed, where it's sturdy enough to withstand the player rolling over it in slumber or knocking it to the floor.

The advent of the lit screen concurrently introduced a temporal opening of the boundaries to the GBA's fictional worlds. While playing stimulating games on the GBA can help relax players before sleep, it also can produce the opposite effect. Thinking back to my own childhood, the lit screen meant that lights-out ceased to impose sleep. My experience of playing videogames was radically altered when I could play until midnight, galvanized by the knowledge that I was transgressing household norms—though I suffered dearly the next morning when I had to wake up early for school. Nowadays, smartphones and computers include built-in night-light settings that tint screens amber to limit the intake of the artificial blue light deemed disruptive to circadian rhythms. The SP has no such feature. Its technological interventions extend the parameters of childhood by allowing the platform to circulate in previously inhospitable play spaces, but it also has the potential to disrupt the primary activity of the bedroom. Again, gameplay is contingent on both context and content—and not all games are suited for every space.

Boktai: The Sun Is in Your Hand

In 2003, Konami launched a peculiar series known as *Boktai,* from the Japanese ボクらの太陽 (*Bokura no Taiyō*). The first installment, *Boktai:*

The Sun Is in Your Hand, follows a vampire hunter named Django the Solar Boy (the name is a nod to spaghetti Westerns) tasked with preserving the world from the undeadening of humanity. Armed with the Gun del Sol, Django must harness the power of the Sun to restore light to a postapocalyptic world. The action-adventure role-playing game (RPG) takes its cues from Hideo Kojima's previous idiosyncratic work on the *Metal Gear* series, in that avoiding enemies is key. But, more important, *Boktai* challenges the way that we think about the spatial affordances of portable play.

Django's ability to navigate cities ravaged by armies of reanimated corpses and his power to put an end to them are both dependent on the Sun. Like *Twisted!*, the transparent cartridge accommodates additional hardware—in this case, a solar sensor—to produce a different sensation of play. Distinct from photometric light sensors that respond to any ambient illumination, the solar sensor reacts specifically to ultraviolet (UV) radiation so that sunshine on the cartridge manifests as sunlight in the game. Beams of light pierce dungeon ceilings to damage undead enemies and allow Solar Boy to recharge his weapon at will. Depending on the strength of the Sun, Django's magic power increases more or less quickly. Without it, he relies on limited banked currency (known as "soll") to purchase goods and sustain his offensive prowess.

Although artificial sources of solar power coupled with stealth-focused navigation allow Django to get by during the dead of night, some aspects of the game make sunlight a necessity. Bosses can be purified only with a solar-powered device known as the Pile Driver, but until such time as they've been eviscerated, their spirits can exert agency. You can defeat a boss at night and drag its remains to the Pile Driver, but you won't be able to use the instrument until your cartridge is in the Sun. In the meantime, the battery-backed real-time clock tracks how long it takes you to return with ambient sunlight. Take too long, and the boss will escape, crawling back to its lair by the time you turn the game back on.

As a result of the game's unique mechanics, the setting is key to *Boktai*. It's rare to find someone playing the game in most of the spaces we might expect to see the GBA. It's ill suited for planes, subway platforms, and waiting rooms, and it's not something that you can easily pick up at night after work for a couple of hours before bed. While you can orient yourself toward natural light indoors, *Boktai* is best enjoyed outside, in parks, backyards, or other open-air spaces. And because the GBA's screen is uniquely suited for direct sunlight (unlike backlit screens, which get washed out), *Boktai* makes the most of the hardware's greatest shortcoming. The hardware's deficiencies become advantages through a clever hardware addition.

By design, *Boktai* is frustrating due to the way it's contingent on uncontrollable variables. Yet the stringent temporal and locative requirements are partly what make it so attractive, as both a game and an object of study. *Boktai* could have used an ambient light sensor, or even structured its mechanics around the real-time clock. Either of these options would have given players more freedom in deciding when and where they play. But the use of a UV sensor rather than an ambient light sensor was no accident. Kojima states:

> Nintendo actually asked us, "why don't you have the sensor detect any light?" and that pretty much defeats the concept. With artificial light we have total control . . . we can turn it on and off whenever we want. The great thing about this concept is that we have no control over sunlight. It might be raining, or it's cloudy, or it's night time . . . you always think about the sun in this game. It's this thing that you have no control over that gives the game its depth.[53]

Although players tend to settle on a game based on how long their commute will be or how comfortable they'll be playing by lamplight on the couch, *Boktai* asks them to look (and play) outside. Weather becomes the deciding factor, rather than transit routes or how much time there is before dinner. A series of rainy, cloudy days means beating a boss is simply off the table. Players must therefore engage in a meta-game of sorts by attempting to squeeze play into narrow windows of time or by playing smarter to maximize how much of the game they can complete before the sun goes down. *Boktai* refigures the player's relationship to agency in that it isn't designed to fit into the player's schedule but rather makes the player's schedule bend to its material demands. It's designed to be approached on its own terms.

Of course, some players armed with determination, creativity, and a stubborn refusal to go outdoors found ways to work around the sensor by using blacklights, which produce light not from heat, like incandescent bulbs, but from long-wave UV light (UV-A). Shrewd players tricked the system into thinking it was sunny by shining a blacklight on the sensor, which worked for the most part. But Kojima had anticipated cheating. Unlike normal meteorological patterns, blacklights don't give the solar sensor a break; so to ensure that the game had to be approached on its own terms, excessive solar exposure causes Django's weapon to overheat, at which point he injures himself whenever he attacks. Users are punished for trying to extend their playing time with smoke and mirrors.

Due to the weather requirements and the ability to overheat the Gun del Sol, play occurs in installments long enough to afford progress, but not too long—you need more than a couple of afternoons to complete the game. But these long-enough sittings come with their own hazards. We generally don't think of playing videogames as something that requires sunscreen, but *Boktai* does. Neglecting to prepare for a session in the world of animated vampires can have hazardous consequences. On a GameFAQs forum, Thunderbird8, reminds users: "If you're going to try [overheating] just for the sake of it, *wear sunscreen* at any cost! I've gotten myself sunburned playing this game without even coming close to the overheat when doing short stints outside."[54]

Because typical home and car windows block most medium-wave UV light (UV-B) rays and a good portion of UV-A rays, the solar sensor registers less power indoors. Play works best outside, but your skin is exposed to low levels of radiation equal to what the sensor registers. So we have another reminder of the embodied nature of gaming and the way that bodies need to protect themselves from ostensibly innocuous activities like playing games on the GBA. As we globally refuse to impose policy decisions that address the growing strain on the ozone layer (which absorbs much of the UV radiation from the Sun), *Boktai* becomes increasingly dangerous to play.

Despite its vexations, *Boktai* invites exploration in and out of the game. Rather than confining play to the transitory spaces of the daily commute or the comforting rooms of the home, it turns us out to sunny patches in public parks. Two sequels followed to prolong this adventure: *Boktai 2: Solar Boy Django* and *Boktai 3: Sabata's Counterattack* (新 • ボクら の太陽 逆襲のサバタ, *Shin Bokura no Taiyō: Gyakushū no Sabata*), both of which preserved the solar sensor.

Once the DS became Nintendo's dominant handheld, Konami rebranded the series as *Lunar Knights* in North America and did away with the core mechanic.[55] Instead, *Lunar Knights* relies on a weather control system called ParaSOL that generates a climate. The reason for this shift was material. Whereas GBA cartridges could accommodate additional hardware, compact DS game cards didn't afford such expansion. So, the clever Konami exploited the DS's continuity with the GBA. Inserting one of the three solar-sensing cartridges into the bottom slot of the DS overrides ParaSOL and reintroduces the delightfully frustrating core mechanic. Continuity within the series reminds us of the interconnectedness of what we like to think of as discrete game generations. The GBA's assemblage circulates temporally, socially, and spatially. And trying to define it is a bit like staring into the Sun.

In the summer of 2018, Nintendo issued a Digital Millennium Copyright Act (DMCA) notice to GitHub, demanding they shut down a browser-based GBA emulator. The JavaScript-powered application in question provided access to over thirty Nintendo games, including titles from the *Super Mario*, *Zelda*, *Pokémon*, and *Fire Emblem* franchises.[1] GitHub was quick to comply, deleting the offending repository and the read-only memory (ROM) images it contained within a matter of days.

Neither the takedown notice nor the Microsoft-owned code-sharing service's promptness is out of the ordinary. In 2015, Nintendo requested that GitHub shut down a similar JavaScript-powered emulator, and in 2014, they issued a takedown notice for Riley Testut's GBA4iOS emulator for iPhone or iPad, which exploited a loophole in Apple's Developer Enterprise Program to allow the user to install the application without jailbreaking the device.[2] Contraventions of the DMCA are obvious enough; in all cases, users were able to access ROMs (i.e., game images that have been extracted from Game Paks) directly from a browser, phone, or iPad. What's more notable, however, is Nintendo's heightened crackdown against unsanctioned emulation and the brazen legal stances they take against their fans.

The 2018 takedown request followed a massive lawsuit that Nintendo had filed at the federal court in Arizona against the operators of two ROM-hosting websites, LoveROMS and LoveRetro, for copyright and trademark infringement.[3] Nintendo alleged that the websites were "among the most open and notorious online hubs for pirated video games" and pointed out that the owners generated revenue through advertising, donations, and cryptocurrency by "trafficking in pirated copies and making unauthorized use of Nintendo's video games, other copyrighted works, and registered trademarks."[4] The suit involved a valuation of $150,000 per ROM image and up to $2 million for each instance of trademark infringement. With over 140 counts of the former and 40 of the latter between the two websites, the defendants faced more than $100 million in damages. In the end, the websites' owners, Jacob and Cristian Mathias, consented to a $12,230,000 settlement and agreed to abide by a permanent injunction barring them from sharing any Nintendo ROMs in perpetuity.[5] Both websites shut down shortly after the suit was filed.

There are reasons why Nintendo targeted these websites. Historically, the company has tended toward cease-and-desist letters and the aforementioned DMCA takedown requests, relying on what's known in legal circles as the "chilling effect"—the discouragement of the legitimate exercise of rights through threats of legal sanction—to keep others from engaging in similar activities. But by filing such an immensely punitive suit, Nintendo made an example of LoveROMS and LoveRetro, broadcasting to other online ROM hosts that complying with takedown requests was no longer enough. In the subsequent weeks, dozens of ROM sites, including EmuParadise—a stable for retro gaming since the turn of the millennium—pulled their Nintendo content out of a sense of self-preservation, without the company having to lift a finger.[6]

Incidentally, the ROM site crackdown occurred in the wake of an announcement of the impending closure of the Wii Shop Channel. Through this online store, users could purchase digital rights management (DRM)–protected versions of games from earlier systems to run via emulation on their Virtual Console.[7] These included not only the Nintendo Entertainment System (NES), Super Nintendo Entertainment System (SNES), and Nintendo 64 (N64), but also systems that predated or competed with the company's consoles, including the Commodore 64, Sega's Master System and Genesis, NEC's TurboGrafx-16 Entertainment Super System, and SNK's Neo Geo. Announced concurrently with the Wii itself, the Virtual Console was an essential part of the platform, promising to "redefine . . . backward compatibility" by allowing users to explore the depths of Nintendo's monumental library—and indeed that of the gaming world more broadly.[8] The Wii Shop Channel's closure effectively cut off players from decades of gaming, ending Nintendo's promise of an accessible back catalog.

Proclamations of the Wii Shop Channel's demise in turn coincided with the relaunch of the NES Classic Edition after the Super NES

Classic Edition enjoyed tremendous market success. These consoles are dedicated hardware objects modeled as miniature replicas of the NES and SNES (and their Famicom counterparts in Japan) that use a Linux operating system to run emulation engines developed by Nintendo European Research & Development (NERD). These emulators provide basic compatibility with the original hardware, in addition to emulating the cartridge chips that allowed developers to expand the system's capabilities later in their life cycles. The Classic Edition consoles came with thirty and twenty-one games, respectively, and were received with such overwhelming and unanticipated success that Nintendo struggled to keep up with demand; scalpers even swooped in to resell them well above the manufacturer's suggested retail price. The extraordinary appetite for these consoles was irrefutable proof of a hunger for Nintendo's retro titles.

It would be naïve to ignore the connections among these three events. Occurring within a span of a few months in the summer of 2018, these corporate decisions are inextricably linked not only temporally, but also by what they say about Nintendo's commodification of nostalgia. The intersection of Nintendo's deluge of lawsuits and takedown notices, the closure of the Wii Shop Channel, and the staggering success of their NES and SNES Classic Edition emulation-based mini-consoles seems to suggest that Nintendo is in the process of reinventing their approach to their platforms and their older intellectual property (IP). After grudgingly tolerating fan production, the company is developing a new business model—one that concentrates decades of user-generated content into a narrow, controlled channel through which they can extract the greatest profit while simultaneously extinguishing cultural practices that don't meet their approval.

Enter the platformization of nostalgia.[9]

Platformizing Mario

In broad terms, "platformization" refers to a transformation of the larger market structures that shape cultural production. As economic and infrastructural aspects of platforms begin to proliferate in web- and app-based ecosystems, it changes the way that cultural content is produced and circulated. Today, we can see how the dominance of the data-driven Alphabet (Google), Apple, Facebook, Amazon, and Microsoft platforms have made them crucial actors in all facets of cultural production, ranging from news to entertainment. The consolidation of interactions into narrow, controlled channels affects the political economy of cultural industries by restricting users' agency as cultural producers. Once you're in the platform, it's very hard to make your way back out.

Platformization lies at the core of a rapidly changing videogame landscape. In their nuanced article on the platformization of cultural production, David B. Nieborg and Thomas Poell observe that through this emerging model, cultural commodities become increasingly contingent—that is, dependent on powerful platforms—as well as incessantly altered and resold based on the data collected from billions of users.[10] As cultural production becomes increasingly platform dependent, it loses its autonomy. Nieborg and Poell say that platformization

> is not only an external process in which platforms transform market structures and curate content, it is also driven by cultural industries actively organizing production and distribution around platforms . . . As cultural producers are transformed into platform complementors, they are incentivized to change a traditionally linear production process into an iterative, data-driven process in which content is constantly altered to optimize for platform distribution and monetization.[11]

As component-based software, videogames have always been platform dependent, but the infrastructure is changing. The industry is moving from direct unit sales of self-contained games to an economy based on in-app purchases, downloadable content, and subscription-based services. Low barriers to entry—particularly in the case of free-to-play (or "freemium") games, where in-app purchases are optional—demand that game developers invest more effort toward improving adoption and retention rather than delivering a polished product. Developers "leverage the contingent nature of games as software by continuously altering, extending, and upgrading game content and functionalities, while simultaneously optimizing its monetization model."[12]

Given the way that Nintendo manufactures nostalgia for their corporate products and IP in their platformization model, understanding the platform as an assemblage is more important than ever. The company has a long history of rereleasing their games on newer platforms, bringing them from one hardware generation to another. But the way that data circulates is changing, and fans' relationship to Nintendo's content is growing increasingly precarious as a result. The company is moving toward an online subscription service that can emulate consoles through a single hardware platform over which Nintendo has both control and oversight. This tactic at once reinterprets and recirculates Nintendo's legacy, and competes with an emulation ecosystem developed by hobbyists over the last few decades. It's becoming harder and harder to uncouple emulation from our idea of what a videogame platform is.

The Case for Emulation

As platforms age, their accessibility decreases as a consequence of their finite, dwindling numbers and increased rates of inoperability. Emulation decouples software from the fallibility of hardware, acknowledging the ephemerality of the platform as object; it blurs the distinction between live hardware and the software that run on it.

Emulators enable one computer system (the host) to behave like another (the guest), allowing the host system to run software designed for the guest system that it otherwise might not be able to access outside of the emulation environment. Host systems can be other consoles, but they can also be laptops, mobile phones, and even web browsers. In this way, emulators make certain software objects more accessible than they might otherwise be; rather than having to rely on dedicated hardware objects like arcade cabinets or portable handhelds, we can experience a vast, curated collection of retro games on a single system.

In many cases, emulators are easy to use and offer supplementary features that are not found in the hardware object they're emulating but that speak to how a player might want to engage with videogame software. For example, one of the most appealing features of many videogame emulators is the ability to save and load a current emulation state, regardless of whether the game provides the player with the ability to save at that moment (or at all). A save state is a snapshot of the configuration of all the memory addresses in the emulated game's random-access memory (RAM) at a particular moment of play and is stored independently of the ROM image. At any time, loading a save state reinserts this data into the emulator to resume the game at the time that the snapshot was taken. Save states allow the player to circumvent saving restrictions, create a backup of their current progress before difficult boss battles, or abuse a game's random number generator (RNG)—that is, the algorithm in videogames that determines random events, such as the chance to land a critical hit or collect a rare item. The feature emerges out of a material community of amateur programmers, who developed these emulators to suit their own styles of play. Save states and other utilities, such as the ability to fast forward gameplay, provide a community-driven solution to what players see as shortcomings of the hardware or software.

Of course, another factor behind emulators' ubiquity is their relative lack of cost. Most browser-based emulators rely on ad revenue rather than subscription fees. Intrepid players that are undaunted by internet service providers' cease-and-desist letters can download games by the hundreds, and these games often come bundled with the emulation programs they need to run on a given host system. Mobile apps equally allow us to run videogames on our smartphones. Emulation plays a significant role in how we play games today, sometimes without us even realizing it.

Despite emulation's prevalence, we don't often consider how it informs the way we interpret videogame platforms.[13] Whether sanctioned by Nintendo, institutionalized by museums, or generated by fan communities, emulators endeavor to preserve an experience of gameplay, but that experience is always mediated. The goal of emulation, as succinctly summarized by Raiford Guins, is:

> to simulate a reliable and easily distributable copy (copies of copies like game software) so that the working program, the experience of game play, can persist in the present (and hopefully for the future) even if experienced on different machines and within different social contexts from those still resonating in the not-so-distant past.[14]

It's worth noting that Guins's objects of study include coin-op arcade cabinets, many of which only exist now as emulators—the fate of the unique machine consigned to mere speculation.

So we can look at emulators as performing a key function in videogame preservation. Questions of preservation and access lie at the root of most emulators, whether they're built into Nintendo's proprietary systems or circulated as grassroots community projects. Decontextualized though they may be, emulators offer insight into what the videogame is and what we *think* it is—that is, the elements of a platform that are included in an emulator or evoked by its features speak to a mediated understanding of what the game is and what we want (or wanted) it to be. As a complex object with contingent definitions, a videogame's functionality and non-functionality both contribute to the sense of what it is. The impossibility of a concrete, catch-all definition forces us to discuss videogames through their relationships to embodied subjectivity and the networks in which they find themselves, even if these networks are emulated.

The resistance to considering emulated afterlives as legitimate components of a platform tends to stem from the anxiety that they cannot reproduce the experience or "aura" of the original.[15] But because hardware objects are mechanically reproduced in the order of millions, there exists no objective hierarchy between manufactured GBAs in the first place. The very democratizing force of mechanical reproduction that makes one GBA equal to the next opens the definition of a platform to emulators as well. Any auratic power that the GBA has emerges more from an imagined ideology of what the object symbolizes than from its plastic and silicon. Like the rest of Nintendo's platforms, the GBA and its software library exist within a vast network of Janus-headed prospective and retrospective objects and cultural contexts. Because Nintendo predicates their design philosophy upon reworking and rereleasing existing hardware, embedding pieces of old consoles into new ones, they render the notion of a platform fungible from the outset. By mirroring the system's code on another platform, both Nintendo (in the case of sanctioned emulators) and their users (in the case of unsanctioned ones) draw on the materiality of nostalgia, all but guaranteeing that the platform will continue long after its life on the market.

Nintendo has strong opinions on emulation that are worth considering if we want to understand the context of GBA emulation. The company says:

> Distribution of an emulator developed to play illegally copied Nintendo software hurts Nintendo's goodwill, the millions of dollars invested in research & development and marketing by Nintendo and its licensees. Substantial damages are caused to Nintendo and its licensees. It is irrelevant whether or not someone profits from the distribution of an emulator. The emulator promotes the play of illegal ROMs, NOT authentic games.[16]

According to Nintendo, any copy of their software is illegal, and the sole purpose of an emulator is to play illegally copied Nintendo software. This position both proposes that even the act of archiving files poses a threat to the videogame industry and dismisses the existence of software created independently for the GBA, such as homebrew games or applications (discussed in chapter 6). For Nintendo, the creative work that artists develop on the GBA is never authentic. The company's legal frequently asked questions (FAQ) webpage equates physical games with authenticity and digital ROMs with illegality, entirely ignoring the platform's function as a creative tool.

It's important to keep in mind that much of what videogame companies declare to be illegal has in fact never been proven in court. Nintendo's FAQ webpage is a prime example of the chilling effect. No matter how absolute Nintendo's language may be on the subject, they are largely stating their preferred outcome. In fact, legal precedence is against them. In 2000, Sony filed suit against Connectix for selling the Virtual Game Station, a PlayStation emulator developed by reverse engineering the console's firmware.[17] The case followed a trajectory similar to *Sega v. Accolade* (discussed in chapter 1): the district court awarded Sony an injunction, Connectix successfully appealed the ruling in a circuit court, and Sony's charges were dismissed. The *Sony v. Connectix* case set a precedent for the protection of emulators, so long as the emulator is the product of reverse engineering. Copyright doesn't extend to an idea—only the *expression* of an idea—so, if the person who creates the emulator reverse engineers the code rather than copying it directly, the emulator falls under the doctrine of fair use. This is why basic input/output system (BIOS) files usually need to be downloaded independent of the emulator itself: the developer holds the copyright over its code (the use by LoveROMS and LoveRetro of Nintendo's BIOS files for their emulators were included among the forty counts of trademark infringement). Although the court acknowledged that Sony would lose profits as a result of Connectix's emulator, they stated that the "Virtual Game Station is a legitimate competitor in the market for platforms on which Sony and Sony-licensed games can be played."[18] The court also noted, "If Sony wishes to obtain a lawful monopoly on the functional concepts in its software, it must satisfy the more stringent standards of patent laws."[19]

In 2012, Nintendo filed a patent for a "software emulator for emulating a handheld video game platform such as GAME BOY®, GAME BOY COLOR®, and/or GAME BOY ADVANCE® on a low-capability target platform (e.g., a seat-back display for airline or train use, a personal digital assistant, a cell phone)."[20] The fact that no such technology has yet manifested at their hands is hardly surprising; the patent is a revision of applications reaching as far back as 2000. Its role is purely to exert control over third-party emulators and to manifest the "lawful monopoly on the functional concepts in its software" that Sony was missing in order to successfully sue Connectix.[21] Despite what Nintendo says, it *is* in fact relevant whether someone profits from the distribution of an emulator—so long as that someone is Nintendo.

Trading Card Emulation

In 2015, Nintendo began releasing a series of *Animal Crossing* Amiibo Cards in randomized sets for the purpose of interfacing with their open-ended life-simulation games. In *Animal Crossing* games, the player assumes the role of a human who moves to a rural village populated by anthropomorphic animals. Games in the series rarely have clear objectives. Instead, the player is invited to take up fishing, gardening, collecting, and home decorating—all while socializing with the other residents. One of the ways to add villagers to the game is to scan an Amiibo card; each card comes with a unique villager and a few items or pieces of furniture.

Like Amiibo figurines—Nintendo's toys-to-life-platform—the Amiibo Cards use near-field communication (NFC) chips to interact with the readers built into the Wii U GamePad, New 3DS, and Nintendo Switch. But where standard Amiibo toys serve the dual functions of transmitting stored data and acting as display figurines, the *Animal Crossing* cardstock collectibles are more likely to end up tucked away in a binder once the data transfer is complete.

The use of paper cards as a vector for videogame content is another instance of lateral thinking—a remix of a GBA peripheral that met with lukewarm success. Over a decade before the series received Amiibo cards, Nintendo released *Animal Crossing-e*, paper cards that interface with the GBA e-Reader to unlock exclusive content in the GameCube *Animal Crossing* game. Like the eventual Amiibo Cards, this content consists of characters and decorative furniture, but also unique audio tracks and special minigames, including fully playable NES titles. Collecting them all became a meta-mission at the time—and, at 66 cents per card and over 300 cards, an expensive one at that.

The e-Reader, released in Japan in 2001 and North America in 2002, is a clunky plastic add-on that inserts into the GBA cartridge slot and receives data from paper cards by way of an optical recognition system.[22] Although NFC technology was commercially available in the early 2000s, components were bulky and expensive. Rather than opt for cutting-edge communication and storage protocols, Nintendo fell back on affordable, withered technology of a kind used in Epoch's 1991 Barcode Battler.[23] Strips of data that were programmed in dot code—a barcode technology licensed from Olympus Corporation—were printed with ink on paper cards. Long bars hold up to 2.2 KB of information, while short bars hold up to 1.4 KB. When the player swipes a card through the e-Reader (just as they might swipe a credit card), an LED sensor in the peripheral scans the encoded data to access the card's contents.

Only a handful of games feature e-Reader support. In *Super Mario Advance 4*, you can unlock thirty-two extra stages, in addition to power-ups and hidden secrets. *Pokémon Battle-e* cards give you special berries and introduce new trainer battles to *Pokémon Ruby* and *Pokémon Sapphire*. But the obvious trouble with this scanning method is that the e-Reader has to be inserted into the GBA to be operational, meaning that you can't run the companion cartridge at the same time as you swipe the cards. Access to this e-Reader content, therefore, requires two GBAs connected via a link cable: one running the e-Reader and the other running the game for which the cards are designed. Hardware demands are somewhat mitigated for the *Animal Crossing-e*, which works with a GameCube game through a multiplatform link cable. However, to make the most of the peripheral, e-Reader users often have to either be dedicated Nintendo aficionados or be able to borrow someone else's system. Again, the GBA becomes a social platform by material necessity.

That said, there is a way to use the e-Reader in a single-GBA, stand-alone mode, and that's to play old NES games. In addition to its card-reading abilities, the e-Reader includes a built-in NES emulator, 64-MB mask ROM, and 1-MB flash memory that can temporarily turn the GBA into a portable NES. Nintendo released thirteen classic games, each sold in packs of five cards that originally retailed for $4.99. Scanning the dot code strips on both sides of all five cards gives you access to single-player versions of familiar NES titles like *Donkey Kong Jr.*, *Ice Climber*, *Mario Bros.*, *Pinball*, and *Excitebike*. Because the e-Reader has limited resources and its long-bar dot code can contain only 2.2 KB of data, all the NES games released for the add-on are among the earliest titles for the NES—those that run on NROM (referred to by hobbyists as "mapper 0") cartridges. As it is, the e-Reader can retain only one NES title in memory at a time. Swapping between games means you have to swipe all ten sides of the cards again.[24]

The e-Reader experienced moderate success in Japan, buoyed by the overwhelming popularity of *Pokémon* and *Animal Crossing*, but it failed to catch on in North America and never formally made it to Europe at all. This failure is partly the result of Nintendo's curious decision to impose a regional lockout on the peripheral, despite the fact that the handheld that it plugs into is region free. Here is another case of Nintendo exploring technical protection measures (TPMs) to regulate the use of their IP. While the e-Reader works in any GBA, the cards' coding delimits a specific set of e-Readers that can scan them, a restriction that is only compounded by the cards' rarity outside Japan. Collecting a complete set becomes challenging, if not impossible, for anyone who didn't have the forethought to have collected them immediately upon their release.

Nevertheless, the e-Reader offers compelling insight into Nintendo's approach to lateral thinking. The printed cards evoke the company's roots as a manufacturer of playing cards—a theme they keep returning to—and highlight early attempts to exploit their back catalog through emulation. Selling old games for $5 on a different system was a way to test the market for classic titles without all the bells and whistles that accompanied most GBA ports. And from the ashes of the e-Reader rose the Virtual Console.

The Virtual Console

In April 2013, Nintendo launched the Virtual Console for the Wii U, a dedicated section of the Nintendo eShop that allows players to "experience some of the top titles from the NES, Super NES, and Game Boy Advance eras," and the successor to the service of the same name for the Wii.[25] Games retail somewhere between $7.99 and $9.99 and exist exclusively as digital downloads. Licensed rereleasing of selected classic games through the Virtual Console can be seen as the company's riposte to videogame piracy and their attempt to retain control over their IP; it provides access to titles currently unavailable through traditional retail networks, even as it acknowledges the ubiquity of software emulation. In a surprising move for the historically insular company, Nintendo hired the Japanese videogame developer M2—best known for their work on the Game Gear emulator and the Sega-published 3D Classic remake series for the 3DS—to work on their GBA Virtual Console emulator. GBA software launched on April 3, 2014, with three titles, *Advance Wars, Mario & Luigi Superstar Saga,* and *Metroid Fusion*, and the library added 71 titles over the following three years.

Given the existence of the 3DS and its own Virtual Console, Nintendo's decision to rerelease GBA games exclusively for the Wii U was met with raised eyebrows by fans who had hoped to enjoy not only the content, but also the portability of the GBA library. The expectation, of course, was that Nintendo would expand on their work with the 3DS Ambassador Program and make those titles available to everyone for a fee on the Virtual Console. The reality was less simple. Recall from chapter 2 that Ambassador games aren't emulated, but rather use the clocked-down GBA firmware preserved alongside the 3DS's backward compatibility with the DS. Simulating a GBA environment necessarily disables the 3DS firmware responsible for background tasks like Wi-Fi capabilities, sleep mode, and locative connectivity. And because Nintendo errs on the side of inexpensive, low-power, energy-efficient hardware, the 3DS isn't powerful enough to run the Wii U's GBA emulator. Rather than revert the 3DS to a GBA or settle for a subpar engine, Nintendo focused their efforts on translating the handheld to the Wii U, a console that had met with a mild response and needed all the help it could get.

As a compromise of sorts, the Wii U's hardware allows emulated GBA games to be marginally portable within the domestic space. Users can send a game from the television screen to the GamePad, the console's primary controller. The GamePad features an embedded touch screen and has a wide-enough radius that players can often reach adjacent rooms with it in tow. (In an IGN thread on the topic, many users expressed particular delight that the signal traveled far enough to allow them to get to the bathroom without having to put down their game.)[26] On the GamePad, visuals are stunningly crisp, thanks to a 1080p perfect pixel mode that scales up the GBA's 240-x-160-pixel resolution by a factor of 6 horizontally and vertically—a more accurate representation of the graphics than the "Screen Smoothing" option, which blends and blurs the pixel edges for a look that often resembles a stained-glass window. With save states and customizable button configurations, the GBA Virtual Console mirrors, absorbs, and reexports many of the desirable features that come out of hobbyist videogame emulation ecosystems.

Perfect pixels aside, the Virtual Console doesn't purport to deliver authenticity. Instead, it operates through a process of self-conscious translation. Games run on the Wii U in a simulated GBA environment that is heavily mediated by the console's affordances and the intervening decade of cultural attitudes toward Nintendo products and videogames more generally. Virtual Console games lack the tactility of the cartridge, but more than that, they also include bug fixes, name changes, edited text, and even enhanced graphics. Many videogames experience slight revisions over the course of their market life, which are indicated materially through the numbers on the cartridge circuitry. But the Virtual Console presents a single, ostensibly canonical reconstruction of the software title without informing users about which version they purchased. The inability to connect a Game Boy Advance Game Link cable to the Wii U also means that the emulator did away with local multiplayer capabilities between multiple systems.

The most notable distinction by far comes from the GamePad's brilliant backlight and the standard illumination of a television screen. In the Virtual Console's emulated environment, there are no options that can simulate the effects of playing on the dim screen of the 2001 GBA, in the hazy glow of the SP's front-lighting, or with the tiny screen of the Micro. M2 had already proved that they could code such hardware limitations into software with their Game Gear Virtual Console, which captured the visual ghosting and motion-blur effects of the low-resolution screen. Without the excuse of challenging programming, it seems to have been a deliberate decision on Nintendo's part to efface the hardware's shortcomings entirely, re-presenting GBA titles as platonic ideals of themselves. Although emulation re-creates the game pixel by pixel, the physical conditions of play—screen size and brightness, input configurations, portability, ergonomics, and so on—are necessarily translated to a new hardware and software ecosystem as the GBA is reimagined and recontextualized.

Emulated Ephemera

When my brother and I were young, my parents would take us to the videogame store to pick out our birthday presents. We would spend the ride home in shivering excitement as we tore into the game boxes and ravenously devoured the contents of the instruction manuals. Our parents knew better than to disturb us as we dived into new adventures even before we got home to power on our console. The instruction manuals were our travel guides, and we had to read them cover to cover before embarking on our journeys.

Ephemera like manuals and box art provide valuable information about a game and console at the time of their release. What instruction manuals say about a game—and, more to the point, what information is presumed to be so common-sense that it *isn't* included—speaks to a set of knowledge protocols that mediate our approach to software and hardware objects. As Lisa Gitelman observes, media are "socially realized structures of communication, where structures include both technological forms and their associated protocols, and where communication is a cultural practice, a ritualized collocation of different people on the same mental map."[27] The protocols associated with technological forms change over time, and while it's impossible to physically return to the sociohistorical context in which a game was released, ephemera allow us to peek into the past to learn about how the media was marketed and circulated. Instruction manuals explain how to interact with the interface, how to win the game, and the point of the game altogether. These "paratexts"—a term that Mia Consalvo borrows from literary theorist Gérard Genette to refer to the peripheral industries and objects around games, including strategy guides, reviews, and advertisements—become integral parts of a game, packaged with the cartridge itself.[28]

As digital titles, most Virtual Console games are stripped of paratexts. Instead, the digital files are often packaged alongside curated images of the software running on the new hardware and an attending paragraph that waxes nostalgic about "unforgettable characters" and "timeless arcade classic[s]" as though players encountering the games need a reminder of who Mario is.[29]

It's a significant departure from the Virtual Console model that GBA games—while still including those reframed game summaries and screenshots—also provide high-resolution, full-color scans of the instruction manuals. By pressing an icon on the GamePad's touch screen, players can access these scans and even keep them open on the touch screen while they play the game on the television. Although the box art remains absent and the manuals lack the tactility of a paper product (meaning no doodled marginalia), the digital manuals activate a form of material nostalgia connected with videogame preservation. Their inclusion alongside the Virtual Console reinserts some of the context of a game's release as though to counterbalance the lack of ownership.

Battery-Powered Memory

The release of GBA games on the Virtual Console in 2013 was strategic not only because it provided an alternative to hobbyist emulation, but also because certain physical GBA cartridges have a built-in life expectancy of ten to twenty years. Before Nintendo began manufacturing GBA Game Paks that used flash memory or electrically erasable programmable read-only memory (EEPROM) to store save data without power, cartridges relied on battery-backed static random-access memory (SRAM). Early GBA Game Paks—like their Game Boy and GBC predecessors—contain small batteries, usually CR1616s or CR2025s, to support save data or maintain time-keeping features. These batteries, while cheap and easy to replace with the right materials and basic soldering skills, will eventually fail. And without a functioning battery, powering down the handheld erases save data (or, in the case of the *Pokémon* games, prevents clock-based events from occurring). By design or default, Nintendo's rerelease of games (and their save data) in digital format on the Virtual Console acknowledges the obsolescence of their cartridges. Battery-backed cartridges available on the Virtual Console include *WarioLand 4*, *Metroid Fusion*, *Metroid: Zero Mission*, *Castlevania: Circle of the Moon*, *Castlevania: Harmony of Dissonance*, and *Kirby: Nightmare in Dream Land*.

The moments where these batteries fail can bring to light perceptions and preconceptions that users elide when the technology or infrastructure functions in the way it should. As Lisa Parks and Nicole Starosielski write: "Infrastructural breakdowns and acts of repair should be thought about as a 'normal' part of technological processes and as opportunities for retooling social relations."[30] The process of replacing a battery carries with it the impulse to consider the object's afterlife, abstracted from its intended use value. Repairing the battery on a cartridge and playing an emulated version are both transformative processes that challenge the obsolescence of videogame hardware.

But this infrastructural breakdown also brings to light the unreliability of the Virtual Console's preservation model, in that its promise of storage remains only insofar as Nintendo maintains its servers. On January 30, 2019, fans mourned the passing of the Wii Shop Channel, through which players could buy Virtual Console games with Wii Points added via credit cards or purchased points cards (on that day, there were a smattering of Wii Shop Channel funeral and vigil videos on YouTube). While users can still play the games they've downloaded, Nintendo announced that the ability to do so "will also stop at some point."[31] Digital game channels will flicker into white noise on the Wii home screen, taking the company's much-lauded preservation model with them. That's because Virtual Consoles fundamentally preclude game ownership. M2's GBA emulator and its downloaded games are designed to be irretrievable to human users. Under the doctrine of first sale, buying a GBA cartridge in 2001 gave you a degree of ownership.[32] You could play or destroy the game, lend it to a friend or resell the physical object you had purchased. But here, all you get is a license to play—and a temporary one at that.

For the time being, we can access dozens of GBA games from Nintendo's historical back catalog through the Wii U's eShop. But the closure of the Wii Shop Channel might give us pause and invite us to reflect on the platform's ephemerality before making a purchase. Nintendo's mode of preservation, platformized as it is, isn't true preservation at all. And, unlike the Wii, the Wii U didn't enjoy outstanding commercial success, so its user base is smaller to begin with. When Nintendo pulls the plug, what happens to those cherished games?

Unsanctioned Emulators

Long before Nintendo released their proprietary Wii U Virtual Console, consumers intervened to reproduce GBA software through emulation, making the source code free to use on nearly any operating system. The prevalence of these emulators belies the labor that went into their development. Because Nintendo restricts their technical documentation to official licensees, the process of developing a GBA emulator required painstaking experiments in reverse engineering, demanding that amateur developers get up close and personal with all facets of the hardware. Many developers exchanged their discoveries with each other, partly in the interest of furthering the community project and partly to show off their own fluency. The progression of these emulators was iterative, leveraging the ongoing breakthroughs that circulated on forums and in chat rooms. Martin Korth's No$GBA (no cash GBA), for instance, began as a freeware debugger for homebrew development before becoming one of the earliest stable emulators (for a discussion of homebrew, see chapter 6). At the time, most developers hadn't yet been able to reverse engineer the BIOS from Nintendo's code. Because reproducing it would constitute infringement (because while content isn't copyrightable, its expression is), most early emulators relied on high-level emulation (HLE) techniques. Early emulators included BIOS clones written in x86 that simulated the BIOS, but at the cost of some accuracy and timing. In this way, Korth and other developers protected themselves from legal sanction while delivering a product that supplied and performed the features that most users needed in a debugger and emulator at the time.

Today, there are dozens of successful GBA emulators that complement and compete with one another. Many of them are designed to run on specific host systems, trading the versatility of being cross-platform for the ability to make the most of the host system's affordances. Each emulator invariably responds to and shapes the way we engage with familiar hardware.

For example, the MyBoy! emulator, a free app (with some paid features), creates the conditions for GBA play on Android smartphones to truly make good on the promise of console-quality gaming *anywhere*. MyBoy! was developed with its players' needs in mind, even as the interface fundamentally changes how we experience the software. The emulator offers two default orientations: a portrait mode with the 4:3 aspect ratio display positioned above a black background with buttons that echo their placement on the SP, and a landscape mode that stretches the image to 16:9 and overlays the controls on top of the picture (figure 5.1).

While pressing phantom buttons isn't unfamiliar to anyone with a smartphone, playing retro games on a buttonless interface requires some mental rewiring. The haptic feedback from the phone's vibrations on supported devices is a nice touch, but it's a poor replacement for the tactile aspect of actual buttons. Fingers can unknowingly slip from their positions while our eyes fixate on the action—a reminder that videogames aren't as intuitive as we might think. Moreover, those of us who are familiar with smartphones must actively work against our impulses to try to drag sprites across the map with our fingers instead of using the overlaid button inputs. We are conditioned to approach games on mobile devices a certain way by the phones' hardware, their operating systems, and the apps developed for them. This embodied knowledge of mobile game interfaces—whether from playing mobile games, from watching others play, or from navigating other mobile apps—actively interferes with the ability to play a GBA game in an emulated environment on a touch screen.

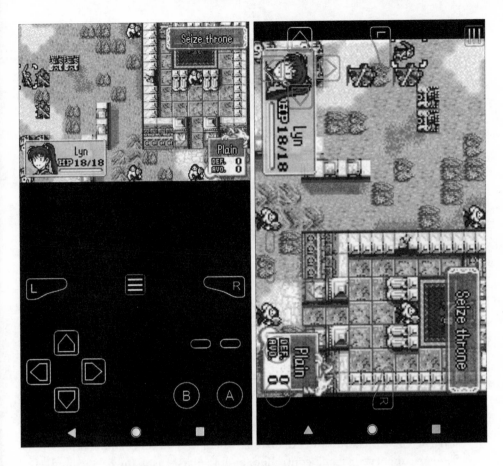

Figure 5.1 Vertical (left) and horizontal (right) layouts on the MyBoy! Android application, running *FE7*. Note the "buttons" superimposed on the screen. Emulated on MyBoy! on a Google Pixel 2.

This kind of emulated play equally reminds us of the mutual relationship between hardware and software that is so key to Nintendo's product development. The GBA's form factor was designed with ergonomics in mind; the position of the buttons on the handheld and the inputs that the software demands are mutually dependent. In *Super Mario Advance 2*, Mario can perform a spin jump whenever you press the R trigger while holding down the A button. This is easy enough to do on all models of the GBA, where your thumbs control Mario's movements and your index fingers, bracing the handheld, can flick the trigger as needed. But when playing on a phone, there's no easy trigger to tap; the L and R buttons are transposed onto the screen where you need to twist your index finger into the correct position—an action made all the more challenging in landscape mode, where the index finger usually braces the phone.

Again, we see the trade-offs and compromises of videogame hardware. MyBoy! exchanges the comfort and familiarity of a button configuration designed in tandem with the platform's software library for the efficiency of running the software on a device that follows many of us around, regardless of whether we want to play videogames. The ability to seamlessly switch from exploring the Minish woods to firing off an email to looking up a recipe for dinner comes at the cost of dedicated hardware. For those of us too busy to sit down and play for hours on end, stolen moments between communication and research may be our only opportunity to escape to the worlds of childhood.

Windows into the Past: mGBA

The mGBA emulator stands as the most complete GBA emulation effort, and a useful one for thinking through some of the GBA's idiosyncrasies. Developed by Vicky Pfau (endrift), mGBA is an open-source GBA, GBC, and Game Boy emulator. Written with the goal of being fast enough to operate on low-end hardware (like netbooks and old phones) without sacrificing performance and portability, mGBA boasts of being the most accurate and universal GBA emulator—and with good reason. It works on Windows, Linux, macOS, PS Vita, 3DS, Wii, Android, and iOS, supports cartridges with hardware expansions—including rumble and motion-sensor support for game controllers and a solar sensor for *Boktai*—and includes a video-recording feature to facilitate competitive tool-assisted speedruns and playthrough sharing. Useful as a developer tool, the multiplatform emulator also enables game debugging via a command-line interface and includes built-in .ips, .ups, and .bps patch support for ROM hacks (discussed further in chapter 6). The mGBA is the emulation equivalent of a Swiss army knife.

Setting mGBA apart from similar software is its ability to play games from the GBA's Classic NES Series. Immediately identifiable by their light gray cartridge shells and simple labels, Classic NES Series games (not to be confused with the NES Classic Edition console) are retro ports of NES games that Nintendo released for the GBA in 2004. The cartridges retailed for $19.99 each. Twelve installments were available internationally and another eighteen were exclusive to Japan. While these were inexpensive compared to most GBA games, Nintendo's pricing sustained significant criticism because most of these titles had already been released for $4.99

as e-Reader cards or were included in the GameCube's *Animal Crossing* as fully playable items that ran via emulation.[33]

Classic NES Series games are seldom compatible with GBA emulators due to a series of unique and often obscure behaviors in their code. Loading one of them in an emulator typically delivers a Game Pak Error screen directing the player to turn the power off and back on without explaining what went wrong. These behaviors include the following:

Memory mapping achieved by copying code into the main RAM and leaping to mirror addresses.

Executing code in video random-access memory (VRAM), the region of RAM usually reserved for graphics.

Unorthodox and clever register manipulation to copy memory from one region to another.

Feigning the save type by pretending to access SRAM even though the games save to EEPROM.

Modifying the ARM processor pipeline.[34]

Classic NES Series games also have a unique way of dealing with sound, in that they use only one of six audio channels (one of the Direct Sound channels). They write 16 bits of audio at a time to one-half of the register rather than 32 bits at a time to input/output registers associated with the channels, so playing them on an emulator that treats them like a standard GBA game results in garbled audio.

According to endrift, the odd behaviors of the Classic NES Series are safeguards designed to dissuade their use on unauthorized systems. She says that Nintendo deliberately employed these methods to prevent players from copying or otherwise interacting with the ROM in ways they didn't sanction. The games weren't just exploiting behavioral relics of the Famicom or relying on a single trick to thwart attempts at reverse engineering; the code was scrambled on purpose, to stymie hackers and hobbyists.

While endrift presents compelling points in favor of this theory, the fact that the games impede attempts at emulation doesn't necessarily mean that they were designed with anti-emulation measures in mind. Rarely are games coded for a hardware object without peculiarities. Sometimes differences are the result of optimization or platform fluency; as programmers grew more familiar with coding for the GBA, they discovered shortcuts to cut down on programming time and maximize performance. At other times, idiosyncrasies arise from lack of familiarity with the ARM processor or with Nintendo's documentation; the GBA was the first of the company's handhelds to adopt ARM architecture, so there was a considerable learning curve concerning the central processing unit (CPU) alone, to say nothing of the improved graphics capability. There might even have been programming accidents that happened to solve bugs and thus were left in.

As a consequence, we might see many of the supposed safeguards against emulation as simply being the result of a game's translation from one console to another. Yes, writing 16 bits of audio to a single 8-bit digital audio channel has the unintended side effect of frustrating emulation, but it's also the result of the old Famicom game not requiring the full functionality of the GBA's sound system. Running code in VRAM is similarly utilitarian; VRAM is the second-fastest memory section in the GBA behind internal work RAM; if the 96 KB of VRAM aren't being used for graphics that harnessed the GBA's potential, why not use them to execute code more efficiently than external work RAM? The Classic NES Series games expose their roots as NES games, not only in the familiar graphics and gameplay, but fundamentally through the code, which looks alien when placed beside the contents of most GBA cartridges. Because most emulators operate under the assumption that all GBA games are created equal and rely on universal shortcuts in the interest of simplicity, issues arise when code suddenly deviates from the expected norm. Without the ability to detect and address idiosyncrasies in the game's code, emulators stumble when attempting to execute a Classic NES Series game. It wasn't until endrift sat down to sift through all the functions of the games' code and address them with targeted fixes to the emulator that they became playable outside their cartridges. Although they seem esoteric, the Classic NES Series games are the result of lateral thinking: withered code tweaked for a new platform.

Still, there's something to endrift's supposition that Nintendo was intentionally trying to obviate emulation, at least through some of the idiosyncrasies of the games' code. Feigning the save type is the hardest feature to see as a relic of NES programming, given GBA's memory protocols and the materials of the cartridge. The code affords all indications that the game saves to SRAM because it includes such a protocol in the 0E memory block. But the cartridge itself includes a chip for EEPROM save storage, the protocols for which exist at the high end of the cartridge's memory in 0D. If the game detects that saving to SRAM has succeeded—as it would if it were played on an emulator that simulated SRAM saves—players are confronted with the Game Pak Error screen. To address this issue, mGBA checks the game code ahead of time to force the save type to

EEPROM. It's difficult to see how feigning the save type would have been desirable purely from a programming perspective.

Here, endrift makes a compelling point when she observes that Nintendo had hobbyist emulation on their minds when coding these games. By the time the Classic NES Series reached retailers, hobbyists had already been playing NES games on their GBA, thanks to the PocketNES emulator developed by Neal Tew (Loopy) and Fredrik Olsson (Flubba). PocketNES runs through a flash cartridge or the GBA Movie Player peripheral—an add-on device that allows you to play movies and music on the GBA using CompactFlash or Secure Digital cards—and began as a way to circulate homebrew NES games on a portable system. There's strong reason to suspect that Nintendo knew about the PocketNES and, moreover, reterritorialized its techniques for their own ends.

In 2002 and 2003, respectively, Nintendo filed for a Japanese and US patent for "a game emulator program that allows a game to be played on a game machine using a display device of a second resolution that is lower than a first resolution for which the game is designed, while reproducing a game image that is close to the original."[35] The document describes an emulator program that translates the 240-x-256-pixel resolution of the NES to the GBA's 160 x 240-pixel resolution without decimating the image. Nintendo claimed that the program was "under development" when the patent was filed. But the method articulated in this patent—eventually granted in 2006—had already been used in 2001 by the PocketNES to great acclaim. PocketNES had managed to preserve the spirit of the games' graphics while fitting them into the GBA screen using a vertical flicker scaling technique. What Nintendo patented wasn't just the idea behind the PocketNES's vertical scaling but the method itself—right down to the flicker.[36]

The decision to enfold copy protection measures into the Classic NES Series specifically is puzzling, considering that Nintendo knew these games had long been playable on the GBA through the work of hobbyists. But even more perplexing is that these protection measures—if at least some of these behaviors were indeed protection measures—actually worked. As it turned out, endrift managed to decipher the games' inner workings and emulate them successfully only a full decade after their release, when she finally took it upon herself to figure out what irregularities had stymied emulators for so long. And yet these features remained exclusive to the Classic NES Series. The most protected IP for the GBA was already two decades old and had been folded into a GameCube game for free. In many ways, the Classic NES Series feels like a purposeful retaliation against hobbyist communities. Nintendo borrowed their classmate's binder to copy their homework and then set fire to the pages when they finished.

Wii Want to Emulate: Visual Boy Advance GX

Not long after the release of the Nintendo Wii, players realized that it was one of the easiest and most efficient consoles to modify at the software level (a practice known as "softmodding") using simple downloadable or game-based exploits. The installation of the Homebrew Channel—a pirate channel in the Wii interface used for loading unsanctioned applications and emulators—offers the ability not only to back up Wii and GameCube games, but also to experience home console systems up to the N64 and handheld systems up to the GBA on one conveniently compact system. With its Virtual Console no longer supported after the Wii Shop Channel's closure, unauthorized emulation through the Homebrew Channel has become one of the only ways to make good on the Wii's promise to provide access to decades of videogame history. Supporting standard 480i and 480p video display resolutions optimized for high-definition television, emulation on the Wii brings many of the same affordances and constraints as playing GBA games on a television with the Game Boy Player (GBP). It similarly opens the screen to communal viewership and welcomes players who might be able to interact with software on a small screen, all while using less hardware. The Wii's built-in controller ports allow players to navigate game worlds with the Game-Cube controller or a GBA connected with the Game Boy Advance Game Link Cable.

But there's another way that the softmodded Wii rearticulates our embodied relationship to the GBA's catalog, and that's through the mimetic interface of the Wii Remote (Wiimote). The Wii hadn't been in development—or even thought up yet—when Nintendo released the GBA, but one of the most exciting aspects of studying a platform years after its market life cycle has ended is being able to see what users do with it in relation to successive technologies. The VisualBoyAdvance GX (VBA-GX) emulator—a Wii-exclusive and optimized port of the open-source VisualBoyAdvance-M—piggybacks on the Wiimote's technical affordances to approximate hardware add-ons included in select GBA cartridges: *WarioWare: Twisted!* harnesses the Wiimote's built-in accelerometer to serve as the game's gyrosensor; and *Boktai* charges the Gun del Sol based on whether the Wiimote is pointed at the sky or the ground (an innovative repurposing of tools that acknowledges how challenging it would be to play the Wii outside in the Sun).[37]

But by far, the most salient reterritorialization comes through the unique and impressive Match Wii Controls feature integrated in the emulator. When enabled, Match Wii Controls translates the expressive affordances of Wii play to GBA games. Titles from series with corresponding Wii installments can exchange GameCube controller inputs for the Wiimote and Nunchuk.

What all this means in practice is that you can play *The Legend of Zelda: The Minish Cap* as though it were *The Legend of Zelda: Twilight Princess*. The little left-handed sprite Link draws and swings his sword when you cut through the air with the Wiimote.[38] Shaking the Nunchuk has him perform a spin attack. With directional movement outsourced to the Nunchuk's analog stick and with a handful of extra buttons to work with, the Wii configuration streamlines play: the Up button on the Direction-pad (D-pad) allows Link to speak to his hat, Ezlo; the 1, (–), and (+) buttons open the Map, Items, and Quest Status screens, respectively; and the infrared pointer function allows the player to select items right from the screen. Mechanically, the game *feels* like *Twilight Princess*, but the distinct, cartoonish graphics are nostalgic reminders that *The Minish Cap* predates the Wii by half a decade.[39] Playing with the Match Wii Controls feature is an anachronism.

The feature presumes a basic familiarity with the Wiimote and Nunchuk, as well as the corresponding Wii title in a given series, a presupposition not held by mainline games. When developers were scrambling to finish the Wii port of *Twilight Princess* by the console's launch date, Shigeru Miyamoto asked the team to extend the time that Link spends in the first village (essentially the game's tutorial) from one in-game day to three. Given how revolutionary—to borrow the language of Nintendo's marketing—the Wii controller was, Miyamoto felt that players should have more time to learn about the new interface, hence the addition of trivial activities like fishing. Such tasks were designed for players to acclimate to new ways of moving their physical and virtual bodies.[40] Evidently, *The Minish Cap* contains no such diegetic activities. The ROM itself remains unaltered.

What does change is the interface. It's worth reminding ourselves that the Wiimote isn't itself intuitive, despite its overall emotional design. Precedent suggests that if Nintendo had released a Wiimote-compatible series of GBA games, they'd have paired it with a series of minigame-based tutorials, akin to what they did with the *NES Remix* on the Wii U eShop. *NES Remix* demanded that players complete simple exercises to familiarize themselves with the retro mechanics before diving into minigames that mixed and matched elements of previous NES titles.[41] These introductory exercises acted as virtual instruction manuals, guiding the player and establishing the rules of engagement. But with Match Wii Controls, there is no such tutorial. Knowledge is tacit. If you're familiar enough with the Wii to have the desire and knowhow to mod it, the assumption is that you also know how to use the controller. Memories—mental and muscle—of playing *Twilight Princess* directly filter approaches to the emulation of *The Minish Cap*. In this way, the feature makes explicit the way that our experience of a videogame is always contextually mediated. Even without the Wiimote in hand, having played *Twilight Princess* invariably changes the way that we think about earlier *Zelda* games.

The VBA-GX's Match Wii Controls feature is exemplary of how fans themselves remix Nintendo's hardware and software in exciting ways. Just as *NES Remix* appropriates the topographies of decades of amateur and hobbyist emulation and ROM hacking—save states, sprite swapping, overclocking, and so on—the Match Wii Controls feature appropriates Nintendo's hardware, commandeering it to function in an environment that exists at the outskirts of the legal system. By using the Wiimote and Nunchuk, players expand the GBA assemblage in Nintendo's own image—lateral thinking in action yet again.

Tool-Assisted Play

As noted, the bulk of the GBA emulators introduce new functions and features that never existed on Nintendo's console. These features include the obvious, like the ability to alter display settings and change controller configurations to accommodate the ways that you might approach the host system. But they also include a wide array of features that, similar to Match Wii Controls, create ways for communities to engage with objects in ways that Nintendo did not intend or predict.

Since the 1990s, players have engaged in a performative metagame known as "speedrunning" where the goal is to complete a game as quickly as possible. Speedrunners approach games differently from most players—on its terms rather than ours—by diligently planning out their routes ahead of time and exploiting programming glitches to skip entire sequences of gameplay (known as "sequence breaking"). A virtuosic speedrunner can complete a game that takes most players tens of hours in a matter of mere minutes. These players often livestream and record their endeavors as proud displays of their technical mastery and gameplay skill. Online communities of speedrunners and the people who watch them keep records of completion time and comb through the videos to ensure that the players followed the rules.

The advent of emulation catalyzed a new, flourishing genre of speedrunning—one that leverages the affordances of an emulator to further decimate clear times. Tool-assisted speedrunning (TAS) combines players' skill with the technological features of emulation by using timed key-presses that, when played back through the emulator, achieves the shortest possible time. Emulators can alter clock speed to slow games down to individual frames for more accurate inputs and then replay the performance at the natural speed, or speed games up to shave off valuable seconds spent watching cutscenes and clicking through dialogue. Through software assistance, speedrunners manipulate mechanics invisible to most users to complete games in an unthinkably short amount of time. By exploiting the emulators' affordances, players engage in a "collaborative form of play based on discovering exploits such as geometry clipping, cutscene skipping, sequence breaking, and memory manipulation," as noted by Boluk and LeMieux.[42]

While unassisted speedruns rely on rigorous practice for perfect physical inputs that become pure reflex, TAS relies on near-limitless knowledge of the game code and the emulator's features. Speedrunners rerun games in segments (from save states, another feature unique to emulated play) hundreds and thousands of times to unearth any error in the game's grammar that might improve their sequence. They use inputs that are prohibitively challenging to perform in real time or physically impossible to achieve outside of emulation (e.g., pressing both the left and right directions at the same instant). In many cases, speedrunners step through the game one frame at a time to optimize their runs to a degree beyond the average player's imagination, overcoming human limitations to perform an impossible playthrough. When we talk about improving TAS clear times, we're often talking about a matter of frames, not seconds. A successful speedrun is a symphony based on incomparable mastery of the game code and knowledge of the affordances of emulation.

Although TAS seems, from the outside, to be a deeply solitary activity whereby individual speedrunners spend hours with their machine until they're fluent in the game's language, it has become a large-scale, multiplayer experience thanks to the emergence of livestreaming platforms like Twitch and massive, structured competitions. In the speedrunning community, "a live audience transforms private play into public performance, breaking up the monotony of repetitive practice through networked intimacies, gamifying the game through community feedback."[43] Unlike electronic sports (e-sports), speedrunning has remained relatively uncommercial, with little corporate backing. Instead, the speedrunning community has developed its own model of collaboration and competition through online marathons where the proceeds are donated to various charities. Games Done Quick, the most famous of these tournaments, holds two annual weeklong marathons where the most accomplished speedrunners come together to display their virtuosity and share their knowledge with others through in-depth commentary over the performances. Over the last seven years, they've raised over $16.5 million and have observed that their marathons are the largest global fundraising events for Doctors Without Borders and the Prevent Cancer Foundation. According to Mia Consalvo, through participation in these events, speedrunners accrue "gaming capital," a dynamic social currency that shapes practices of play and the future of the gaming industry, through elegant displays of their technical knowledge.[44] On speedrun.com, the community keeps records of assisted (and unassisted) speedruns based on uploaded videos or livestreamed playthroughs, where the moderators are always careful to verify that a speedrunner who has set a record followed the rules.

It might be strange to think about speedrunning as a practice with specific and enforced sets of rules, in light of the fact that they're based around exploiting glitches inherent in the code. But the community recognizes a distinction between cheating and exploitation. Consalvo explains that exploits "don't involve a player actively changing code in a game or deceiving other players; instead, they are 'found' actions or items that accelerate or improve a player's skills, actions, or abilities in some way that the designer did not originally intend."[45] In order to preserve accuracy and to focus on players' mastery of the game code, the community prescribes the use of certain emulators and bans the use of others. Bizhawk, a multisystem emulator made by the people who run TAS Videos, a community dedicated to publishing gameplay "superplays," is the favored emulator, while Visual Boy Advance is approved but not preferred. Although the emulator facilitates TAS, it's players' mastery over the game code that's meant to be displayed; the emulator falls away when the process is complete.

On April 1, 2018, a speedrunnner named Biospark discovered a new exploit in *Metroid Fusion*, a side-scrolling adventure game released for the GBA in 2002 that follows bounty hunter Samus Aran as she explores a planetary surface rife with parasitic organisms. The trick uses the relationship between the blocks in the game world and the way that the game saves data. Blowing up certain blocks out of bounds using power bombs overwrites key values in the save data to fool the game into thinking that players have progressed much further than they have. Within two days, the memory corruption exploit allowed the speedrunner JRP2234 to shave 21 minutes and 18 seconds off the world record.[46]

The discovery of this exploit occurred at a time when a *Metroid Fusion* tournament was ongoing. So as not to undermine the strategies that the speedrunners had carefully practiced beforehand, the new trick was banned for the tournament. What's more, it also occasioned the development of a new category of *Metroid Fusion* speedruns: "Any% No Memory Corruption." This isn't new in and of itself. Most games have various brackets built around the different percentages of the game that speedrunners have to complete for it to count as a clear ("Any%" means that so long as players get to the credits, it counts). But it's interesting to witness a community change the rules of the game to preserve the existing records of *Metroid Fusion* speedruns, even though the practice will be indelibly altered going forward. Even after all this time, players are still discovering new ways to push the GBA's games to their limits. To believe that we understand everything about the platform is not to understand it at all. As an ongoing, ever-mutating assemblage, the GBA is constantly shaping and being shaped by vast communities of users.

Emulation enables a wide range of playful metagaming practices beyond speedrunning, many of which give rise to their own communities with their own rules, aesthetics, and experts. One of the most explicitly playful metagaming practices is the use of a randomizer to create unexpected forms of play, troubling the logic of a given game and, more broadly, of the platform in creative ways. "Randomizers" are patching applications or executable programs that create surprising gameplay experiences by randomizing features of a game, shuffling characters, equipment, and settings around so that each playthrough is as unexpected as the last one was. The patch or program modifies the ROM (as discussed in chapter 6), and the game is run through an emulator.[47]

Yune: A Universal Fire Emblem Randomizer is a patching application designed by Lushen124 (OtakuReborn) that rearranges dozens of variables in any of the three GBA *Fire Emblem* games. *Yune* alters character recruitment order, growth points, classes, weapon power, and out-of-battle rewards. A mage, a class known for high magic and high resistance, might end up with good defense and suddenly be capable of leading the charge against the enemy army. A slow knight might become unexpectedly speedy, but very weak. Rather than telling characters what to do based on an inherited knowledge of the tropes of fantasy classes, players suddenly have to defer to what their randomly generated units want. By rearranging familiar touchstones, randomizers disrupt the game's flow. As such, according to Michael Iantorno, they "have essentially created a new genre of speedrunning, where technical prowess is paired with meta-knowledge of game logic and systems."[48] Players can't fall back on muscle memory or encyclopedic knowledge of glitches to complete the game; instead they have to adapt to the changes as they come. Randomizer communities organize themselves around Let's Play videos, Twitch livestreams, Discord servers, and community-specific forums. The resulting playthroughs are often characterized by humor and delight and the collective experience of surprise.

Perhaps the most notable disruption of a videogame's intended flow is an unexpected social experiment called Twitch Plays *Pokémon* (*TPP*), a crowdsourced attempt to play the *Pokémon* games. In February 2014, an anonymous Australian programmer scripted a bot in Python to capture select messages from the Twitch stream's chat room (↑, ↓, ←, →, A, B, Start, Select) and direct them to the Visual Boy Advance emulator, which was running *Pokémon Red* on Game Boy. Over the course of 16 days, millions of people tuned in from around the world to get the bot to catch, name, train, and compete with *Pokémon*. The result was a breathtaking cacophony of inputs—chaos of the highest order. But somehow Twitch beat *Pokémon*. And then it did it again. In March, Twitch turned to the GBA's *Pokémon Emerald*, where participants, usually numbering upward of 15,000 at any given moment, set off on an adventure with the fire Pokémon Torchic. *TPP* changed handheld interactivity. *Pokémon* had always been a game that required people to come into contact with each other to exchange their little monsters. But this was sociality on a whole different scale.

These are the kinds of play experiences that arise once hardware and software are in players' hands. Although speedrunning, randomizing, and Twitch playing seem to be abstracted behind the computational processes of emulators, randomizers, and Python bots, these weird, creative experiences nevertheless display a meeting between the machine and the human. These experiences are at once medium specific and profoundly universal. These are at once procedural events and dynamic performances, social commentary and personal entertainment, archives of play and histories of the platform. They're what happens when players gamify games. They're the vibrant, delirious, and stubborn afterlives of the platform.

There's No Way of Owning

In the wake of Nintendo's recent assortment of lawsuits, DMCA crackdowns, and the Wii Shop Channel's closure, videogame researchers have reflected on the company's commodification not only of their own past, but also of the past and present that fans and hobbyists have produced in concert with them. Whether the company wants to admit it or not, emulation and homebrew ecosystems have long been imbricated in Nintendo's corporate decisions. Indeed, Frank Cifaldi, the founder of the Video Game History Foundation, openly attributes the resounding success of Nintendo's back catalog through the Virtual Console and the Classic Edition consoles to the popularity of free emulators and online ROM sites:

> I don't think the business I'm in exists without emulation . . . the video game community would have totally moved on if it wasn't easy to access old games. I don't think Nintendo's Virtual Console would exist. It proved the market was there.[49]

Robust communities of speedrunners, randomizers, and fans provide proof of market for the Virtual Console, as well as for objects like the NES and SNES Classic Edition. What's more, emulation plays a crucial role in the preservation of and access to videogame history and the GBA in particular. For many users, browser-based tools and downloadable apps are the most—if not the only—accessible ways for them to form a relationship to the IP that Nintendo released for the GBA.

To play a GBA game by legitimate means, a player must own a GBA (discontinued in 2010), a Nintendo DS (discontinued in 2013), or a Wii U (discontinued in 2017). A legal way to purchase and play a GBA game through Nintendo's official channels no longer exists; users must instead hunt down functional secondhand devices in pawnshops or online, where the profit is no longer going to Nintendo anyway. With no promise of GBA games coming to the Switch yet, users who want to explore early titles in their favorite series are left in legal limbo.

As a global study of online piracy shows, the effectiveness of enforcement measures like DMCA takedown notices and punitive lawsuits is uncertain. "Instead," the authors write, "it might be sensible to search for the answer to piracy elsewhere—in the provision of affordable and convenient legal access to copyright-protected content."[50] With Google and Apple both having recently announced their own browser-based videogame streaming services—a sort of multiplatform Netflix equivalent for games, consistent with the platformization of cultural commodities—it's clear that some companies are rethinking our relationship to videogames and ownership. Under the duress of convergence, Nintendo's handheld competitor has already shifted from Sony to Apple. The landscapes of portable and console gaming are veering toward the mobile and the browser-based, and Nintendo seems to be rethinking the way that they commodify their nearly forty-year-old library.

If we look back to the valuation of each ROM image in Nintendo's lawsuit against LoveROMS and LoveRetro, the $150,000 price tag may in fact be justified by a rationale that involves plans for the creation of pres-ently nonexistent revenue streams. Nintendo supposedly has no plans for a GBA equivalent to the NES and SNES Classic Editions, but neither did they have plans to enter the mobile gaming market in the early 2010s; reversing that stance has proved to be one of the most profitable deci-sions in their corporate history.[51] Moreover, although the Switch has yet to receive a Virtual Console of its own, its online subscription service allows players to stream NES and SNES games.[52]

When, in January 2019, data miners discovered evidence of SNES games slated for future release, they also found code that suggested the addition of two more emulator cores.[53] So, it's possible that Nintendo is preparing a robust streaming service of their own. Still, this service is markedly different from its hardware counterpart. Beyond their imma-teriality and lack of accompanying ephemera, digital games—as we have seen with the Virtual Console—are fundamentally transient.

Articulating their stance on emulation on their website, Nintendo emphasizes how lateral thinking is at the heart of their software develop-ment process, expressing concerns that emulation detracts from their potential profits:

> Nintendo is famous for bringing back to life its popular characters for its newer systems, for example, Mario and Donkey Kong have enjoyed their adventures on all Nintendo platforms, going from coin-op machines to our latest hardware platforms. As a copyright owner, and creator of such famous characters, only Nintendo has the right to benefit from such valuable assets.[54]

The difficulty is that the company does little to preserve each incarnation or, indeed, their aging hardware. Nintendo is right in noting how famous their IP is, which only serves to make its preservation more critical for future scholars of videogame history. Shutting down the Wii Shop Channel and making vast libraries of old games inaccessible to players reminds us that digital ownership is ephemeral and the infrastructures that sustain it are designed for obsolescence. The film industry learned this lesson the hard way: proprietary publishing models and a lack of active preservation resulted in the loss of half of American films produced before 1950 and over 90 percent made before 1929.[55] In many ways, videogame piracy has become preservation.

The thing that Nintendo seems to forget about nostalgia is that, as much as nostalgia is attached to their IP and embedded within the com-pany's hardware objects, it fundamentally exists within people. Nintendo has long endeavored to present a friendly and inviting public image to entice gamers of all backgrounds to their products, but these recent decisions might reveal cracks in the façade; chilling lawsuits don't inspire feelings of warmth and goodwill toward a brand. Tendencies toward platformization, therefore, have significant implications for Nintendo's consumers and their historical engagement with the company's creative works through a flourishing participatory culture that sustains and elevates the cultural cachet of the Nintendo name.

That said, we don't return to a platform like the GBA just out of nostalgia for our childhood—we return to it because there's still more to explore, understand, and glitch. Cutting off access and stymying preservation efforts fail to acknowledge the things that we love most about the platform and the reason that it has such staying power. Of course, love for the characters and the brand continues to capture our imaginations, but the platforms are also areas of potential. The GBA remains a platform for playful exploration—with or without Nintendo's help.

In 2003, hybrid media artist Paul Catanese produced a three-channel Game Boy Advance (GBA) art installation titled *Super Ichthyologist Advance*.[1] Inspired by *Pokémon*'s ethos of entrapment and collection, he turned the real-world Pokédex into a virtual repository for digital echoes of endlessly looping koi. Played back across a triptych of white GBAs, the installation mused on containment and visual perception. But it also spoke more broadly to the unexpected artistic affordances of Nintendo's handheld.

Catanese hadn't intended to adopt the GBA as a key component of his creative practice. While he had tangential experience with game development, he came to the GBA not as a player or programmer, but as an artist frustrated by inelegant and inflexible technological solutions to video installations. One of his previous projects had required that he weave numerous cables through the venue's walls and ceilings in order to loop a video on a 3-inch display. Not only did this excess of cables make for a time-consuming and laborious setup, it also required physically modifying the gallery space.[2] While Catanese searched for a self-contained video player as an alternative to wrangling with cords, an unrelated conversation with a friend involved in the GBA homebrew scene alerted him to the ability to program for the GBA without license from Nintendo, thanks to the work of hackers who had reverse engineered the platform's hardware and code. Compact and portable, the GBA proved to be an ideal vessel for intermedia art. Venue installation involved little more than ensuring that spare batteries were on hand. Although *Super Ichthyologist Advance* is not a game by any stretch of the imagination, the system nevertheless displays the Nintendo logo on start-up, imbuing the project with some of its cultural cachet. What began as a workaround for the constraints of video playback in the early 2000s became a burgeoning interest in rethinking the GBA's uses. "I find myself imagining galleries that fit in your pocket," Catanese writes, "personal hand-held theatres, digital Cornell boxes and electronic books imbued with the intimacy of Chinese scroll paintings."[3]

Super Ichthyologist Advance and Catanese's subsequent GBA installations highlight how a videogame platform's uses often exceed what developers intended, sometimes in surprising ways. Despite two decades of intervening technological innovations, the GBA endures in art installations, executable files tucked away on laptops, and damaged Nintendo DS Lites rescued and repurposed to play GBA games. Players revisit the games of their youth, motivated not only by nostalgia, but also by a desire to discover previously unknown features of the software and of the platform on which it runs. Nintendo may have quietly discontinued the hand-held in 2010, but its fans have not been willing to let the platform descend into obscurity.

In an invitation to enrich the platform studies framework through media-archaeological methods, Thomas Apperley and Jussi Parikka ask "to what extent do the practices of the users of platforms form and inform the platform studies archive?"[4] In other words, how significant are the everyday practices of a community of users in shaping the way that we think about a platform as a cultural and computational object? Many of the books in this series, including this one, produce a materially grounded discourse about a given platform by using an archive of publicly available secondary media, including promotional materials, developer interviews, gaming magazines, and end user responses. But what can we gain by expanding this archive to consider the actual and everyday experiences of a community of users, even if (or especially because) these practices run counter to how Nintendo expected that their platform would be used?

Homebrew, hacking, and modding practices contribute to the GBA's lasting popularity and its residual impact on culture. These unsanctioned software and hardware afterlives make visible the recursive relationships between media platforms, the bodies of their users, and their cultural and material contexts. They speak to a different kind of videogame development—one that refuses the regime of planned obsolescence and gives agency to consumers in an increasingly platformized commodity culture.

Due to these afterlives' lack of corporate legitimacy, many studies of videogame platforms refrain from considering amateur or fan interventions as being vital to the platforms' continued existence. And yet we have already seen how hobbyists' innovative lighting solutions helped shape Nintendo's approach to the SP's development (see chapter 2). Players' interventions into the GBA's hardware performed a crucial role in the handheld's adoption and gave rise to a set of cultural protocols around its use. Playful acts of experimentation and repurposing are therefore fundamental to what the GBA is, two decades after its release. Incorporating the audience's expressive engagements with the object into the platform studies archive can deepen our understanding of the platform and of its place in our cultural imaginary.

To that end, this chapter takes up Siegfried Zielinski's invitation to perform a media *an*archaeology as an approach to thinking about the audience's uses of a videogame platform outside the bounds of corporate media industries. In lieu of producing an archive with the aim of discovering a unified, standardized object, media anarchaeology "privileges a sense of the multifarious possibilities over their realities in the form of products."[5] These possibilities include disassembling, reverse engineering, and other forms of tinkering connected to do-it-yourself (DIY) culture. Zielinski's anarchaeology invites us to think about how experimentations with media technologies can alter our sensory and affective experiences of engaging with the object. Studying the playful and disruptive meetings of media and humans allows us to better understand how the participatory communities around the GBA shape and are shaped by the platform.

This chapter looks at three creative approaches to the platform: homebrew, hacking, and hardware modding. All of these practices offer insight into a material community of users who gather around the platform, connected by a shared interest in exploring the system's material and aesthetic possibilities. These interventions remind us that videogame platforms are not defined solely by the uses Nintendo prescribes. They are equally defined by the possibilities that exist beyond their intended functions. Amateurs, hobbyists, enthusiasts, and players pry open the black box of technology to produce an unofficial record of what the platform continues to be in the present.

GBA Homebrew and the Aesthetics of Mastery

The term "homebrew" refers to software developed for closed platforms rather than for systems that support user programming. The GBA has attracted a sizeable homebrew community not only due to its popularity as an object of nostalgia, but also because of the relative ease of programming creative works for the system. Collectively, hobbyists have released hundreds of games that vary in length and purpose. While some are meant for play, others are merely designed to demonstrate a programmer's accrual of technical knowledge. Regardless of the intention behind them, most of these games circulate online without expectation of payment because the economy of homebrew is primarily cultural rather than financial.

In 2005, Brett Camper produced an exceptional master's thesis on GBA homebrew, in which he examined how hobbyist videogame development arises in dialogue with the commercial gaming industry.[6] This document, "Homebrew and the Social Construction of Gaming: Community, Creativity, and Legal Context of Amateur Game Boy Advance Development," remains the single most comprehensive account of the GBA's homebrew community, and indeed of the social, legal, and discursive positions of homebrew more generally. Consequently, Camper's work is an essential reference document for this chapter's consideration of homebrew.

Camper wrote at the zenith of GBA homebrew, which ironically coincided with the moment at which its future was most precarious. The Nintendo DS had recently been released, and homebrewers were both intrigued by and apprehensive about the idea of migrating to the new touch-screen-capable platform with its three-dimensional (3D) polygons.[7] "Will the GBA ever acquire the kind of fierce amateur loyalty the Atari 2600 enjoys, twenty years after its heyday?" Camper wondered. He speculated that the GBA lacked the staying power to sustain homebrew development due to broader shifts in the industry.[8] As it turns out, the GBA did manage to capture and retain fan loyalty. While hobbyists may not be developing for the handheld in the numbers they did during the community's heyday in the early 2000s, the GBA nevertheless continues to enjoy modest popularity as a system for playful exploration, particularly for beginners seeking to learn about the intricacies of videogame development through technically specific experimentation.

It isn't just nostalgia for the GBA aesthetic that keeps its homebrew scene alive—although retro fetishism certainly plays a role—but also nostalgia for a simpler age, when a single person could program an entire game. The GBA is one of the last widely popular dedicated gaming platforms for which solo or small-team game development is feasible. It's for this reason that DS homebrew and hacking never enjoyed the same cultish fanaticism, despite the wealth of open-source resources that circulate. The DS's 3D graphics and touch-screen interface are often beyond the scope of what a single hobbyist can code during spare time after school or work.

The more technically advanced the platform, the more it requires a bigger team, specialized labor, and higher-level programming. At a certain point, the technology becomes too large for a single person to grapple with in stolen moments. While indie development for Android and iOS offers the promising return of small-team hobbyist programming, it doesn't bring the technical and hardware specificity of dedicated gaming consoles, where single individuals or small teams of friends could release games into the community as a form of self-expression, receive constructive criticism, and acquire technical expertise.

As participatory culture—that is, an environment in which audiences become cultural producers themselves—homebrew and hacking are at odds with the capitalist model of platformization.[9] Consequently, hobbyist development operates within a layered environment of barriers to access that Nintendo imposes through technical, legal, and discursive maneuvers. Foremost among them is, of course, the need to circumvent their technical protection measures (TPMs). Nintendo uses a refined digital rights management (DRM) system that conflates trademark and patent infringement in order to prevent unlicensed developers from programming for their hardware (as discussed in chapter 1). Because Nintendo doesn't sanction homebrew development, GBA games that place their logos in the read-only memory (ROM) header—a requirement for the GBA's boot cycle—enter a murky area of legal legitimacy, even if the works themselves have nothing to do with Nintendo's intellectual property (IP). Sometimes this transgressive element is part of homebrew's allure.

The second challenge relates to the accessibility—or lack thereof—of programming information. On December 8, 2016, an archive.org member uploaded version 1.1 of Nintendo's *AGB Programming Manual* to the Internet Archive, unveiling the platform's technical architecture and programming instructions for all to see. Prior to this moment, official GBA programming information had been reserved for parties who signed and adhered to Nintendo's license agreement. Hobbyists had to suss out the intricacies of the system through tedious reverse engineering, meticulous observation, and code-based trial and error. Online communities came together to compile exhaustive records about everything from the GBA's basic input/output system (BIOS) to the structure of its ROM images, which circulate through detailed and laborious documentation projects like *Tonc* by Jasper Vijn (Cearn) and *GBATEK* by Martin Korth. Comparisons between these projects and Nintendo's official programming manual reveal the extent of hobbyists' efforts; they comprehensively and accurately exposed the platform's internal workings for anyone to access.

Finally, the platform's technical specifications impose limitations on the types of creative works that hobbyists can produce: graphics are primarily limited to two-dimensional (2D) sprites and tiles, audio is restricted to two digital-to-analog converters (DACs) and the four legacy channels from the Game Boy, mechanics can only rely on the Direction-pad (D-pad) and six other buttons, and so on.

But there are also additional demands—sometimes self-imposed—at the level of programming language. In programming, the term "language" refers to a vocabulary and set of rules that are used to instruct a computing device to perform specific tasks. High-level, object-oriented programming languages like C and C++ are more readable to human users (they bear some similarities to everyday grammar) and more portable—a word that here refers to the ability to migrate to other operating systems (i.e., porting) rather than movement through space. These languages, as well as scripted languages like PHP, are much more abstract than the lowest level of programming: "machine language," made of raw numbers that the CPU decodes into executable instructions. One abstraction layer above machine code is "assembly language" (sometimes abbreviated as "asm"), which is specific to a given computer architecture. Each line of assembly code for the GBA's ARM processor consists of a three-letter mnemonic representing an instruction ("MOV" to move numbers between registers, "LDR" to load a value from a memory address, "SDR" to store a value, etc.), followed by a register identifier or numerical value. The instructions are then converted into executable machine code by a utility referred to as an "assembler."

One of the ways homebrewers express an interest in returning to the materiality of the machine is by coding in assembly language. This is partly in the interest of the code's efficiency. With a 16.7 MHz central processing unit (CPU) and less than 1 MB of working random-access memory (RAM), coding GBA software in high-level languages often comes at the cost of program size and runtime speed. Although one of the GBA's selling features, as far as developers were concerned, was that most of the programming could be done in C (colloquially referred to as "portable assembly" because it can still work directly with memory), inefficiency can be costly. Some processes demand assembly programming in order to maximize each cycle.

There are also material and aesthetic reasons for homebrewers' interest in low-level programming. Because there's a one-to-one relationship between machine code and assembly language, programming in assembly requires intimate knowledge of the GBA's ARM processor. Programmers can't just rely on a compiler that benefits from safety features; they have to tinker directly with the numerical values or bits in the CPU's registers and write in something closer to the machine's own language. This type of low-level work is tedious—a simple instruction in C requires multiple lines in assembly—and requires precision to prevent accidentally disturbing the other bits in a given register.[10] But it also gives programmers a great deal more control over the hardware.

The lack of abstraction between code and silicon makes writing in assembly language attractive for programmers invested in the aesthetics of technical mastery. As Cearn notes in his GBA documentation project, one of the reasons to program in assembly "is just for general coolness. . . . The very fact that it is harder than higher languages," he writes, "should appeal to your inner geek, who relishes such challenges."[11] GBA programming, therefore, occasions a return to a largely obsolete form of independent, hands-on videogame development and brings with it a particular kind of geek elitism, one that is grounded in a familiarity with the GBA's computational architecture.

Through a focus on the GBA's underlying hardware, homebrew developers often seek to perform a particular kind of technologically literate identity. This phenomenon is not unique to videogame communities but rather is part of a longer history of amateur production that can be traced back to radio hobbyists in the early 1920s. Susan Douglas argues that, as social and economic changes rocked the United States and the workplace became increasingly bureaucratized and hierarchical, radio introduced a technology "that some men felt *they* could control."[12] Amateur tinkering with wireless radio became a symbol of social status for a particular (and exclusive) group of middle-class men who felt anxious about the changing face of their country and struggled to develop a concrete sense of identity at a moment when upward mobility became harder to imagine. Douglas writes:

> Working-class boys with neither the time nor the money to tinker with wireless could not participate as easily. Neither could girls or young women, for whom technical tinkering was considered a distinctly inappropriate pastime and technical mastery a distinctly unacceptable goal. This fraternity, whether self-consciously or accidentally, brought together roughly similar men in a region uninhabited by those so different from them.[13]

These technical communities are defined as much by who can participate as by who is systematically excluded—women, people of color, and working-class boys with little opportunity to acquire knowledge of electronics. Camper observes strong parallels between the radio and GBA hobbyist communities—both are examples of hands-on pastimes dominated by young, white, middle-class men seeking to build social, cultural, and professional reputations. Most hobbyists developing for the GBA are boys and men between high-school and college age, many of whom are pursuing computer science or similar degrees.[14]

In both cases, the drive for technical mastery operates within obliquely gendered discourse. Consider homebrewer ScottLininger's explanation for why he programs: "I started GBA programming about a year ago after my wife bought me an SP and I fell in love with the thing." Or look at notb4dinner's description of homebrew's appeal: "I bought my GBA SP to kill time on the train, and it was just such a cute little machine I couldn't help but have a go at programming it. Pleas[a]ntly it's just as cute on the inside as outside."[15] The language of cuteness feminizes and fetishizes the technology. It displays an almost erotic desire to probe within the plastic casing. If we recall how cuteness is related to both objectification and dominance (see chapter 4), then it's clear that the impulse for technical mastery is at least somewhat about control and ownership over the system.

While Camper explains that the homebrew community welcomes beginners, there are nevertheless unspoken social and cultural barriers to entry that revolve around questions of identity and diversity. We would do well not to forget these, even as we consider how hobbyists develop unique aesthetics and applications outside what Nintendo envisioned for the GBA.

Demos, Games, and the Pleasures of Competition

The clearest example of technical mastery is the "tech demo," a liminal object that is neither playable game nor art piece. Rather, as its name suggests, it's a short demonstration of a hobbyist's technical literacy and programming skill through impressive visual, audio, or gameplay effects. Although many tech demos accept user input, interaction is usually exploratory rather than goal oriented; there are no conditions for winning or losing, no scores, and no records. Instead, the tech demo's audience might attempt to recognize, understand, or mentally rewrite the programming behind the effect they see on their screen.

One of the more common effects featured in GBA tech demos is the execution of Mode 7, a complex technique that creates a perspective view similar to what could be programmed by way of the famous Mode 7 in the Super Nintendo Entertainment System (SNES). In order to create a pseudo-3D effect through the illusion of depth, each of the screen's scanlines—that is, each horizontal row of pixels that composes a raster scanning pattern—is scaled progressively larger.[16] The SNES produced this effect through a hardware graphics mode, but the GBA requires that the programmer calculate the scaling factor for each scanline and then write out code to instruct the GBA to apply that degree of scaling as the screen is drawn in real time. Andrew May's *Mode 7 Demo* shows off a pseudo-3D racetrack that is navigable with the D-pad, but there are no sprites to manipulate and no races that occur. Debray Matthieu's *Demo Mode 7: Waterfall* is similarly intended to demonstrate his competence at executing this challenging visual effect. The demo is interactive only insofar as the user can alter the waterfall's size and velocity and change their viewing angle. Erik Rounds's *Raycast Technology Demo* shows how this advanced graphics technique can be used to create pseudo-3D environments for first-person action games. It uses Mode 7 as a rudimentary raycaster—a fast, real-time rendering technique that creates 3D perspectives by programming vertical extensions on a 2D horizontal plane.

We can trace the way that commercial game aesthetics inform these tech demos' treatments of their virtualized environments: May's perspective-based track can easily become the setting of a racing game; Matthieu's waterfall can become a background feature in a role-playing game (RPG); and Rounds's raycast environment communicates its indebtedness to first-person shooters. But these demos stand as their own objects with their own goals. The GBA was both lauded and condemned as a portable SNES. Here are hobbyists testing how far that comparison extends by reproducing the most significant graphics effect of the SNES through skillful and meticulous programming.

Other tech demos may fit less cleanly into existing videogame genres. For instance, Jimmy Mårdell (Yarin)'s *Fractal* is a rudimentary fractal generator for the GBA that allows the user to explore three kinds of fractals with customizable color palettes. Offering the ability to zoom without losing precision and save fractals and palettes to static random-access memory (SRAM), *Fractal* feels like a complete, self-contained object. But it is decidedly not a game and, much like a fractal itself, resists easy classification. In this way, Yarin expands the system's abilities beyond dedicated gaming, highlighting its underlying use as a platform for other forms of computing and creative expression.

Despite their heterogeneity, tech demos cohere around a shared interest in thoroughly exploring and exploiting the GBA's affordances, emphasizing the programming process more than the resultant product. Often, the goal in releasing a tech demo is to invite feedback from more experienced members of the community or to share discoveries to accrue reputation and cultural capital within the scene. To that end, the homebrew community values the free circulation of information.

Although process-focused demos make up the bulk of homebrew development, many hobbyists use their skills and technical expertise to create their own games. These are usually short puzzle or action games, which Camper calls "small worlds":

> Small world games harness the built-in features of the GBA hardware that minimize the programming of game infrastructure; they resist the temptation towards indulgent programming to encourage a focus on the implementation of gameplay. Their design is also often cognizant of the on-going nature of homebrew development, in which additions are made in pockets of time snatched during late nights or vacations. In short, they are an effective response to homebrewers' technical and social restrictions.[17]

While RPGs carry expectations of a compelling narrative and lengthy duration of play, small games have greater replay value and are less likely to be held to the standards of their commercial counterparts. Somewhat ironically, the homebrew scene becomes a hub for the kinds of videogames that are often dismissed as "casual games" for their relative simplicity—games like *Tetris*, top-down arcade style shooters, and puzzle games. In the context of GBA homebrew, where hobbyists are intimately familiar with the hardware components and aware of all the complexity of coding in assembly language, these small world games are recognized as rich explorations of the GBA's expressive potential.

gbadev.org and the Economy of Homebrew

The heart of the GBA's homebrew community is gbadev.org, a website that emerged not long after Nintendo announced the handheld's release. Its "About" page reads: "It started as a website aiming to share development information about the then unreleased GBA system. Here we are 19 years later, doing the same thing. Who would have thought?"[18] Over the course of two decades, more than 500 developers have contributed material to the site—a number that doesn't even include the many untracked guests who have used its wealth of resources. The website hosts everything from emulators to tools for manipulating ROM images to forums for exchanges of technical information and troubleshooting questions. The esoteric nature of GBA programming has given rise to a small but close community willing to share information and encouragement. Members help resolve setup errors, explain the intricacies of the system's graphics and audio hardware, and collectively create an environment of informal mentorship.

On July 11, 2008, gbadev.org celebrated five million visitors and eight years online. To mark the occasion, SimonB and Krom, the website's administrators, invited members to reflect on their experiences with the community. The responses highlight how programming for the GBA enables participants to acquire technical knowledge and hone a diverse set of programming skills, which contributes to both personal and professional development. ScottLininger writes:

> My skills as a GBA developer led to a freelance project back in 2005 that helped me make the decision to "jump ship" from the corporate world I'd been working in. Wow, that's just crazy to think about . . . My life would be totally different today without this forum. . . . My experiences on the GBA gave me a bunch of knowledge that helped me with the big, hairy series of interviews that I had to go through to get my current job. It's funny how hobbies can do that.[19]

He's not alone in having found employment as a result of his participation in the gbadev community. DekuTree64 says, "Without this forum, there wouldn't have been the wonderful coincidence of events that led to my employment."[20] Keldon notes that personal homebrew projects contributed to their eventual employment. And gladius credits obtaining their first game programming job to the help they received on the forum. In many cases, a drive for professionalization and the creation of a supportive social network provide the motivation for spending hours or days tinkering with the obscure memory registers of an ostensibly obsolete system.

While these posts touch on an important aspect of hobbyist game development—namely, the accrual of cultural capital and professional skills—they also speak to how the GBA homebrew community, as a form of participatory culture, understands itself in relation to the videogame industry. GBA homebrew largely circulates in an online "gift economy," where, "in the absence of states or markets to mediate social bonds, network communities are instead formed through the mutual obligations created by gifts of time and ideas."[21] Although the GBA's technical architecture doesn't necessarily invite the civic engagement, informal mentorship, and social connection characteristic of participatory culture (quite the opposite), the online milieu of GBA homebrew affords the circulation of the requisite technical knowledge to program for the platform, encouraging synchronous creation and consumption.

In her formative work, Tiziana Terranova explores the valences of free labor in the digital economy, pointing to the blurred territory between production and use, work and cultural expression.[22] Most saliently, she posits a connection between the digital economy of participatory culture and the "social factory," which harnesses low-cost labor from social rather than industrial agents. While free labor isn't unavoidably exploitative—it may be conceded willingly in exchange for the pleasures of communication and artistic expression—it often becomes subsumed within the larger regime of capitalist commodity culture.[23] Far from establishing a socialist utopia of free circulation, homebrew often cements the primacy of Nintendo's corporate brand.

The idea that hobbyists treat the GBA as the last dedicated gaming platform for which a kind of technically driven homebrew development is possible speaks to a mutual relationship between hobbyists and Nintendo. Even in the early 2000s, other platforms were eminently more accessible from a programming perspective, including Flash. The Korean Game Park 32 (GP32) handheld console—also released in 2001—deliberately used SmartMedia cards rather than proprietary cartridges to encourage amateur development.[24] Users who registered their hardware on Game Park's website received a suite of free developer tools so that they could create their own applications and games. But despite its open architecture, the GP32 is culturally unremarkable: Nintendo's GBA has the name and the nostalgia. Homebrew occurs without Nintendo's explicit approval, but it also reifies the handheld's position in culture. The people making the most money from homebrew, however tangentially, work for Nintendo.

The obvious reason why hobbyists decline to profit from this production, of course, is due to the technological, legal, and discursive contexts in which the games arise. While developing games without Nintendo's consent is ostensibly legal, the appropriation of their logo in order to enable the system's BIOS to recognize a game is questionable at best. As we saw in chapter 1, there are historical reasons for Nintendo's efforts to restrict unlicensed development, namely the videogame crash of 1983. Moreover, the videogame industry has often been described through the metaphor of "razors and blades," where razors (the hardware) are sold at or near a loss and blades (the program's software) generate the bulk of the company's profits.[25] So Nintendo's TPMs produce a hostile legal environment for the circulation of homebrew.

As a result, homebrew games are typically circulated digitally, where they're either played on an emulator or loaded into a flash cartridge (flashcart) and then inserted into the GBA.[26] Flashcarts are intermediary hardware objects shaped like Game Paks that use built-in flash memory or Micro SD cards to enable the transfer of game software between a computer and the proprietary GBA. To nobody's surprise, Nintendo doesn't sanction flashcarts. They refer to these objects as "Game Copying Devices," a term that occludes their origins as amateur developer tools. On their legal frequently asked questions (FAQ) page, Nintendo writes:

Are Game Copying Devices Illegal?

Yes. Game copiers enable users to illegally copy video game software onto floppy disks, writeable compact disks or the hard drive of a personal computer. They enable the user to make, play and distribute illegal copies of video game software which violates Nintendo's copyrights and trademarks. These devices also allow for the uploading and downloading of ROMs to and from the Internet. Based upon the functions of these devices, they are illegal.[27]

Even if we forget homebrew for a moment, there *are* legal reasons to make a copy of a game. Title 17 of the U.S. copyright code states that copying a computer program isn't an infringement, provided that it's copied for archival purposes.[28] Owners of digital content are permitted to duplicate it for protection against damages, and game copying devices are the only way to do this. Consequently, what we have here is another case of Nintendo exercising the chilling effect, attempting to preclude the use of such devices through legal intimidation. Flashcarts' primary function is arguably to enable noncommercial hobbyist development by providing a way for the programmer to move files between a computer (where they're created) to the handheld (where they're meant to be played). Through careful legal framing, Nintendo obscures the distinction between non-licensed homebrew development and illegal videogame piracy to corner the market.[29] According to the language on their website, a digital ROM is always an illegal file.[30]

In some rare cases, homebrew games might circulate in limited runs of physical cartridges. One of the main vectors for homebrew sharing is the competition (or "compo"). These often have a technical or thematic constraint, like using a particular graphics mode or following a particular aesthetic. Compos serve as an evaluative mechanism by which developers accrue cultural capital based on the technical mastery that their games exhibit. Occasionally, rewards are material, such as when ten games from the 2004 Mbit Compo were distributed on a labeled game cartridge sold at cost. This event significantly extended the games' reach beyond the participants of the compo; their 500-cart print run sold out on preorder.[31] However, these material circulations—and, by extension, homebrew's mimicry of the commercial videogame industry through the distribution of physical cartridges—are the exception, not the rule. Compos are driven by the motivation to finish a game, the pleasure of sharing hours of labor with others, and the enjoyment of participating in a communal event.

There are reasons beyond legal concerns for why hobbyists might not want to circulate their work for profit. Writing on participatory culture, Henry Jenkins notes that the distaste for profiting from fandom comes more from the desire to create forms of cultural production and distribution that "reflect the mutuality of the fan community" than out of political or economic resistance to capitalism.[32] The upward mobility that comes from the accrual of a diverse skill set is often presumed to be sufficient reward. Members of the social collective are encouraged to give back to the community that made their knowledge possible. On the aforementioned anniversary forum, silent_code writes:

> you guys helped me a lot!
> Now I am invloved [sic] with some serious stuff, but I still like to work on my homebrew and help people on the forum whenever I can. :^)[33]

The community sustains itself through a cycle of knowledge formation and sharing that helps professionalize young developers. Encouragement and constructive criticism come naturally to some members of the community, who vividly recall how they also had to start from the beginning, exploring Nintendo's proprietary hardware and software through trial and (more often than not) error after error. The development of technical knowledge is, above all else, community driven.

Both homebrew and commercial game development for the GBA are subject to its material constraints, but they openly differ in form and motivation. For homebrew developers, the end goal is rarely to produce a polished game. Rather, it's to probe the limitations of the platform's hardware and share the creative results of their explorations with a community of people who are equally interested in the aesthetics and mechanics of GBA programming. The homebrew scene, for all its focus on the platform's technical components, is a highly social setting.

Rewriting the ROM

The development of a set of knowledge protocols that emerge out of the homebrew community leads to a cocreative practice known as "ROM hacking," the modification of the file images of videogames. ROM hacks are a type of fan production in which dedicated enthusiasts of a preexisting IP consolidate their programming, storytelling, and design skills to create noncommercial works that tend to circulate within a gift economy without the commercial game developers' cooperation. Unlike homebrew, where hobbyists code a game from scratch, ROM hackers repurpose existing software assets to translate familiar narratives, parody popular games, or tell new stories altogether. This creative practice uses commercial games as scaffolding, but it nevertheless requires a thorough understanding of the workings of Nintendo's hardware and software. In a comprehensive guide to GBA ROM hacking, FAST6191 defines the process as "the editing of ROM images . . . with the intent of changing how underlying game code or the assets of it function *in a useful way*. Simply changing sections of an image without rhyme or reason is not ROM hacking as ROM hacking is usually the end result of a measure of reverse engineering."[34] There are clear aesthetic and purposive elements that distinguish a competent ROM hack from dilettantes playing around in the files without knowing what they're doing. For FAST6191, ROM hacks are deliberate and meaningful rather than chaotically disruptive.

Much has been written about mods for massively multiplayer online role-playing games (MMORPGs) in recent years.[35] But there are important distinctions between mods and GBA ROM hacks at the material and discursive levels. GBA ROM hacks, like homebrew, occur close to the silicon. The qualities that make for an accomplished ROM hacker often overlap with those of skilled hardware modders: patience, boundless curiosity, and a desire to pull things apart. Many ROM hackers are thoroughly familiar with the GBA's technical architecture.[36]

This section is not a ROM hacking tutorial (for that, I recommend looking at online guides), nor is it a complete history of the practice. Instead, this section surveys the materiality and technical mastery behind GBA ROM hacking, as well as the political economy and IP laws that simmer around these activities. My goal here is to think about some of the unofficial ways that GBA software circulates and how this circulation influences and is influenced by our ideas of what the GBA platform is. As media archaeologist Erkki Huhtamo posits, "the seams are left visible" through these practices. He writes: "instead of beating an illusion with another illusion, the aim [of ROM hacking] is to make the cracks in the facade visible, to focus attention on the manifold processes looking for an outlet behind the ideologies of uniformity."[37] In other words, ROM hacking is a way of testing the platform's limits not just technologically, but also culturally. In the discussion, I use the *Fire Emblem* ROM hacking community as a case study to consider the symbiotic relationship between

Nintendo and ROM hackers. Although it is neither the largest nor the most prolific community, the hobbyists who hack GBA-era *Fire Emblem* ROMs play a key—albeit niche—role in the history of a series that has enjoyed unprecedented success in the last couple of years.

Knowledge Protocols, Hex Editors, and Patch Distribution

The process of ROM hacking ostensibly begins with the physical game cartridge. Before digital copies of GBA ROMs can circulate online, they need to be extracted from the plastic housing designed to protect the printed circuit board (PCB) and the thirty-two gold-finished pins from accidental damage. Here again, we see the way that Nintendo takes measures to prevent hobbyists from accessing their hardware: each cartridge is fastened with a small tri-wing security screw. Reaching the Game Pak's internals requires the proper tools.

Prior to the accessibility of flashcarts, early ROM hacking required decoupling the ROM chip from the PCB by way of desoldering. Soldering creates a permanent connection between metals—in that, unlike gluing or taping, it causes a chemical reaction that creates a new alloy with the ability to transfer electricity—but it can also be reversed. Desoldering severs the connection between the ROM chip and the circuit board, thereby changing the original cartridge from its initial electronic assembly. Jaime Lee Kirtz argues that desoldering effaces the work of the laborer who put the cartridge together by removing traces of these connections.[38]

Today, opening the cartridge to access the PCB isn't necessary because most ROMs are sourced from copies circulating online. But opening the cartridge is nevertheless useful for seeing what it contains. PCB design varies between games, especially as it concerns memory. Three types are used in GBA cartridges: flash memory, battery-backed SRAM, and electrically erasable programmable read-only memory (EEPROM). It's in part due to these hardware discrepancies that fully playable bootlegged GBA games often struggle to retain saves. Knowing where to store save files allows hackers to ensure that save data doesn't get corrupted when the ROM hack is played.

GBA ROM hacking is complicated by the fact that, outside of some homebrew contexts, the GBA doesn't have what we would consider a file system. Hackers can use an advanced technique known as "tracing" to find where data is located in the ROM image, but there's no all-purpose file browser. Instead, once they have a viable ROM image, hackers manipulate the code primarily through a process called "hex editing," which relies on dedicated programs that display binary software data in hexadecimal notation. There's an overdone joke about binary in computing circles that boils down to the ambiguity of numeral bases. The joke goes: there are 10 kinds of people in the world—those who know binary and those who don't. This plays on how the binary 10 is equal to the decimal 2, but it also exposes the way that a simple misunderstanding of the set of numbers can completely alter semantic meaning. If I ask for the answer to the question of 8 + 2, you might immediately say 10. While correct in decimal, this answer could ruin a hack in hexadecimal notation, where the solution is A. Thus, even if ROM hacking seems to be cutting corners compared to homebrew games created from the ground up, technical mastery is still at play. Edits require that the hacker has knowledge not only of hexadecimal notation, but also of the GBA's architecture, the command line, and a set of debugging procedures.

The processes behind ROM hacks typically break down into four categories: graphics editing, text editing, sound editing, and game logic alteration. Each type of hack requires its own tools and skills. General hex editors reveal software patterns, but they don't actually display graphics, text, or musical notation in a way that the human reader can easily understand. For graphics, hackers often use a tile editor, which is a development utility for creating or modifying sprites, tiles, and bitmaps. These tools also often include a map editor for level design and a palette editor to alter colors within the GBA's 15-bit color limits. To edit text, hackers have to account for how Nintendo's developers adopted custom decoding and display engines to produce text more efficiently than storing it as graphics. These text engines often force hackers to rely on tables containing lengthy lists of hexadecimal values and their corresponding representations in readable text to find the right text in the ROM image. Audio hacks equally use their own software. Sappy became one of the more popular multiseries GBA audio ripping and inserting tools because it's able to work with most games that use the tracker-style audio format that Nintendo provided for licensed developers (called "Sappy" in ROM hacking circles, hence the tool's name). The program can convert Sappy tracks to musical instrument digital interface (MIDI) format, which can then be edited in a music tracker.[39] In all cases, these tools grew out of the idiosyncrasies of GBA ROM images, thanks to the curiosity and experimentation of hobbyists.

Graphics, text, and audio edits form the bulk of most ROM hacks, but hackers often want to change the mechanics or logic of the game as well. Ostensibly, this means working in assembly language, and many hackers continue to prefer this low-level programming. However, over the years, community members have developed a range of bespoke toolsets for specific games or series that afford the ability to alter levels, stats, and mechanics. For instance, Hexator's Java application FEditor Adv is a robust editing tool that allows the ROM hacker to customize almost all facets of any of the three *Fire Emblem* games released on the GBA (it also supports a much more direct text-editing feature to minimize reliance on obscure tables). *Pokémon, Zelda,* and *Super Mario* platformers have equally given rise to their own custom software tools. These programs benefit from consistencies within the ROM images of games in a given series, but they also respond to the particularities of the community using them. The limited flexibility of the system's hardware leads to idiosyncratic creative approaches that cohere into visible aesthetic preferences and cultural protocols. What this means in practice is that, while many of the underlying concepts behind graphics, text, audio, and logic hacks are the same, creating hacks for *Fire Emblem, Pokémon*, or *Super Mario* requires specialized technical knowledge and vocabularies that often seem arbitrary in nature but result from the game's engine and nearly two decades of collective creative exploration. This additional layer of specialization acts as a way for hobbyists to build a technically specific sense of self through the ability to navigate the code patterns and community protocols of a given IP (this is the fan hacking response to Nintendo's "Who Are You?" advertisement). Mastery of these custom toolsets necessarily requires participation in the community; what appears on the surface as a solitary pastime invariably involves "standing upon the shoulders of others all the time."[40]

ROM hacks circulate online as patch files, codified checklists of the differences between the original game and the hack. Distributing hacks as patches serves a practical purpose, in that patch files are much smaller than a full ROM image (a factor more important twenty years ago, when digital storage was less plentiful). But it also serves a crucial legal purpose. By only circulating records of differences, patch files don't reproduce any data or game assets. Even if a fair use defense protects the resulting software object (especially in the case of a parody game), circulating the entirety of the code could be a contravention of copyright.

To play the hack, users must obtain a copy of the original ROM image, either by extracting the file from the Game Pak or downloading it from the internet. But the author of the ROM hack does not technically break the law in circulating this creative work. Once both files are obtained, there are two forms of patching the hack onto the original game: soft patching and hard patching. The former doesn't alter the ROM image itself; instead, an emulator opens both files and runs them concurrently, preserving both. The latter uses a dedicated program like LunarIPS or NUPS to apply the patch to a clean (unmodified) ROM image. Players can then engage with the patched file on an emulator or load it onto a flash-cart to play it on their GBA. Most patches circulate on romhacking.net, the largest ROM hacking site, or else through dedicated communities for a given series.

Early GBA ROM hacks primarily used the Internal Patching System (IPS) file format, consisting of location length, payload, and a signal for the end of the file. As time went on, most hobbyists began to adopt its more efficient successor, the Universal Patching System (UPS). Unlike IPS, the UPS format can support files over 16 MB. The reason why this matters has to do with the original game size and the system's hardware limitations. GBA *Fire Emblem* ROMs are exactly 16 MB. With IPS, this leaves no room for expansion, so cocreators are limited to transforming the game's existing assets. With UPS patches, they have more freedom to explore larger adventures with new graphics, soundtracks, and objectives.

ROM Hacks and the *Fire Emblem* Fandom

On August 18, 2012, a prolific ROM hacker known online as Blazer announced a complete patch for *The Last Promise*, a hack of the first *Fire Emblem* game localized for North America (*FE7*).[41] On the modified title screen, the credit line reads "© 2012 Blazer/Intelligent Systems," signaling that Blazer sees this work as having been coauthored, even if Intelligent Systems didn't so much as partner with Blazer as unknowingly produce the assets, mechanics, and engine that Blazer used to craft this hack.

The product of four years of labor, *The Last Promise* introduces an entirely new narrative, a cast of original characters, and completely rede-signed maps based around *Fire Emblem*'s core mechanics. At the time of its release, Blazer was eighteen years old; the game was the product of hours of work done in his spare time after high school classes.[42] While his lack of experience crafting a game-length narrative shows through the dated storyline and cheesy writing, *The Last Promise* is unparalleled among *Fire Emblem* ROM hacks for the sheer amount of content it contains. All facets of the game—graphics, music, script, maps, character classes, animations weapons—have been modified (this type of project is often called a "total conversion"). Not only is it a full game that rivals the length of all three official GBA installments in the series, but it also contains a substantial postgame, not unlike what Intelligent Systems would later offer in the 2015 *Fire Emblem: Fates*, all while working within the ROM image's limitations. Despite *The Last Promise*'s flaws along the lines of narrative, map design, and game balance, it's exemplary of a kind of labor of love recognized not only by the ROM hacking community, but by *Fire Emblem* fans more generally. Here are some of their comments:

> **Xigdar**: Some obscure mechanics . . . some really questionable decisions. . . . But it's also efforts. Lots of efforts poured into it. No matter how the result may end, you can see how much time was put into it. It even had voice acting!

> **PompomRenaldo**: It's an important game, and if you're into the progression of romhacks, it's cool to see the kinds of things that [*The Last Promise*] did, and how it improved over time. You can tell it was made with a lot of love even if the end product has clear flaws.

> **Nefftron**: Outdated or not, it's actually FINISHED and has everything a full FE game would have, and for that it deserves tremendous applause.

> **ColinWins**: I like it better than a couple of actual FE games, so there's that.[43]

Not all ROM hacks are as comprehensive as *The Last Promise*; they vary in goal and intricacy. Katie's *FE8 Creature Campaign Reverse Recruitment*, for instance, tweaks a single feature to reverse the recruitment order of playable characters in *Fire Emblem: The Sacred Stones*. Most of the story and the gameplay remains true to the source material, but players can now use characters that are typically only unlocked late in the game, which restructures their engagement with the cast.

Other games reshape the narrative to make a social or political statement. *Restoration Queen*, a *Sacred Stones* script edit ROM hack by lizzledpink and glitteringworlds, makes minor edits to the game's dialogue to give its female characters a greater sense of subjectivity. The original plot of *Sacred Stones* follows the royal Renais siblings Eirika and Ephraim in two separate campaigns as they fight to protect their homeland. Fans of the series have long waged the critique that Eirika's story is less developed than her brother's, and that she is often placed in the role of the "damsel in distress." *Restoration Queen* is, in its hackers' words, "a way to re-experience *Sacred Stones* in a more actively female (and queer) positive manner." They go on to explain the impetus behind the project:

> We (Liz and Glitz) love Sacred Stones, but we don't love a lot of the sexist writing and content that went into its making. In particular,

Eirika was our inspiration, as we felt she was short-handed by her route. We didn't want to change the heart of the plot or the characters; they're what we fell in love with in the first place. But we saw a lot of room for improvement, and chased it.[44]

The textual alterations are intended to be enjoyed without being overtly noticeable. "You there, with the girl. Tell me, would that be the wayward princess of Renais?" (a phrase directed at Eirika's knight bodyguard) becomes "You there, girl. Tell me, are you the wayward princess of Renais?" (a phrase directed at Eirika, allowing her to speak for herself instead of being spoken for). A conversation between two sorcerers changes from "Lute, please, it's dangerous outside the walls. Stay here in the village" to "I need you to stay and protect the village." By narrative necessity, Lute needs to remain in the village because the player cannot yet deploy her in battle, but the altered text shifts her position from girl in need of protection to the villager's protector. These changes are subtle, but the result is a profoundly different affective experience for the player.[45]

The fan website Serenes Forest preserves a directory of *Fire Emblem* ROM hacks in various states of completion, which continues to get updates even to this day. Despite the release of new *Fire Emblem* titles, its GBA section lists more than seventy active and completed hacks and another seventeen on hiatus—a reminder that hobbyists create these hacks in their free time and sometimes abandon projects as a result.

Like many mods, most *Fire Emblem* ROM hacks are usually thematically conservative, while remaining mechanically proximate to the original. Technologically savvy fans often produce these games with a deep appreciation for the series because they just want more of it: new characters, longer campaigns, fresh stories. We often think of the hacker as a pseudosocialist hero, resisting capitalist hegemony to reproduce game commodities in a unifying appeal to class consciousness, as "a critical subject formed in antagonist relation to systems of intellectual property, one who challenges and interrupts the cohesion of rule systems embedded within technological commodities."[46] While there certainly might be a subversive element to the act of extracting a ROM image from its cartridge, modifying its content, and circulating alterations, to see such an act as antagonistic seems to discount the spirit of collaboration inherent in many ROM hacking practices. Much of what actually occurs is, in Henry Jenkins's words, "dialogic rather than disruptive, affective more than ideological, and collaborative rather than confrontational."[47] Despite the adversarial, deviant, or subversive connotation of the term "hacker," the people who perform ROM hacks appropriate official content out of a fondness for the game and the system on which it runs. Even a hack like *Restoration Queen*, which critiques the source material for its relatively lackluster depiction of women, expressly does so out of love. ROM hackers don't want to destroy the IP of Nintendo and Intelligent Systems; they want to learn from it and engage with it in creative ways.

The audience for *Fire Emblem* ROM hacks almost completely overlaps with the people who will inevitably pay Nintendo for the next installment in the series. Despite using unofficial tools to exploit weak points in Nintendo's technical and legal frameworks, these hobbyists continue to support the company financially. ROM hacks sustain the series during periods of low official activity, supporting the lengthy development processes at Nintendo and Intelligent Systems.

After the lukewarm commercial reception of *Fire Emblem: Radiant Dawn*, released for the Wii in 2008, the series' fate was uncertain. Intelligent Systems then took five years to produce the next and ostensibly final installment—a long wait for fans who had grown used to a new game each year.[48] ROM hacks became a way for the most dedicated series aficionados to scratch their itch, bringing with them the nostalgic pixelated aesthetic of the GBA's 2D maps at the moment when the series began to migrate to 3D. Announcing the release of the complete patch for *The Last Promise*, Blazer wrote: "In many ways, it's like a completely new game, and Fire Emblem fans in the west haven't had one of those in a while."[49]

An important subgenre of ROM hacking when it comes to fans' relationships to the series is the "translation hack," through which hobbyists produce unofficial versions of a game in a language other than its original. Given Nintendo's tight control over their IP and their regulations over who they allow to produce games for their platforms, it's not entirely surprising that some games never traveled from Japan to the rest of the world. The process of readying a videogame for an international audience extends beyond translation; it requires localization, the process by which a game's story, cultural references, and gameplay are adapted to ensure that the game retains its coherence and relevance in other regions.

Given how time-consuming and expensive localization can be, many early RPGs remain unofficially region-locked to Japan by way of the language barrier. Most translation hacks produce full-script translations from Japanese to English to allow fans to partake in installments that never made it across the (linguistic) ocean, but the practice also allows enthusiasts to make games accessible to people who don't speak either of the two languages that Nintendo typically privileges. Although Nintendo and Intelligent Systems never released *Fire Emblem: The Binding Blade* outside Japan, many North American and European fans have played it, thanks to the efforts of hackers who have reverse engineered and modified the ROM image. Released unofficially as *Fire Emblem: The Sword of Seals*, the patch has altered many players' understanding of the series more broadly.[50]

In *Atari to Zelda*, Mia Consalvo outlines the history of videogame localization as a combination of official and fan labor.[51] While it's now part of the industry and undertaken by large companies (like Nintendo's in-house product development division, Treehouse), fans have been translating videogames since the 1990s, seeking to play titles that Nintendo had decided were not worth the cost to localize. Unlike localizations, fan translations typically don't make gameplay adjustments or censor game content, but that doesn't mean the process doesn't involve effort.

The technical demands of hacking the ROM image and painstakingly translating hours' worth of text, character by character, go beyond the immediately visible. Because ROM images don't store text in a format that is legible to a human reader, hackers need to use hex editing and tables to read and alter text.[52] These and other esoteric programming skills come into play in ways that often go unnoticed to the player, who downloads a patch from somewhere on the internet. As Consalvo points out, fan translations are as much an art as a masterful display of computer science knowledge. They require creativity to account for romance languages' more literal meanings compared to kanji or to convey humor, tone, and specific cultural references that a Western audience might not understand. Moreover, while kanji's structure makes it easy to deliver a substantial amount of text on a single screen, the Roman alphabet demands considerably more space—not just visually, but also in terms of the number of bytes allotted. Narrative-heavy games like those in the *Fire Emblem* series sometimes require fans to exercise their judgment in deciding what to cut to make the text fit. Even ostensibly simple transliterations of names need ROM hackers to get creative by moving assets around the character portraits to fit them within the limited menu space.

Members of translation hacking communities blur the distinction between consumer and producer in undertaking labor that the industry neither sanctions nor remunerates. Translation hackers engage in a metagame of their own, playing with the language of the narrative and of the machine itself in projects that often take months or years to complete.

Commodifying Labors of Love

For all that Nintendo attempts to foreclose the possibility of decoding their software, they inevitably profit, however tangentially, from ROM hacks and fan translations. In 2017, Nintendo and Intelligent Systems released *Fire Emblem Heroes*, a free-to-play mobile *gachapon* (*gacha*) game featuring characters from across the series. Gachas, much like loot boxes in massively multiplayer online games, encourage players to spend in-game currency for a randomized chance at acquiring characters. When a player runs out of the free currency that they can accrue simply by playing the game, they can supplement their stores of in-game funds with pricy in-app purchases. Although players can complete the entirety of the game's content without spending a dime, *Fire Emblem Heroes* generated $300 million in gross revenue within its first year alone and has steadily remained one of Nintendo's most profitable properties. The mechanic of collection in *Fire Emblem Heroes* operates as the incentivizing factor behind such astronomical profits; players often want to recruit their favorites from across the series' many titles. We can therefore see how translations of *The Binding Blade* may unwittingly aid Nintendo and Intelligent Systems' efforts to capitalize on fans' nostalgia for and devotion to the series. The translations introduce a cast of characters to a much wider international audience rather than keeping it restricted to Japanese-speaking players. Although only a limited number of *Fire Emblem Heroes* players have encountered the translations, they are often among the most dedicated fans of the series and the most vocal on forums. For these players, unlicensed *Fire Emblem* ROM hacks play an important role in their understanding of the GBA era and of the series altogether.

Here, we can return to the fraught nature of participatory culture. Writing on mods, Renyi Hong and Vivian Hsueh-Hua Chen note that "while corporations gain market value from the activities of co-creators, the co-creators themselves are devoid of intellectual property rights to their productions and are often offered little or no monetary reimbursement."[53] Weeks, months, and even years of fan labor are easy for companies like Nintendo to profit from, in part because of the legally gray area in which it all takes place. ROM hacks and translations typically exist without direct legal intervention, provided that the hobbyists aren't making money from them. Omni, who is working on a *Fire Emblem: The Binding Blade* ROM hack titled *Fire Emblem: Maiden of Darkness*, writes the following in an FAQ:

Is this Fanfiction?

Yeah, basically. All romhacking to any extent is fanfiction, and I fully accept that MoD is my own fanfiction of FE6.

How can I support you?

You can't. I don't accept donations and there's no Patreon. If you have talent as an artist, you can offer to lend a hand. But other than that there's no way to support me. I could open up donations and the like, but it's murky legal-wise and I don't feel right taking peoples [sic] money for fanfiction.[54]

Fans are willing to acknowledge both the legally gray aspect of fan labor and their own discomfort with capitalizing from what they see as fanfiction. Meanwhile, companies are willing to quietly allow fans to play with their content and profit from their output.

A more complicated situation arises when the profiting company isn't Nintendo but other hobbyists, who have developed a cottage industry around the sale of reproduction cartridges (or "repros"). The product of reverse engineering the Game Pak, repros allow you to play fan hacks on GBA hardware without a flashcart, just as you might play any licensed game. By burning the patched ROM image of the hack onto a chip and connecting it to an adapter that matches the GBA cartridge's pinout, repro sellers enable a return to materiality.

Many of the most popular GBA fan hacks and translations circulate as repros today, with a large number of them emerging from the *Pokémon* and *Fire Emblem* communities. For $70 plus shipping, you can purchase a physical copy of *Fire Emblem: The Sword of Seals* and *Fire Emblem: The Last Promise* from Retro Gamer US.[55] These cartridges come with high-quality custom labels and their own boxes, replete with artworks, game screenshots, forged Entertainment Software Rating Board (ESRB) ratings, and even a reproduction of Nintendo's official seal. They sell on Etsy, an online marketplace known for handmade jewelry, vintage crafts, and, increasingly, modified videogame software and hardware.

It's clear that a great deal of effort went into making these facsimiles. The attention to detail in the box art alone is exciting for collectors of curios and material ephemera. But there's also an elegant form of piracy at play. Retro Gamer US mentions that these games are fan hacks in their product descriptions, but never credit the hackers by name. Instead, their marketing makes them look like the creators. While most ROM hackers are understandably upset to see repro sellers profiting off their patch files with neither permission nor credit, they have little legal recourse. Going after the repro seller would involve taking ownership of the hack. Given the complicated legal nature of ROM hacking, it's not surprising that they seldom wish to do so. As a way to navigate this legal quagmire, some ROM hackers have begun adding screens with messages along the lines of, "if you've paid for this product, you've been scammed," or protecting their work by technological means to ensure that their credit screen can't be removed.

Fraught as they are, repros resist the dominant rhetoric of technological progress and generational videogame history. Manufacturers may declare the end of a platform's lifecycle and may cease producing new games for a system, but hobbyists and hackers continue to appropriate this residual hardware for their own artistic endeavors. To say that *Rizumu Tengoku* was the last game to be released for the GBA is true only in a narrow sense. Nintendo's production of official games ceased in 2006, but hackers and hobbyists continue to release new games for a system that has been thought of as commercially obsolete for over a decade.

The Nostalgia of the Hardware Mod

Just as nostalgia is fundamentally embedded in Nintendo's approach to hardware innovation and software development, it is also responsible, at least in part, for fans' interest in preserving these material objects against the ravages of time. Consider Charles Kelso's personal retrospective, in which he identifies a white 2001 GBA running *Pokémon Sapphire* as having been *the* defining object of his youth.[56] As a ten-year-old, Kelso gave his GBA to a younger cousin—a gesture that seems at once profoundly generous and unfathomably foolish. Confronted with an urge to return to these childhood memories as an adult, he resorted to scouring local game stores in a desperate bid to replace his lost handheld and the accompanying cartridge that had so shaped his encounter with it. But at the climax of his quest, he realized a fundamental truth about nostalgia: "Things are almost always better in memory than in reality once you revisit them."[57] He goes on to explain:

> This had nothing to do with the game itself, but the Gameboy Advance [sic]. And not this Gameboy Advance, but all of them. As a kid, not having a backlit display wasn't even something that I considered. I don't think I was really capable of understanding that it was a drawback, it just was what it was. Trying to play on the Gameboy Advance's unlit, reflective display now? A nightmare.[58]

Here's where we can see Svetlana Boym's distinction between reflective and restorative nostalgia most clearly. As we saw earlier in the introduction to this book, restorative nostalgia presents the desire to re-create the lost home and relive special moments from our childhood. This is what Kelso attempted to do when he discovered that "a part of [his] childhood was missing." He sought to replace it with something that was as close as he could get to the objects that left an indelible mark on him. Restorative nostalgia ignores imperfections. But erasing the imperfections of a videogame platform works only when you don't immediately turn on said platform and try to use it in all its imperfect glory.

Restorative nostalgia disappoints us. It's traitorous for the way that it exposes our tendency to aestheticize that which we are nostalgic for, sometimes beyond recognition. With nineteen intervening years of technological innovation, the GBA's lack of a backlight—a feature that we've come to expect on everything from our stoves to our washing machines—is inconceivable, an inconvenience we've effaced entirely from our rose-tinted reminiscence of the handheld's expressive affordances (figure 6.1).

In contrast to restorative nostalgia, what Boym defines as "reflective nostalgia" acknowledges the past's pastness and allows us to reflect on our memories without necessarily trying to re-create them. The fact that past experiences are irretrievable is effectively what makes them pleasurable. For Kelso, the nostalgia that eventually fulfills him is the reflective kind he feels after his girlfriend buys him a modded GBA for Christmas. With a backlit screen and a glass lens, *Pokémon Sapphire* looks as good as he remembered—despite it never having looked that way at all. Kelso calls the modded device "a completely useable and perfectly preserved relic from [his] childhood," evident alterations be dammed.[59] Reflective nostalgia is evoked by hardware modding.

Figure 6.1 A built-to-order Retro Modding GBA that cannibalizes the AGS-101's backlit screen (left) beside an unmodded 2001 model with its default dim screen (right). Both display the same scene in *FE7*.

Broadly, there are two groups of people who play on modded GBAs: users and modders. Writing in the mid-1990s, Sherry Turkle identified a move in computing history from the active hardware and software manipulation of hackers and hobbyists to the passive reception of users. The emergence of the user in the 1970s and early 1980s coincided with the popularity of user-friendly applications on personal computers (PCs) that provided "a scintillating surface on which to float, skim and play."[60] Diving beneath the surface to explore the inner workings of the software and hardware became *verboten*. Users, in Turkle's sense of the word, want the handheld to look and function a certain way, but are content for it to remain a black box through which they can enjoy the videogames from their childhood without necessarily understanding what happens within the machine. Conversely, modders want to bring their technical and design expertise to the hardware or want to master their software by learning about the technological infrastructure that powers it.

There are compelling—albeit hazy—distinctions between videogame preservation and hardware modding along the lines of aesthetics, performance, and economics. On the one hand, hardcore preservationists might see modding as transgressive, as stripping the aura from the object and making it something other than what Nintendo intended. On the other hand, modding often extends the platform's life by replacing defunct components. At the end of the day, the fact that people are still carrying the GBA around is a kind of preservation in itself.

The 2020 Game Boy Advance

The object with which I open the introduction to this book, the made-to-order GBA built by Montreal-based Retro Modding, is useful for thinking through the preservation-use paradox. The custom handheld includes a backlit display, a voltage regulator with digital brightness control, an audio amplifier, a glass lens, and a 14-hour universal serial bus (USB) rechargeable battery pack, none of which existed in the 2001 GBA. Rather than reproduce an ineffable experience of playing on the "original" system, Retro Modding uses a combination of new and residual hardware to craft an object that captures the affective sensations of a 2020 GBA.

The Retro Modding warehouse is a remarkable sight. Rows of candy-colored cases line the back walls, bracketing stacks of boxes containing hundreds of GBA and SP screens and PCBs. There's a soldering station near the back row, meticulously tidy, with all the necessary materials in labeled boxes. Cleanliness is a prerequisite for the challenging and time-consuming task of applying the aftermarket glass lens to the screen without getting dust, dirt, and grease all over the display. When I first visited, eighteen custom GBAs rested on their worktable waiting for quality assurance testing. Each sported a unique combination of shell and button colors to meet the preferences of their eventual users.

Retro Modding's GBAs highlight the broader cultural and contextual assemblage that mediates and is mediated by experiences of play. Olivier, who runs the company, observes that his customers are usually men between twenty-five and thirty-five years old—people who had first encountered the Game Boy or GBA as children. Indeed, Olivier's own foray into modding finds its origins in childhood recollections of playing with Nintendo's handhelds.[61] A prime example of Boym's reflective nostalgia, the Retro Modding GBA does the work of recognizing pastness by isolating the constraints of the 2001 GBA and making alterations to improve its appeal and accessibility. Users can enjoy the physical and embodied experiences of interacting with the chassis while also benefiting from the affordances expected of a gaming device today.

Just like homebrew and ROM hacking, hardware modding consists of a variety of practices, some more technically demanding than others. Part of the appeal of console modding is the act of making the old feel new again. While a subset of mods exist solely to improve the aesthetics by changing the existing shell or buttons for another color (a practice known as "case modding"), the majority of mods are concerned with allowing the hardware to perform functions that the manufacturer didn't intend. Popular alterations include amplifying the audio by bypassing the GBA's own amplifier and carving the plastic shell to make space for a USB-rechargeable lithium-ion battery pack (figure 6.2).

By far the most significant and transformative hardware intervention is the backlighting mod, whereby the modder removes the unlit GBA screen from the console and replaces it with a backlit alternative. The process typically follows one of two protocols developed and circulated by prominent community experts. The older of the two is the "AGB-101" protocol, a portmanteau of internal codenames for the GBA ("AGB") and the backlit SP revision released in 2005 ("AGS-101"). Modders carefully transplant the SP's liquid crystal display (LCD) into the GBA. Technical complexity arises as a result of proprietary hardware. These LCDs don't connect to the handheld's PCB by way of a universal port, so community experts developed custom ribbon cables to translate the signal. Because Nintendo manufactured so few AGS-101 units, most AGB-101 mods use aftermarket screens, which Retro Modding markets as "new old stock." These are screens manufactured by Sharp—the same company that produced those that went into the SP—but that were never used in a handheld.

Figure 6.2   The back of Retro Modding's GBA, showing the custom USB-rechargeable battery back and the company's logo where the barcode used to be. The transparency of the shell simulates an aesthetic of technical mastery.

In recent years, there has been a simmering anxiety around the finitude of the AGS-101. As the number of people modding the GBA continues to grow, the supply of 2005 SPs and the new old stock screens is dwindling. In May 2019, the Chinese manufacturing company Funny-Playing released an in-plane switching (IPS) LCD kit, introducing the second protocol. The kit relies on the withered technology of cheap 3.2-inch (8.1-centimeter) screens produced by LG in 2012 for use in mobile phones, and includes a custom ribbon cable that interfaces with the PCB for a solder-free installation.[62] With its robust color reproduction, wide viewing angle, and high resolution, the IPS LCD produces a sharp, vibrant image. We can use FunnyPlaying's product as a way to think about the changeability of modding protocols and the way that technology is co-created by its makers and users.

The popularity of both backlighting mods says several things about the GBA. First, it speaks to the nostalgic and aesthetic appeal of the 2001 form factor. The easiest and most affordable way to enjoy GBA software on a backlit handheld is to buy an SP, or even a DS. But there's something about the shape of the 2001 handheld that seems to capture players' fascination more than the clamshell revisions. Out of the 1,400 handhelds that Retro Modding sold in their first year and a half, 800 were GBAs while only around 100 were SPs—a startling inversion of the actual market success of both products.[63] More saliently, the desire to backlight the GBA speaks to the expectations we have of our electronics in the present moment. We can no longer imagine playing videogames on dim screens. Context always mediates our approach to a platform.

With both the new old stock AGS-101 and the IPS LCD available on their website, Retro Modding often receives questions about which screen is "better." This looks, on the surface, to be a technological question, but it's really about taste. If we look at the modding community, it's clear how skills and techniques for performing particular technological practices are transferred from the experts to the nonexperts: video- and text-based tutorials, product descriptions, and social media marketing strategies are ways by which adepts cement themselves as experts and strategically share their knowledge. What is less easily transferred, as Carolyn Marvin says, "is the specific cultural setting and worldview that gives significance to these practices from the point of view of the bequeathers."[64] The choice of whether to mod one's GBA with one of the AGS-101 screens or with an IPS LCD is socially and culturally specific. And while most community experts have an opinion, there is no universal consensus.

Retro Modding's response to the question has been to distinguish between the "authentic AGB-101 mod" and the "sleek, modern IPS LCD," a tactical framing of the two protocols as being equal but different. In reality, neither mod is authentic or truly contemporary. The very fact that a GBA is backlit precludes it from being authentic to Nintendo's 2001 object, and the fact that we're working with residual media means it's not "modern" media at all. What is and is not considered genuine and what is and is not considered new are not technologically but socially constructed questions. This is what makes modding so compelling as a cultural practice.

Retro Modding has developed a profitable business out of creating bespoke devices for users who don't have the time or expertise to do so themselves. Olivier explains: "When there are makers that build a new mod, we try to master it as much as possible and find a way to optimize our use of it on a larger scale." Often, Retro Modding shares their protocols as instructional DIY posts in the tutorials section of their website. Within the GBA modding community, ideas are consistently evolving as modders tinker with the components.

There's a precariousness to this work. The judgment in the case of *Nintendo of America Inc. v. King* sets a frightening precedent for corporate control over what users are allowed to do with the hardware they purchase, much as the platformization model discussed in chapter 5 attempts to throttle the circulation of digital ROM files.[65] Jeramie Douglas King owned Go Cyber Shopping, an electronic components retailer based in Waterloo, Ontario, that sold flashcarts compatible with the DS and Nintendo 3DS; mod chips for the Wii (chips that, long before the suit was filed, had been rendered obsolete by the ease of software modification); and hardware tools facilitating technical protection measure circumvention. Canadian courts rejected Go Cyber Shopping's argument that these devices had a fair dealing defense based on the interoperability of computer programs (referring to the vast corpus of homebrew applications developed for Nintendo's handhelds and consoles), stating that the market for "illicit and infringing activities" far surpassed their theoretical uses with homebrew.

Although the case failed to receive the same notoriety as Nintendo's suit against LoveROMS and LoveRetro, it has had far-reaching implications for the way that it expands the definition of what constitutes a TPM: "A user without one of the Applicant's consoles is also unable to access a Nintendo Game on a genuine game card. It is therefore clear that the physical configuration is an access control TPM as contemplated under the Act."[66] If, according to Canadian legislation, any physical configuration is an access control TPM, then simple acts of repair could be interpreted as TPM circumvention and punished accordingly—noncommercial and noninfringing uses be damned.

DIY Modding

As noted, not everyone wants to buy a modded handheld. In many cases, there is also an underlying interest in technical mastery, in the satisfaction of taking the machine apart to see how it works and putting it back together in new ways. It's the hardware equivalent of cleverly exploiting a game's programming to create a ROM hack.

In the introduction to *Game Console Hacking*, Joe Grand observes that hardware modding is "about creativity, education, experimentation, personalization, and just having fun."[67] Modding as a *cultural technique* acknowledges the passage of time and puts into conversation the material object, with all its attending processes, and the body of the player encountering its agency and affective potential. Indebted to Foucault's foundational work on cultural archaeology, cultural technique theory sees technologies as assemblages that include memories, experiences, thoughts, and other nontechnological acts.[68]

Hardware modding results in a material object, but it's also a way of being with technology. Much of hardware modding's appeal comes from bringing personal identity to the platform. As Grand notes, modding "gives us a sense of ownership a faceless company can't provide."[69] The resulting product is not only unique, but also created on the player's terms, by the players hands.

Freeplay Tech's retro videogame handhelds encapsulate the DIY aspect of hardware modding most clearly. Rather than use Nintendo's original hardware, these handhelds use Raspberry Pi, a series of small, affordable, single-board computers. The Freeplay Zero and Freeplay CM3 kits combine a Raspberry Pi Zero or Raspberry Pi Compute Module 3, respectively, with a custom PCB and miniature LCD in a GBA housing.[70] These projects draw on a history of makers who developed innovative creations using pieces of original GBA hardware and who posted the details of their projects on modding forums like Sudomod. In their Kickstarter, the Freeplay Tech team says:

> This project was born out of the landscape of "homebrew" console creators. . . . Often these would have a Rat's Nest of wiring on the inside and were difficult for most people to replicate. Furthermore, if something went wrong, finding the problem could be a nightmare for anyone without serious electronic experience.
>
> We decided to build our own retro handheld console in a way that other hobbyists/enthusiasts could also use to build one for themselves. One thing we are very good at is creating circuit boards to fit specific requirements, so we chose a well-known and readily available retro game console shell that we love and built our circuit board to fit it.[71]

Think of the Freeplay kits as walkthroughs for hardware modding. Both kits come with a preprinted circuit board, a 3.2-inch (8.1-centimeter) LCD, a built-in brightness controller, and an assortment of parts specific to the build. Freeplay Tech partnered with Retro Modding to source the GBA shell and buttons, and it's up to the modder to supply the Raspberry Pi, lithium polymer battery cell, and Micro SD card. Their website hosts detailed build guides, as well as troubleshooting tips and a community forum where modders can show off their builds, discuss their projects' development, and ask for help. These mods are comprehensive in their scope: the plastic GBA housing needs to be cut with an X-Acto knife to resize the LCD opening and accommodate the battery pack; two holes need to be drilled into the shell to hold X and Y buttons; components need to be soldered to the custom PCB; and the Raspberry Pi needs to be properly configured to run the operating system. Most hobbyists can easily acquire the skills necessary to put the kit together, but the projects require time and patience. For many beginner modders, the Freeplay Zero and Freeplay CM3 are as much about learning new skills as they are about the finished product.

Both the Freeplay Zero and the Freeplay CM3 are designed to run more than just GBA games—hence the need to drill holes for the X and Y buttons. The $5 price tag of the Raspberry Pi Zero belies how powerful the computer is. Its technical specifications boast a 1-GHz single-core CPU and 512 MB of RAM. (Recall that the GBA's CPU is measured in *megahertz* and its RAM in *kilobytes*.) The Raspberry Pi 3 is even more powerful with a 1.2-GHz CPU and 1 GB of RAM. Using RetroPie, a front-end management application based on a preconfigured Linux distribution, the Freeplay Zero and Freeplay CM3 can emulate handheld and home consoles up to the PlayStation and the Nintendo 64 (N64). In many cases, fear and a lack of tools are all that stand between thinking that you can't complete the project and doing it. This fear isn't only cultural; it's something that companies like Nintendo deliberately cultivate through the aura of their products.

The 3D printed GBA XL created by dbak85 is precisely the kind of innovation that led to the Freeplay Zero.[72] The GBA XL is based on the shape of the GBA, but it is large enough to contain a 5-inch High-Definition Multimedia Interface (HDMI) screen. As dbak8 states, "the GBA is just too small for what I want," so the solution was to print a custom case with a 3D printer. It follows in the style of the 3DS XL line, deterritorializing Nintendo's approach to innovation. Between the physical act of taking the hardware apart and putting its components back together, hardware modding produces that feeling of technical mastery and empowers players to create the platform they want.

Many mods highlight the cultural practices of use that change or go beyond gaming. Division 6's GBA accelerator is a chip that modders can solder on the PCB between the ARM processor and the cartridge connector. By pressing three GBA buttons at a time (whichever three were connected during the installation process), they can then switch the GBA's speed to one of four modes: normal (1x), fast (1.5x), ultrafast (1.75x), and slow-motion (0.85x). The accelerator reconfigures players' relationship to gameplay by allowing them to "fast forward" through text-heavy sections of games or slow down difficult action sequences to complete them more easily. It also allows the handheld to run homebrew games that use faster processing power; the GBA's CPU can run much faster than the GBA typically runs it, so some homebrew games developed for emulators would feel slow on the GBA hardware without the accelerator.

Most recently, voltage regulators designed by the Australian modder BennVenn and by Retro Modding have added sleep functionality to the hardware. Recall that the GBA line of handhelds doesn't have a true sleep mode. But a handful of games, including *The Legend of Zelda: The Minish Cap* come with a software-based sleep mode, accessible via an in-game menu, that turns off the display and audio while maintaining the game's progress to save the battery. Pressing the L, R, and Select buttons at the same time restores the session. The difficulty with this sleep mode is that, because it's based in software rather than hardware, it has no effect on the handheld's backlight. Putting an AGS-101 or modded GBA into sleep mode results in a lit backlight without an image, meaning that it still consumes an alarming amount of battery in low-power mode. The voltage regulators made by BennVenn and Retro Modding shut off the backlight when the game is sleeping. Years after the SP's release, modders have fixed what they saw as a problem of inefficiency, while realizing a feature that Satoru Iwata had hoped to include in the original hardware.

The embodied experience of playing on modded handhelds certainly differs from the experience of engaging with the 2001 hardware. But it is also worth considering that playing on the original hardware is ultimately a different experience today than it was twenty years ago. Even perfect reproduction cannot reproduce the cultural and historical contexts of the early 2000s, or the eleven-year-old's hands that first picked up the console. Kelso's experiences chasing after the white GBA certainly suggests as much. Picking up that same console today can't strip away the intervening years. The very fact that cultural expectations dictate that handhelds are rechargeable and backlit mediates any return to the 2001 GBA, just as the experience of watching a recent computer-generated imagery (CGI) film mediates the experience of watching CGI from twenty years earlier.

"We Don't Do Nintendo, We Do Mods"

One of the consequences of many hardware mods is the erasure of the "Game Boy Advance" name from its centralized position beneath the handheld's screen. When Olivier and I spoke about the logo's absence on many of his products, he explained that, while there's a market for the logo, Retro Modding aims to stand out in an aftermarket saturated with cheap knockoffs. Their brand is effectively the lack thereof—an attempt to reproduce a similar quality as Nintendo's tooling while acknowledging that they're doing something different from the official manufacturer. As he explained to me, "We don't do Nintendo, we do mods."

In doing mods at a short remove from the cultural cachet of the Nintendo name, professional modders and hobbyists participate in debranding practices that are not unlike the act of removing manufacturers' emblems from cars, a process referred to as "debadging." A study of consumer creativity and market forces in debadging circles considers these car owners as "unruly bricoleurs" who, through the removal of brand signifiers, negotiate their relationship to brand identity and find empowerment in reappropriating their cars.[73] In particular, it examines the discursive frameworks that give rise to such a practice. While some car modders simply want their cars to appear sleeker, many see debadging as an act of reclamation and identity formation. Some hope to trick others into assuming their cars are more prestigious than they are. Thus, debadging is a way of accruing social and cultural capital by excluding those who are unfamiliar with the aesthetic and mechanical differences among cars. One participant in the study wrote, "If you can't figure out [what the car is], I don't care to tell ya."[74] Between the technical knowledge of how to debadge and the postulate that, if nonexperts cannot identify a car without its emblems, they have no right to know what it is, car modders participate in layered economies of social distinction.

Similarly, debranding points to hardware modders' criticism of contemporary branding practices even as it acknowledges the brand's imbrication in their sense of identity. Removing the words "Game Boy Advance" from beneath the screen is partly linked to issues of trademark and materiality. But it can also point to a critique of a society that often conflates social status with the display of visible brand markers. It's a rebellion against closed, proprietary hardware. Of course, the GBA's design is recognizable enough as one of Nintendo's handhelds. But even as a purely aesthetic gesture, debranding nevertheless carries a certain amount of social and cultural weight.

The comparison between videogame hardware modding and car modding communities is neither accidental nor novel. Writing about the practice of overclocking a computer system—that is, increasing computational components' processing speed beyond the limitations set by the manufacturer—Bart Simon calls PC modding "hot-rodding for geeks."[75] Both communities, he argues, share an interest in performance, technical mastery, and the aesthetic presentation of the machine.

But there's another key area of overlap in addition to these material ones: the feminization and fetishization of the machine.[76] Judy Wajcman notes the car's privileged position in hegemonic male culture: "A fetishized object for many men, cars symbolize for them individual freedom, self-realization, sexual prowess, and control."[77] Hot-rodding and debadging offer men immediate opportunities to exert this control by manipulating the object—a phenomenon mirrored in the gendered discourse of consumer electronics. Wajcman observes that engaging with technology is seldom simply a question of acquiring skills because these skills "are embedded in a culture of masculinity that is largely coterminous with the culture of technology."[78]

It's worth considering the language that we use to talk about technology. The gendered name of the platform itself is not uniquely embedded into Nintendo's marketing conventions, but rather is part of the larger negotiations of networked contact: "Male-to-female connectors configure all electronic information exchange as electrifying heterosexual intercourse."[79] The motherboard is a PCB capable of expansion through daughtercards; the terms "master" and "slave" are used to describe a communication protocol where one device controls others—even as the production of chips, circuit boards, capacitors, and other technological components upon which consumer electronics depend are already contingent upon a history of colonialism and gendered violence. The naturalized discourse of computational technologies belies the ability to tell a neutral technological history; therefore, attention must always be directed to the ways that hardware and software reproduce ideologies of power.

In line with this body of research, Jaime Lee Kirtz has written on who is invited into modding communities and who is not. She addresses the assumptive design practices behind tools for repair and construction, positing that "screwdrivers and power tools have become 'a symbol of masculinity' that helps cultivate 'masculine legitimacy of skilled labour.'"[80] The symbolism of the material tools required for hacking, the gendered and sexualized language of computer parts, and the technical competence that many people see as incompatible with femininity converge to systematically exclude women from modding circles.[81] The familiar riposte, "If you don't know how to mod, you shouldn't be doing it" belies the fact that modding competence always has to be learned.

In many ways, GBA hardware modding continues to reproduce the same distinctions as homebrew communities. Women are increasingly identifying as gamers or videogame players, but my own experience in modding circles reveals that gender parity has not quite reached hardware modding. From troubleshooting installation to sourcing parts, most amateurs will encounter established male modders during the process.

All this brings us back to the context in which these platforms circulate and the discourse that surrounds them. There are paradoxes at play here. On the one hand, homebrew, ROM hacking, and modding remain male-dominated activities. But the relatively open circulation of knowledge protocols and the anonymity of the internet introduce greater opportunities for entry than radio did in the 1920s. Nintendo's original audience for the GBA in 2001 was predominantly boys. And yet the modded handheld effaces this constant reminder. It is no longer the gamer boy's advanced handheld—it belongs to anyone and no one.

Game (Is Never) Over

As I've argued throughout this book, the historical approach to videogame platforms that identifies a platform as a stable configuration of hardware and software elides the embodied experiences of its users and ignores the myriad ways that people continue to engage with the objects during and after their market availability. Homebrew, hacks, and mods remind us that, much as platforms are designed for their users (often with a narrow, prescriptive set of functions), those same users continuously push against the platform's constraints to create something new. The drive for technical mastery that arises from probing the platform's inner workings leads to a network of professionalization and shared social and cultural experiences. The material communities that persist or grow around the GBA give the platform new kinds of "zombie" lives that revitalize and reshape the handheld and its position in popular culture.[82] The GBA exists as much in the present as it does in the past.

Calling for a move from consumption to creative production, Zielinski writes: "The only effective form of intervention in this world is to learn its laws of operation and try to undermine or overrun them. One has to give up being a player at a fairground sideshow and become an operator within the technical world where one can work on developing alternatives."[83] There are things we can't learn about the GBA just by playing it the way it was designed to be played. Try as they might, Nintendo can never have complete control over what happens to their handhelds once they leave the warehouse. In trying to sell the GBA, Nintendo once asked us: "Who Are You?" Now, we show them. The GBA is out there, and we have made it our own.

Conclusion: After Afterlives

Joe Heaton, a UK-based product designer and a prolific modder, fashions bespoke Game Boy Advance (GBA) handhelds out of defunct Nintendo DS Lites. Known as the "Neon Advance," Heaton's creation is a remix of Nintendo's hardware, a cut-up DS that doesn't play DS games, a futuristic GBA with sharp edges and a neon glow. His creation is certainly a beautiful reimagining of Nintendo's hardware, but its value lies in more than just its aesthetics. The Neon Advance has a lot to say about the fate of our consumer electronics.

The Neon Advance emerged from the remains of damaged handhelds. While reshelling broken DS Lites, Heaton observed that most of their problems stemmed from broken hinges, faulty top screens, and unresponsive resistive touch pads (the DS's bottom screen is a touch screen). All these features are necessary for DS games but are entirely extraneous to GBA backward compatibility. For the most part, the bottom halves remained functional for GBA play.

Rather than dispose of working technology, Heaton reanimates the corpses of discarded DS Lites, riffing off earlier Game Boy Macro mods that filed off the top screens to turn the DS into a functional GBA. The trouble with Game Boy Macro mods was always the fact that sawing off the hinges is time consuming and inelegant. So Heaton preserves them as they are and instead adds a custom-colored light-emitting diode (LED) acrylic rod between them to create a visual flair that sets the device apart from its kin. To address the fact that the DS's speakers are housed in the top half of the clamshell design, Heaton embeds a speaker in the space where the stylus used to be, because it's no longer necessary once he removes the touch screen's digitizer. The DS still runs its own firmware until it boots a GBA game, so users can access the settings with the Direction-pad (D-pad) and the A button to make sure that the game loads in the bottom screen rather than the absent top screen. In this way, Heaton cocreates a GBA with the DS to address the fallibility and constraints of both hardware objects.

Emerging out of a refusal to discard operative technology, Heaton's Neon Advance invites consideration of e-waste, the afterlife to which most (and eventually, all) technology is consigned. Residuality confronts consumers with what happens after a piece of technology breaks. Lack of knowledge about the workings of consumer electronics means that most users overlook acts of repair and repurposing in favor of disposal, even when the repair is simple enough to execute, as with the Neon Advance. This is partly by design. Manufacturers rely on a combination of technical protection measures (TPMs) and threats of voided warranties to prevent users from tinkering with their hardware. When a handheld breaks, Nintendo offers a simple solution: buy a newer, better one.

Like most videogame consoles, neither the GBA nor the DS is forward compatible. Despite the company's acknowledgment that consumers don't want to lose the time and money they've invested in Nintendo products, the GBA and DS necessarily participate in the broader regime of planned obsolescence. Planned obsolescence is the logic of consumer electronics cycles, and it is based on designing products with an artificially limited life span to encourage additional consumption. Given the mutual relationship between videogame hardware and software, planned obsolescence is always part of the platform by virtue of its lack of forward compatibility with the software for the next hardware object. By manufacturing a platform with the knowledge that an upgraded system will replace it in a matter of years, Nintendo invests in a profitable future, contingent upon the brand loyalty that they inspire in their consumers, who will not only buy the next handheld but also the ports and remakes that Nintendo releases for it. That's the thing about new media: it will become old one day.

Of course, there are material considerations at play in the regime of obsolescence. It's bigger than just consoles. As technology evolves at a rapid pace, circuit boards and other electronic components become increasingly compact while being able to store ever-larger games that run on ever-more-powerful engines. Nintendo's software storage migration from cartridges to discs to their current ultraslim Game Cards is as much about planned obsolescence and TPMs as it is about adapting to more efficient technologies that have reached an affordable price point. If they want to continue to enjoy a stream of revenue, companies can't simply churn out new software for old hardware in the way that Nintendo did for a decade with the Game Boy. Consumers expect more powerful and more efficient hardware, with improved graphics capabilities, practically from the moment the technologies are unveiled. But the inability to engage with new software on old hardware tends to foreground technological advancements without considering what gets left behind.

This is the increasing problem of e-waste that we're left with, which doesn't seem to be going away anytime soon. E-waste is the most toxic and the fastest-growing subset of waste in North America. It's also the most wasteful in another sense: approximately two-thirds of all the consumer electronics that people dispose of in the United States are still functional.[1] We often rely on the logic that these residual-but-not-yet-obsolete technologies will be recycled by local organizations to be used in new technologies, but this is the case only rarely. As Lisa Parks explains, the majority of consumer electronic e-waste ends up in the hands of electronics salvaging firms, which have developed lucrative and profitable business models based on structured obsolescence.[2] Behind the veneer of ecofriendly, waste-minimizing efforts, these multinational companies exploit the labor of prisoners and migrant workers to turn a profit.

In the end, most hazardous e-waste merely moves from landfills in North America, Europe, and Australia to parts of Asia that have few or no environmental regulations. Little meaningful recycling takes place. When e-waste remains in postindustrial parts of the world, governments ensure that it is invisible to upper- and middle-class (mostly) white people; they deposit waste near low-income neighborhoods or Indigenous communities.[3] Waste disposal, Parks notes, almost always intersects with racial- and class-based politics.

The material residue of media is waste. As noted by Jennifer Gabrys, "Electronic waste, chemical contamination, failure, breakdown, obsolescence, and information overload are conditions that emerge as wayward effects of electronic materiality."[4] Focusing on waste demands that we consider temporal materiality, infrastructure, soil, and water. Gabrys adopts the word "fossils" to describe the material and imaginative residues of electronics. As fossils, e-waste traces the imprints of lives—both Nintendo's corporate life and the actions and appropriations of the consumer. But over time, they degrade and fall apart. As new electronics render the old obsolete, they begin to accumulate dust through disuse. Indeed, most GBAs and DS Lites collect dust in boxes in basements or drawers, largely forgotten and seldom powered on. Gabrys offers a compelling argument that dust offers a more accurate sense of media objects than narratives of technological progress.

Acts of modding or repairing consoles seek to prolong the platform's life cycle; brushing off the dust revives the object, if only temporarily. Heaton's intervention in the DS Lite's obsolescence by repurposing it to run GBA titles emphasizes the materiality of the object. Yes, part of this is a nostalgic return to old technology (it's through the lens of nostalgia that the Neon Advance received the most coverage on gaming news sites). But at the same time, salvaging consumer electronics is a way to make visible the usually invisible manufacturing labor that many of us have the privilege not to think about.

Platforms are neither environmentally nor politically neutral. Just as the burden of e-waste disposal is disproportionately placed on classed and racialized bodies, media infrastructures are contingent on the underpaid labor of those who manufacture consumer electronics, often in deplorable and dangerous working conditions. According to Parks and Nicole Starosielski, media infrastructures "have historically been used in efforts to claim and reorganize territories and temporal relations. Their material dependence on lands, raw materials, and energy imbricates them within issues of finance, urban planning, and natural-resource development."[5] Mimi Nguyen notes that digital freedom and excess impose an equal and opposite reaction on the "bodies of Asian and Asian American immigrant women workers (in sweatshops and factories of varying working conditions) [that] provide the labor for the production of . . . circuit boards, those instruments of identity play, mobility, and freedom."[6] The fact that players can take pleasure in the mobility and freedom of their portable platforms is contingent on other people not enjoying these same things in a world structured by postindustrial capitalism.

It's often easy for us to elide the environmental and social imprint of technology. Thinking about the corpses of fish decaying on shores of contaminated bodies of water near the lithium mines that the SP, Micro, and DS relied on for their rechargeable batteries hardly constitutes the kind of play that Nintendo promises its consumers. The user's enjoyment of a videogame relies on the refusal to consider the material ramifications of engaging with media technology. Technology and leisure have become coterminous, in that our free time is often categorized by a retreat into our handhelds, smartphones, or computers. But this approach to so-called free time depends on a kind of rigid ecodenialism—a refusal to think about what it means for our leisure time to depend on these objects and the sheer number of resources that go into their manufacturing. If play is a form of escapism through which we evade quotidian responsibilities, it behooves us not to think about the ecological costs of such an escape. But this is precisely the ideology that safeguards the practices that corporations undertake to generate a profit from the sale and disposal of hardware objects.

We do a disservice to everyone affected by the manufacturing processes by *not* acknowledging all the lives touched (and sometimes besmirched) by these products. The plastics, circuits, and batteries have *already* had a social and ecological impact during their extraction, refining, and final manufacturing. Their existence has already relied on large quantities of water and oil. And they will continue to have an impact once they're left behind. The ARM chips nestled within the GBA's chassis are the products of a global semiconductor industry, which relies on the cheap labor of a "low-paid, predominantly female work force, recruited specifically for its supposed docility and disposability and subjected to ferocious work discipline."[7] These women work under conditions known to cause lung and heart failure due to repeated exposure to dangerous materials.

Because Nintendo is notoriously secretive about their position in the global manufacturing system, it's difficult to trace the origins of the microprocessors, screens, wires, and other components that make up a GBA. And without concrete evidence, most of our suspicions about labor practices remain just that: suspicions. But in a 2001 article, Nick Dyer-Witheford lifted the veil on a labor dispute that took place at the Maxi-Switch plant in Cananea, Mexico, located in the *maquiladora* zone; the term *maquiladora* refers to a manufacturing plant run by a foreign company that assembles products free of duties and tariffs and exports the finished products to that company. The plant in question employed young girls in their teens to work 10 hours a day, at the end of which they took home a mere $3.50. In response to the low wages and poor ventilation— ambulances would visit the factory three or four times each day in the summer after workers collapsed on production lines—the workers began to unionize, led by a woman named Alicia Perez. Owners fired Perez after company employees assaulted her in retaliation for her efforts. "The Maxi-Switch incident was exceptional," Dyer-Witheford writes, "because workers' struggles tore the cloak of invisibility that companies such as Nintendo . . . draw over the manufacture of their products."[8] The Maxi-Switch plant produced Game Boys.

While the Maxi-Switch incident is remarkable in that it offers a rare moment of insight into the political economy of videogame production, it would be naïve to think that this was an isolated incident. In 2012, investigations into Foxconn, an electronics manufacturer working with Nintendo, revealed that children as young as fourteen were working 11- or

12-hour shifts in the Chinese manufacturing plant that produced components for the Wii U. The production line's foreman refused to let them leave until they completed all the work they'd been assigned each day.[9] Alerted to this exploitation of child labor, Nintendo launched their own investigation, determining that Foxconn had violated the terms of their agreement and declaring that Foxconn would be "taking full responsibility" for the incident. Previously, Foxconn's subsidiary, Q-run, was responsible for 34 percent of the GameCube's assembly, a console manufactured concurrently with the GBA.

Recognizing that "their toil equals our play," to borrow the equation that Dyer-Witheford adopts to express the division between the consumption by those wealthy enough to enjoy consumer electronics and those who have little choice over how these electronics are produced with their labor, has the potential to change how we think about our hardware. We would do well to consider the way that companies frame these technologies when presenting them to us. By Nintendo's account, the 2001 GBA came into the world fully formed, the product of the brilliance of the male engineers and developers who worked at Nintendo. This is, at least, the narrative we get from the fun, scripted *Iwata Asks* interviews that Nintendo produces to promote their brand. Rarely do we see the hands that solder the boards together. This framing is a product of the ideology of technological progress, which often effaces process and production.

The violent thread in videogames is not found in its content, but rather in the violence of the alienated labor of capitalist material production. The regime of planned obsolesce renders this violence ouroboric. Here was the Game Boy Advancing into the new millennium. But what about the millions of Game Boys and Game Boy Colors (GBCs) that came before it?

Over the years, Shigeru Miyamoto has often likened the world of Hyrule and its surroundings to a "miniature garden," a translation of the Japanese *hakoniwa*, a tiny, dense version of natural landscapes comprising stones, plants, proportionally scaled architecture, and sometimes tiny figures—all intricately put together by dextrous fingers.[10] *Hakoniwa* involves nature that has been curated, controlled, and aestheticized, just as the world of Hyrule is carefully constructed pixel by pixel, tile by tile. Miyamoto's metaphor of the miniature garden mediates between Japan's traditional image of itself and emerging (and unsustainable) ecological practices:

> In the good old days, Japanese children had fields and meadows they could run around in, but nowhere in our cities today will you find such

places. . . . Adults have lost them too. It is no longer a simple matter for people to "play with nature."[11]

Playing with nature becomes *play* itself—that is to say, digitally mediated play. While Western audiences come to the experience differently than Japanese players by way of different cultural contexts, they can nevertheless appreciate how videogames, especially those populated by idyllic landscapes like *The Legend of Zelda* offer "immediate access to unlimited 'meadows,' a new 'nature.'"[12] Parents and grandparents have myriad stories to tell of their adventures in and out of the city, but children today are seldom allowed to explore the outdoors alone for a range of social, cultural, and environmental reasons.

Within *The Minish Cap*, there's no sight of modernization—no heinous reminder of the output of industrial waste. Construction materials are locally sourced: Western Wood and Mount Crenel provide the building blocks (literally the graphics tiles) for artificial infrastructure. No matter what lurks in caves and dungeons, the sunny overworld evokes all the imagery of a Romantic poem. As people play *The Minish Cap* during their commute, passing strip malls and crumbling infrastructure, they can look down at the screen and wander through a pastoral landscape. And yet this topography nevertheless relies on mining silicon and rare earth metals, and on the devastating effects of a globalized transportation industry. Even as the game promises a utopian landscape, the material object held in a player's hands reminds us of the cost of such an escapist fantasy.

Playing GBA is contingent on material, temporal, and financial privilege. While the GBA was more affordable than its competitors, its $100 price tag could cover school lunches for a month, to say nothing of the supplementary cost of individual games. The hours spent on whimsical journeys through the Minish forest presume that demands on the player's time are minimal, or at least flexible. The ability to own a GBA suggests certain securities: that the money required to purchase the console isn't needed for other expenses, that people can spend time on the luxury of play.

So, beyond questions of nostalgia, there are material and ecological reasons to consider the GBA's afterlives as vital articulations in the platform's assemblage. Heaton's revival of dead DS Lites implicitly values the social, material, cultural, economic, and environmental contexts in which the handheld was produced, distributed, and eventually purchased. Instead of looking to newer media forms, it reclaims the everyday objects of the residual, even when the inner workings of these objects were intentionally engineered to be impenetrable, or at least obfuscated.

Modding the platform is a fundamental refusal of planned obsolescence, in more ways than one. Planned obsolescence is discursive and, as Garnet Hertz and Jussi Parikka put it, "takes place on a micropolitical level of design."[13] The language that Nintendo uses to frame their platforms is certainly part of the regime (the GBA will let the player live "life, advanced"; the Wii is a "revolution").[14] But materially, planned obsolescence shows itself as plastic enclosures that are hard to get into, proprietary chargers and adapters, and unique battery packs. Modding begins with a refusal of the black box. It starts by opening up the shell to tinker with the object. The desire to breathe new life into residual hardware and to repurpose it for a context external to the regime of e-waste lies at the heart of many modding practices.

As Nintendo continues to manufacture new handhelds, they exhibit a curiously bifurcated attitude toward the ownership of their platforms. On the one hand, they seek to exercise complete control over how consumers use their hardware and software, funneling their intellectual property (IP) through proprietary channels and leaning on legal judgments around their TPMs to regulate use (as discussed in chapter 5). Consumers are expected to buy the platform, play licensed games, and buy the next handheld when this one breaks. Under no circumstances are they to take the handheld apart. On the other hand, Nintendo doesn't seem to mind that disuse means that 81.5 million GBAs will make their way to overflowing landfills like the millions of Game Boys before them.

These concerns about sustainability are part of Retro Modding's larger agenda. Reflecting on Nintendo's ambivalent approach to platform ownership, Olivier says, "It's like they lose responsibility as soon as they release it and it gets to the consumer's house." He's resentful of the fact that Nintendo attempts to exert control over their platforms without taking accountability: "They shouldn't be restrictive about how that stuff is handled afterwards. . . . We're talking about millions of Game Boys, all that plastic and all those PCBs with strange chemicals."[15] The reshuffling of electronics components from urban areas to low-income rural landscapes has tangible effects on the water and soil; plastics and printed circuit boards (PCBs) leach carcinogenic chemicals into environments deemed less important by the privileged elite of North America.

In the summer of 2019, Retro Modding launched a console trade-in program that promises to "give your old handhelds new life." This is part of a growing tradition of modders exchanging cash or store credit for spare PCBs, screens, plastics, and conductive silicone button pads that otherwise would collect dust in a basement or make their way to a salvaging firm. Hardware modding of the kind that Olivier is in the business of performing confronts users with the unpleasant realities of consumer electronics. The hundreds of GBA boards and shells that line Retro Modding's warehouse have had their voyage to a landfill momentarily deferred. Instead, they'll journey to the homes of players eager to revisit or discover the GBA. While not used in the way Nintendo intended, these modded devices nevertheless preserve the work that went into mining, extracting, refining, and assembling the components that make up the platform's hardware. This element of reuse and repurposing leads Oliver to see his work as a type of preservation—not preservation of the hardware as Nintendo once created it, but preservation of the platform nonetheless.

The reabsorption of the DS into the GBA's assemblage by way of the Neon Advance is emblematic of Nintendo's own design philosophy, predicated upon the reappropriation of residual media for new ends. More generally, the fact that we're still talking about the GBA—let alone buying revamped versions of it to return to its vast library of software titles—speaks to the materiality of nostalgia and the desire to keep enjoying, exploring, and creating with the platform.

Revision has always been part of Nintendo's approach to both hardware and software development, inextricably linked as they are through mutual relationships of affordances and constraints. The company's patents lay bare the continuities among their platforms: the Game & Watch inspires the Game Boy; the GBA contains the guts of its predecessors; the DS looks back to all three; and the Wii U and Switch revisit GBA-GameCube connectivity. Nintendo's failures, such as the nauseating 3D of the Virtual Boy or the touch-screen overlay for the SP prototype, eventually reemerge in the stereoscopic 3D and resistive touch-screen technologies of the 3DS line of handhelds. All the while, continuity between machines operates symbiotically with familiar characters' reappearances in software titles for each system. This is less linear progression than lateral thinking—ideas are reworked, put aside, and then later revisited.

Amateur programmers, game designers, and artists equally continue to return to the GBA. As one of the last bastions for solo game development, the GBA remains an important platform for creative expression and for the accrual of a set of hardware-specific programming skills. Fans revisit and reinvent the worlds of the GBA's software, motivated by nostalgia, fondness, critique, or some combination of all three. Beyond the realm of games, musicians harness the handheld's hardware to make chiptunes, a genre of music produced using the sound chips or synthesizers in early computers and videogame consoles, by combining the GBA's innate ability to use samples with the synthesized sounds of the four 8-bit channels inherited from the Game Boy. Artists create retro-aestheticized works from GBA bitmap modes, use the GBA to display their oeuvres in a gallery setting, or create miniature succulent gardens out of damaged and discarded shells. Hackers try to figure out what makes the hardware tick, delving into the intricacies of an outmoded assembly language to display their own technical mastery. In sum, users find all sorts of things to do with the device that Nintendo never could have predicted, proving that hardware obsolescence is not synonymous with platform obsolescence.

The GBA platform is more than a precise configuration of hardware and software—more than an aesthetic object that signifies a particular embodied, branded cultural identity. It is at once static object and complex, ever-mutable assemblage. It is under continuous construction by those who engage with it in and counter to the ways Nintendo intended. Emulating, hacking, translating, modding, deconstructing, rescuing, reusing, sharing, donating, and disposing of the platform all speak to the way that its residue remains visible in the interventions and memories of its users, carried forward on a current of nostalgia, aestheticization, and technological innovation. The GBA exists and persists because of and through its players. And its fluidity invites us to keep asking, "Who are you?"

Acknowledgments

The trouble with monographs is that they so often obscure the fact that authorship isn't a single-player game. I can say with certainty that *Who Are You?* wouldn't exist without the influence and assistance of a wonderful assemblage of family, friends, colleagues, modders, researchers, and others.

First and foremost, I owe an immense debt of gratitude to my parents, Sandra Giuliani and Jack Custodio, for unwaveringly supporting my research and writing. A special thank-you also goes to my brother, Matthew, for bringing home a secondhand Game Boy Advance (GBA) all those years ago, and for continuing to hunt Pokémon with me even to this day.

This project never would have happened without my supervisor and mentor, Darren Wershler, whose knowledge, direction, and encouragement have been instrumental to my growth as a scholar. My profound thanks to Stephen Yeager, for his thoughtful revisions on the (way too long) master's paper that morphed into this book; to Jesse Arseneault, Susan Cahill, and Andre Furlani for their guidance during my time at Concordia University; and to Lori Emerson and Jussi Parikka for co-teaching the course that planted the seeds. My master's research project was supported by the Social Sciences and Humanities Research Council of Canada (SSHRC) and the Fonds de Recherche du Québec—Société et Culture (FRQSC).

At the MIT Press, I want to thank acquisitions editor Douglas Sery for his trust and his support of this project; series editors Nick Montfort and Ian Bogost for their invaluable comments on my initial pitch and for paving the way; manuscript editor Virginia Crossman and copy editor Susan McClung for their careful reading and thoughtful comments; the three anonymous peer reviewers whose generous feedback guided the development of this book; and Noah J. Springer for answering all my questions, often before I even asked them.

I'm indebted to everyone who took the time to revisit and share their GBA memories with me: Bailey Cohen-Krichevsky, Evan Brown, G-stant, Jake, Nick, Andrea Wahba, Carolyn, Geneviève Paris, Gaetan, and Abbie "spoopy" Rappaport, who is also my creative collaborator at the Residual Media Depot. Equally important are the dedicated members of gbadev.org who compiled a vast corpus of technical information about the handheld's hardware and code. Although I've never met them, their careful documentation has been crucial. I also owe thanks to Michael Iantorno for sharing his knowledge of ROM hacking and to Olivier and the team at Retro Modding for opening my eyes to the GBA's scintillating afterlives. My work on hardware modding is supported by Mitacs through the Mitacs Accelerate Program.

Thanks go as well to Carolyn Dooge, for donating her careful proofreading skills and her Game Boy Advance SP; Craig Melhoff, for shawarma and Nintendo news; Katheryne Morrissette for her sage wisdom; my dearest friends Reveena Rothman-Rudnicki and Alex Xanthoudakis, for their endless love and encouragement; and my extended family, Anna Giuliani, John Robertson, and Ron Giuliani, for their much-appreciated reassurances at Sunday dinners. Finally, I want to thank my partner, Travis Wall, who is always there when I most need courage.

Who Are You? was written on the traditional and unceded territory of the Kanien'kehá:ka nation.

Notes

Introduction

1. Arsenault, *Super Power, Spoony Bards, and Silverware: The Super Nintendo Entertainment System,* 193–194.
2. Jones and Thiruvathukal, *Codename Revolution: The Nintendo Wii Platform* (esp. chapter 6).
3. Altice, *I AM ERROR: The Nintendo Family Computer/Entertainment System Platform,* 7.
4. Juul, *A Casual Revolution: Reinventing Video Games and Their Players.*
5. Here, I follow the definitions articulated in Nieborg and Poell, "The Platformization of Cultural Production: Theorizing the Contingent Cultural Commodity," 4276.
6. The term "affordances" is borrowed from the field of human-computer interaction (HCI) studies and describes the perceivable uses of an object. Affordances are materially realized by an object's users.
7. See esp. Raiford Guins, *Game After: A Cultural Study of Videogame Afterlife.*
8. Williams, *Marxism and Literature,* 122.
9. Carolyn Marvin emphasizes the recursive quality of technological innovation: "New media . . . are always introduced into a pattern of tension created by the coexistence of old and new, which is far richer than any single medium that becomes a focus of interest because it is novel." Marvin, *When Old Technologies Were New: Thinking about Electric Communication in the Late Nineteenth Century,* 7–8.
10. See Acland, "Introduction," xx; Hertz and Parikka, "Zombie Media: Circuit Bending Media Archaeology into an Art Method," 429.
11. See Ryan, *Super Mario: How Nintendo Conquered America.* Ryan is far from the only one to reflect on the sheer number of ports the GBA witnessed. Threads on gaming forums frequently feature players complaining about Nintendo being too busy porting games to create new ones.

12. Despite its Greek-sounding name, nostalgia's origins reach only as far back as seventeenth-century Switzerland, when medical student Johannes Hofer introduced the term in his 1688 dissertation to describe what was understood to be an ailment caused by physical displacement from one's homeland. Similar to paranoia and melancholia, its migrant and imprecise symptoms included anxiety, loss of appetite, fainting, cardiac arrest, and even an inclination toward suicide. Fortunately, Hofer determined the condition was curable. Its remedies included leeching, opium consumption, and a return to the Swiss Alps. A prescription to return to retro Nintendo titles sounds altogether more appealing. For a history of nostalgia, see Boym, *The Future of Nostalgia*, esp. 3–8.

13. Boym is not alone in this work; numerous scholars, theorists, and cultural critics have sought to understand the nostalgic attraction to the past that motivates contemporary cultural production. See Benjamin, "The Work of Art in the Age of Its Technological Reproducibility," Baudrillard, *Simulacra and Simulation*, and Adorno and Horkheimer, *Dialectic of Enlightenment: Cultural Memory in the Present*.

14. Boym, *The Future of Nostalgia*, 49.

15. Crigger, "Searching for Gunpei Yokoi."

16. Crigger, "Searching for Gunpei Yokoi."

17. deWinter, *Shigeru Miyamoto: Super Mario Bros., Donkey Kong, The Legend of Zelda*, 15.

18. deWinter, *Shigeru Miyamoto*, 15.

19. Crigger, "Searching for Gunpei Yokoi."

20. deWinter, *Shigeru Miyamoto*, 14.

21. Jones and Thiruvathukal, *Codename Revolution*, 12.

22. It's important to acknowledge that the *Iwata Asks* interview series conducted by Satoru Iwata was produced by Nintendo for the explicit purposes of public relations and marketing. That said, Nintendo is notoriously secretive about their internal history, and these interviews—carefully curated through they may be—nevertheless offer us insight into their hardware and software development processes. Itoi, "Iwata Asks: Super Mario Bros. 25th Anniversary Volume 1."

23. Sheff, *Game Over: How Nintendo Zapped an American Industry, Captured Your Dollars, and Enslaved Your Children*, 51–52.

24. This is my translation. For the full interview in French, see Miyamoto, "Miyamoto, la Wii U et le secret de la Triforce."

25. Iwata, "Iwata Asks: The Legend of Zelda: Ocarina of Time 3D."

26. Miyamoto, "Miyamoto, la Wii U et le secret de la Triforce."

27. *Ocarina of Time* is second only to *Super Mario 64* in offering the clearest examples of the N64 controller's affordances. *Super Mario 64* was developed concurrently with the controller. In fact, for the first six months of the game's creation, there was no controller. Programmers worked instead on Indy emulator boards with a simple serial port that allowed them to control Mario by way of keyboards and modified Sega joypads. Of this process, Nintendo coder Giles Goddard reflects on how *Super Mario 64* and the N64 controller are indebted to each other. While the controller wasn't designed for one game, *Super Mario 64* created a world in which the developers could test-drive what Goddard estimates to have been at least 100 prototypes. See Goddard, "The Making of *Super Mario 64*—Giles Goddard Interview (NGC)."

28. Iwata, "Iwata Asks: *The Legend of Zelda: Ocarina of Time 3D.*"
29. Iwata, "Iwata Asks: The History of Handheld *The Legend of Zelda* Games."
30. Nintendo, NES Classic Edition.
31. For Louis Althusser, ideologies address or hail people, offering them an identity that feels innate or naturalized. Through the ritual of recognition and response, he posits that we become the subjects we always already are. He refers to this process as "interpellation." See Althusser, *Lenin and Philosophy and Other Essays.*
32. Peckham, "Next Link May Not Be a Girl, But He's Androgynous by Design."
33. The dangerous side to this advertising campaign is the way that it anticipates Gamergate, which happens when playing videogames is leveraged into being a gamer as an ontological statement. Women who then identify as gamers—the identification that Nintendo attempts to foster through something like the "Who Are You?" campaign—are then construed as threatening the spaces that white men have come to see as their own, based on historical overrepresentation in the videogame industry. See Chess, *Ready Player Two: Women Gamers and Designed Identity;* and Shaw, *Gaming at the Edge: Sexuality and Gender at the Margins of Gamer Culture.*
34. In 2012, Iwata acknowledged that Nintendo users are split evenly between men and women. See Nintendo, "72nd Annual General Meeting of Shareholders Q&A."
35. Jacobson, *Raising Consumers: Children and the American Mass Market in the Early Twentieth Century*, 114.
36. In a useful study of intended audiences, Adrienne Shaw examines gamer identity through Althusser's concept of interpellation. Specifically, she explores the politics of gaming identity by considering who responds to the hail "Hey gamer." If players don't believe they've been addressed even while they're playing a game, lack of identification with the hail points to a lack of diversity and representation. See Shaw, "On Not Becoming Gamers: Moving Beyond the Constructed Audience."
37. Video Games Central Wikia posted a compilation of the "Who Are You?" GBA SP commercials, including the Japanese-only commercial on June 9 at 2014, which can be found at https://www.youtube.com/watch?v=dfd-71Ty-JU.
38. Lynch, *Loving Literature: A Cultural History*, 22.
39. Turkle, "The Things That Matter," 5.
40. Nakamura, "'Words with Friends': Socially Networked Reading on 'Goodreads,'" 240.
41. Nakamura, "'Words with Friends,'" 240.
42. Henrik, "Wait what?"
43. Chien and Tai, "The Design of a Portable ECG Measurement Instrument Based on a GBA Embedded System," 1782.
44. Rhode, "Portable Modular Diagnostic Medical Device," US Patent 5,876,351.
45. See Montfort, "Continuous Paper: The Early Materiality and Workings of Electronic Literature"; and Kirschenbaum, *Mechanisms: New Media and the Forensic Imagination*, 31.
46. See Hayles, *My Mother Was a Computer: Digital Subjects and Literary Texts*, 108 (emphasis in original).

47. See Winner, "Upon Opening the Black Box and Finding it Empty: Social Constructivism and the Philosophy of Technology," in which he offers a critique of social constructivist approaches to technology.

48. Bogost and Montfort, "Platform Studies: Frequently Questioned Answers."

49. The idea of layers is fundamental to the field. In 2002, Lars Konzack presented a paper at the Computer Games and Digital Cultures conference, in which he outlined a seven-layer "bottom-up" approach to analyzing computer games. These layers formed the basis for the five-layer model that Montfort and Bogost would come to articulate in the afterword of *Racing the Beam: The Atari Video Computer System*: reception/operation, interface, form/function, code, and platform. See Konzack, "Computer Game Criticism: A Method for Computer Game Analysis."

50. See Zielinski, *Deep Time of the Media: Toward an Archaeology of Hearing and Seeing by Technical Means*.

51. Apperley and Parikka, "Platform Studies' Epistemic Threshold."

52. Parikka, *What Is Media Archaeology?*, 2.

53. Parikka, *What Is Media Archaeology?*, 3

54. Williams, *Television: Technology and Cultural Form*, 19.

55. Crigger, "Searching for Gunpei Yokoi."

Chapter 1

1. Between its hardware revisions (DS, DS Lite, DSi, and DSi XL), the DS line sold 154.02 million units. See Nintendo, "Consolidated Sales Transition by Region (as of March 31, 2018)."

2. Peter Main, "Gerard Klauer Mattison Press Conference Presentation."

3. See, for example, Nostalgia Nerd, "Was the GBA Just a Super Nintendo?"

4. Okada, "In the Chair: Satoru Okada," 95.

5. Okada, "In the Chair," 95–96.

6. Okada, "In the Chair," 96.

7. Altice, *I AM ERROR: The Nintendo Family Computer/Entertainment System Platform*, 4.

8. Pan of Anthrox et al., *Game Boy CPU Manual*.

9. Nintendo, "Technical Data: Game Boy, Game Boy Pocket, Game Boy Color."

10. Sheff, *Game Over: How Nintendo Zapped an American Industry, Captured Your Dollars, and Enslaved Your Children*, 295–296.

11. Sheff, *Game Over*, 340–341.

12. Sheff, *Game Over*, 294.

13. Kent, *The Ultimate History of Video Games: From Pong to Pokémon and Beyond—the Story Behind the Craze that Touched Our Lives and Changed the World*, 416.

14. *Electronic Gaming Monthly*, "Nintendo's 32-Bit Color Portable 'Project Atlantis' to Be Ready in Fall"; and *Next Generation*, "Nintendo's New Color Handheld."

15. Okada, "Okada on the Game Boy Advance."

16. Tobin, "Introduction," 6.

17. Okada, "Okada on the Game Boy Advance."

18. Nintendo, "Game Boy Advance Developer Team Interview."

19. van Tilburg, *Curiosity: 30 Designs for Products and Interiors*, 7–9.

20. Nicolas's design partner, Reiko Miyamoto, sees the image of a lion in the handheld. In her eyes, the speakers and their asymmetrically mirrored Start and

Select buttons resemble whiskers and the shoulder triggers look like ears. With a white shell, it's easy to see where the panda comparison comes from. Whether lion or panda, the abstracted comparison to an animal seems to make the hand-held more alive.

21. Nintendo, "Game Boy Advance Developer Team Interview."
22. Nintendo, "Game Boy Advance Developer Team Interview."
23. Nintendo, "Game Boy Advance Developer Team Interview."
24. van Tilburg, *Curiosity*, 108.
25. van Tilburg, *Curiosity*, 108.
26. Nintendo of America, *Nintendo Power: Subscriber Bonus*, 2.
27. By "plays all games," Nintendo means all Game Boy and GBC games.
28. The ARM7TDMI name can be broken down as follows: it runs **ARM 7** code (an implementation of ARMv4T architecture) and has a **T**HUMB mode, a **D**ebug mode, and a **M**ultiplier.
29. ARM Limited, *Technical Reference Manual Revision r4p1*.
30. Nintendo of America, *AGB Programming Manual*, version 1.1.
31. In an interview in the *Nintendo Power Subscriber Bonus*, Steve Okimono, developer relations manager for Nintendo of America, and Dan Kitchen, vice president of handheld development for Majesco, discussed the differences between the Game Boy and the GBA's CPU in such terms.
32. ARM Limited, *Technical Reference Manual*.
33. Okada et al., "Memory for Video Game System and Emulator Using the Memory," US Patent 7,445,551 B1; Korth, *GBATEK*.
34. Okada et al., US Patent 7,445,551 B1; Korth, *GBATEK*.
35. Okada et al., US Patent 7,445,551 B1; Korth, *GBATEK*.
36. Nintendo, "Game Boy Advance Developer Team Interview."
37. Nintendo, "Game Boy Advance Developer Team Interview."
38. Okada, "Okada on the Game Boy Advance."
39. Okada et al., US Patent 7,445,551 B1.
40. Okada et al., "Gaming Machine that Is Useable with Different Game Cartridge Types," US Patent 6,810,463 B2.
41. Crigger, "Searching for Gunpei Yokoi."
42. Korth, *GBATEK*.
43. Okada et al., US Patent 7,445,551 B1.
44. Okada et al., US Patent 7,455,551 B1.
45. However, you can stick a toothpick down there to see the switch flip down.
46. Ernst, *Digital Memory and the Archive*, 61.
47. Ernst, *Digital Memory and the Archive*, 55.
48. Okada et al., US Patent 6,810,463 B2.
49. Okada et al., US Patent 6,810,463 B2.
50. Okada et al., US Patent 6,810,463 B2.
51. Korth, *GBATEK*.
52. Korth, *GBATEK*.
53. Korth, *GBATEK*.
54. Collins, *Game Sound: An Introduction to the History, Theory, and Practice of Video Game Music and Sound Design*, 76.
55. Arsenault, *Super Power, Spoony Bards, and Silverware: The Super Nintendo Entertainment System*, 92–93.

56. Nintendo of America, *AGB Programming Manual*, 25.
57. Although the GBA is often said to support 16-bit color (not to be confused with its 32-bit processing), the sixteenth bit is unused. We can write out the bit pattern as "xbbbbbgggggrrrrr" where "x" is the unused bit and "b," "g," and "r" stand in for blue, green, and red, respectively. It is also more accurate to say that GBA color palettes are written in BGR (blue-green-red) notation rather than the standard RGB (red-green-blue), so, while red is represented as 255, 0, 0 in RGB, it would be written as 0, 0, 255 in BGR. This becomes very important when you decide to program your own GBA game. If you unthinkingly input RGB values for the color teal (82, 181, 165) without swapping the red and blue values, you'll end up with olive green. SNES graphics also used BGR notation.
58. Nintendo, "Changing the Color Palette on Game Boy Advance Systems."
59. Nintendo of America, *Nintendo Power Advance* 1, 10.
60. Nintendo of America, *AGB Programming Manual*, version 1.1.
61. Nintendo, "Technical Data: GameCube."
62. The appropriation of the GBA's retro aesthetic is part of a long tradition of appropriating residual technologies for contemporary artistic practices. In her chapter in *Residual Media*, Michelle Henning cites the politically significant example of the Lomo camera, produced in 1980 by a Soviet optics company, which has experienced a revival as a fashion statement. "Through its renewed fashionability," she writes, "the Lomo becomes, not obsolete or residual, but 'new' in the sense that it enables one to stay ahead in the game of social distinction, and it allows one to feel 'alternative' and different without necessarily taking an oppositional or critical stance." Producing pixel art or cross-stitched portraits in the style of the GBA aspires to render its aesthetic new in terms of social and cultural distinction, even as it appropriates the aesthetic trappings of residual media. See Henning, "New Lamps for Old: Photography, Obsolescence, and Social Change," 57.
63. Nintendo of America, *Nintendo Power Advance* 1, 10.
64. Kline, Dyer-Witheford, and de Peuter, *Digital Play: The Interaction of Technology, Culture, and Marketing*, 169.
65. Korth, *GBATEK*.
66. Takata and Tanaka, "Security System Method and Apparatus for Preventing Application Program Unauthorized Use," US Patent 7,089,427 B1; Okada, "System for Preventing the Use of an Unauthorized External Memory," US Patent 5,134,391.
67. Altice, *I AM ERROR*, 90.
68. Sheff, *Game Over*, 60–70.
69. United States Court of Appeals, *Atari Games Corporation and Tengen Inc. v. Nintendo of America Inc.*
70. United States Court of Appeals, *Sega Enterprises Ltd. v. Accolade, Inc.*
71. United States Court of Appeals, *Sega Enterprises Ltd. v. Accolade, Inc.*
72. United States Court of Appeals, *Sega Enterprises Ltd. v. Accolade, Inc.*
73. Altice, *I AM ERROR*, 111.
74. Altice, *I AM ERROR*, 111.
75. Kohler, "The Secret History of *Super Mario Bros. 2*."
76. Kohler, "The Secret History of *Super Mario Bros. 2*."
77. Outside Japan, the FDS's *Super Mario Bros. 2* became known as *The Lost Levels*.

78. Iwata, "Iwata Asks: Super Mario Developers."
79. Suzuki, Tezuka, and Kimura, "Super Mario Advance."
80. Suzuki et al., "Super Mario Advance."
81. Suzuki et al., "Super Mario Advance."
82. Suzuki et al., "Super Mario Advance."
83. Arsenault, *Super Power*, 107.
84. Arsenault, *Super Power*, 123.
85. Vijn, *Tonc*.

Chapter 2

1. Main, Teleconference Call, my transcription.
2. Main, Teleconference Call, my transcription.
3. I borrow the term "assemblage" from Deleuze and Guattari, *A Thousand Plateaus: Capitalism and Schizophrenia*. The word is a rough translation of the French *agencement*, but for simplicity, I choose to stick with the vocabulary most often used in English translations.
4. In considering technology within this framework, Jennifer Daryl Slack and J. Macgregor Wise state: "Technology as articulation draws attention to the practices, representations, experiences, and affects that constitute technology. Technology as assemblage adds to this understanding by drawing attention to the *ways that these practices, representations, experiences, and affects articulate to take a particular dynamic form*." Slack and Wise, *Culture and Technology: A Primer*, 129 (emphasis in original).
5. Here, "deterritorialization" refers to the disconnection of articulations while "reterritorialization" refers to the formation of new ones. Deleuze and Guattari, *A Thousand Plateaus: Capitalism and Schizophrenia*, 233.
6. Nintendo, "Consolidated Sales Transition by Region (as of March 31, 2018)."
7. Sugino, "Interview: The Man behind the GBA SP."
8. The quote has since been changed on the *Iwata Asks* webpage to "the hardware is just a box you buy only because you want to play games which run on the hardware." The change from "Mario games" to "games which run on the hardware" is revealing about the way that the company has since begun to focus on a broader range of properties. Iwata, "Iwata Asks: Nintendo 3DS Volume 5: Asking Mr. Miyamoto Right Before Release."
9. Norman, *Emotional Design: Why We Love (or Hate) Everyday Things*.
10. Moore, "Cramming More Components onto Integrated Circuits," 114.
11. Mills, "Hearing Aids and the History of Electronics Miniaturization," 74.
12. Sugino, "Interview."
13. Sugino, "Interview."
14. Sterne, "The mp3 as Cultural Artifact," 826.
15. A dozen years before the SP, Sega's Game Gear used a fluorescent tube to facilitate play in low-light conditions. The trade-off was that it used up batteries at an alarmingly rapid rate. Furthermore, Nintendo released a backlit Game Boy in 1998, though it never made its way to retailers outside Japan. The "indiglow" screen (as it was affectionately termed) used an electroluminescent backlight well suited to a monochrome or single-color LCD. But this technology would have caused massive color bleed on the GBC's screen, so backlighting was abandoned until the AGS-101 SP emerged in 2003.

16. Yoshino, "Development of the Lithium-Ion Battery and Recent Technological Trends," 5.
17. At the time, mobile phones often used four LEDs to light the display. To reduce battery drain and avoid having to increase the size of the chassis, the SP used a single LED to create the front-light effect.
18. These elements included the front-lighting system, a thumbwheel potentiometer (for brightness control), black and red wires, a sheet of reflective film, and a resistor.
19. Sugino, "Interview."
20. AGS was the SP's internal name, continuing from the AGB of the previous model. The introductory 2003 model used the code AGS-001. The AGS-101 had two brightness levels, the lowest of which was still brighter than the front-lit AGS-001.
21. At the time of this writing, smartphone users are similarly bitter about Apple, Google, and Samsung's decision to remove the 3.5-mm headphone socket on their mobile phones, replacing it with a USB-C dongle that prevents simultaneous charging and headphone use. Mobile phone users, however, have recourse to Bluetooth technology, whereas SP users were confined to cheap adapters.
22. Iwata, "Iwata Asks: Nintendo 3DS Volume 1: And That's How the Nintendo 3DS Was Made," section 4.
23. Iwata, "Iwata Asks: Nintendo 3DS Volume 1," section 3. They also included stereoscopic 3D support in the GameCube. *Luigi's Mansion* was developed to use this feature, but 3D televisions hadn't yet gained enough popularity to make it cost effective, so nothing came of it (though *Luigi's Mansion* did enjoy a port on the 3DS to realize its initial vision).
24. Kutaragi, Sony E3 2003 Press Conference.
25. The term "console wars" refers to the fierce competition that occurred between Sega and Nintendo in the early 1990s. See Harris, *Console Wars: Sega, Nintendo, and the Battle That Defined a Generation.*
26. Okada, "In the Chair: Satoru Okada," 97.
27. Okada, "In the Chair,"
28. Okada, "In the Chair,"
29. Inoue, *Nintendo Magic: Winning the Videogame Wars,* 168. Yamauchi is often misquoted as having said, "If the DS succeeds, we will rise to heaven, but if it fails, we will sink to hell." His proclamation was not just about the DS, but about their business more generally.
30. OSDL, *A Guide to Homebrew Development for the Nintendo DS.*
31. Iwata, "Interview with Nobuo Kawakami and 4Gamer."
32. Fils-Aime, Nintendo E3 Press Conference.
33. Fils-Aime, Nintendo E3 Press Conference.
34. Jones and Thiruvathukal, *Codename Revolution: The Nintendo Wii Platform,* 28. Inoue makes a similar point in *Nintendo Magic,* 107–112.
35. Iwata, "Iwata Asks: Nintendo DS Volume 4: Asking Iwata."
36. Sugino, "Interview with Game Boy Micro Developer Kenichi Sugino."
37. Fils-Aime, Nintendo E3 Press Conference.
38. Sugino, "Interview with Game Boy Micro Developer."
39. Ngai, *Our Aesthetic Categories: Zany, Cute, Interesting.*
40. Fils-Aime, Nintendo E3 Press Conference.

41. Fils-Aime, Nintendo E3 Press Conference.
42. Nintendo, "Corporate Management Policy Briefing 2006 Q & A. June 7, 2007."
43. Nintendo, Consolidated Sales Transition by Region; Eng, "Game Boy Advance Breaks Sales Records."

Chapter 3

1. DeSpira, "Pac-Man: The Untold Story of How We Really Played the Game."
2. See Gregersen and Grodal, "Embodiment and Interface"; Jones and Thiruvathukal, *Codename Revolution: The Nintendo Wii Platform*; Giddings and Kennedy, "'Incremental Speed Increases Excitement: Bodies, Space, Movement, and Televisual Change.'"
3. Simon, "Wii Are Out of Control: Bodies, Game Screens, and the Production of Gestural Excess."
4. Rambusch, "It's Not Just Hands: Embodiment Aspects in Gameplay," 72; Gallagher, "Body Schema and Intentionality."
5. See Gallagher, *How the Body Shapes the Mind*.
6. Shaun Gallagher observes a distinction between the body image and the body schema. According to Gallagher, the body image is a system of perceptions, beliefs, mental representations, and attitudes relating to one's own body. Conversely, the body schema is a system of sensorimotor abilities and habits that function without awareness or monitoring (Gallagher, *How the Body Shapes the Mind*, 24–25). Given this conceptual distinction, Andreas Gregersen and Torben Grodal posit that playing a videogame "may lead to a sense of extended embodiment and sense of agency that lies somewhere between the two poles of schema and image—it is an *embodied awareness in the moment of action*, a kind of *body image in action*—where one experiences both agency and ownership of virtual entities" (Embodiment and Interface, 67; their emphasis).
7. See Merleau-Ponty, *Phenomenology of Perception*.
8. Studies have found an explicit relationship between tool use and the body schema. According to neuroscientific research, the neurons that respond to somatosensory and visual stimulation can integrate tools within the field linked to the part of the body using the tool. This expansion allows us to perceive the tool as part of our own bodies. See Maravita and Iriki, "Tools for the Body (Schema)."
9. James Paul Gee posits that we effectively *become* virtual characters in a virtual world by way of a "projective stance." While I agree with the proposition that Link becomes an *extension* of ourselves as we navigate Hyrule, I want to be careful in suggesting that he does not become the sum of our experiences with the game world and its hardware. Our auditory, visual, proprioceptive, and somatosensory systems always undergird virtualized experiences. See Gee, "Video Games and Embodiment," 253.
10. *Electronic Gaming Monthly*, "Game Boy Advances," 86.
11. Lateral thinking strikes again with the GBP. Its purpose echoes that of the Super Game Boy peripheral developed in 1994, which offered players the ability to run Game Boy cartridges on their SNES. Because the SNES had neither the Game Boy's native hardware nor the ability to emulate software at full speed, the Super Game Boy cartridge included its own CPU; the SNES was purely there as a conduit for input and output.

12. Nintendo has evidently realized that the size of their handhelds limits their audience to people with healthy vision; the release and commercial success of the 3DS XL line demonstrate that they're looking at a more accessible model to broaden their consumer base.

13. It's amusing to note that the GBP recursively allows ported SNES games to return to console form on an entirely different system. This move foregrounds technological continuity, even while exposing the programming alterations in the game code necessary to their migration to the GBA. The fungibility between home console and handheld device finds its pinnacle in the design of the Switch.

14. See Grodal, *Embodied Visions: Evolution, Emotion, Culture, and Film* (esp. chapter 7), and Grodal, "Stories for Eye, Ear, and Muscles: Video Games, Media, and Embodied Experiences."

15. This doesn't even account for regional refresh rates. While the NTSC standard has a refresh rate of 59.94 Hz, European Phase Alternating Line (PAL) televisions draw their frames at 50 Hz, which has a massive impact on graphics rendering and timekeeping. To account for the GBA's region-free standard, the PAL GBP boot disc has the option to play games in 50 or 60 Hz.

16. Currently, one Amazon seller had the cable listed for around $1,400.

17. As evinced by Extrems's homebrew software intervention, the Game Boy Interface (GBi), which replaces the boot disc, the GBP's latency isn't solely a television problem. Some of it comes from the boot disc software itself, which engages in a process of translation between the GBP and the GameCube. Initially, Extrems found that the standard GBi delivered two to three frames of input lag (32 to 48 ms) on top of what the television display already added—which was more than what the GBP's default boot disc produced. So Extrems developed low latency (at 240p) and ultralow latency (at 480p) to correct for the lag by adjusting refresh rates to match the GBA's 59.73 Hz more closely. Unfortunately, any innate zooming and scaling were sacrificed in the process, making PDP and LCD display reliant on an upscaler, a popular peripheral used by retro videogame players to scale the original resolution of a console up to the resolution of a modern television—yet more hardware on top of the substantial investment in official Nintendo products.

18. Theorists often evoke the parallel of "real" and "virtual" worlds when discussing the relationship between input and in-game action. However, given that the body and mind are really present in the interaction between player and game, I prefer the distinction of "physical" and "virtual."

19. Gregersen and Grodal, "Embodiment and Interface," 69.

20. Rambusch, "It's Not Just Hands," 74.

21. Gregersen and Grodal, "Embodiment and Interface," 71; Norman, *Emotional Design: Why We Love (or Hate) Everyday Things*.

22. This is the default keyboard configuration for the mGBA emulator, for instance.

23. For example, the GBA has four face buttons, two shoulder triggers, and a single D-pad, while the PlayStation Portable (PSP) brings eleven face buttons, two shoulder triggers, a D-pad, and an analog nub similar to those found on some laptops.

24. Swalwell, "Movement and Kinaesthetic Responsiveness: A Neglected Pleasure," 78. See also Morris, "First-Person Shooters—a Game Apparatus," 87.

25. See Fernández-Vara, Zagal, and Mateas, "Evolution of Spatial Configurations in Videogames," 161–164; they note the example of the maze from *The Minish Cap* but provide incorrect directions to complete it.

26. See Rambusch, "It's Not Just Hands," 72; Clark, *Being There: Putting Brain, Body, and World Together Again*.

27. Clark and Chalmers offer the example of Otto, who has Alzheimer's disease and consequently relies on environmental information to structure his life. His notebook, in which he records new information and retrieves old information, performs the role of long-term memory ("The Extended Mind," 12–13).

28. Grodal, *Embodied Visions*, 175.

29. See Lindblom, *Embodied Social Cognition*; Newman, "In Search of the Videogame Player: The Lives of Mario"; Roth, "From Action to Discourse: The Bridging Function of Gestures"; Simon, "Wii Are Out of Control"; Swalwell, "Movement and Kinaesthetic Responsiveness."

30. Newman, "In Search of the Videogame Player," 415.

31. Nintendo of America, *Nintendo Power Advance*, 1, 8.

32. To say the game is Japanese-exclusive is to say that it was never translated. The game runs on any GBA, though, given its lack of region-lock.

33. Iwata, "Iwata Asks: Rhythm Heaven." See also Schultz, "Rhythm Sense: Modality and Enactive Perception in Rhythm Heaven," 267.

34. Iwata, "Iwata Asks: Rhythm Heaven."

35. Schultz, "Rhythm Sense," 254–255.

36. Kaneda, "*Rhythm Heaven*: Video Games, Idols, and Other Experiences of Play," 436.

37. Harris, "WarioWare Twisted Reviewed on GBA."

38. Iwata, "Iwata Asks: WarioWare: Smooth Moves."

39. Juul, *A Casual Revolution: Reinventing Video Games and Their Players*, 10.

40. Iwata, "Iwata Asks: WarioWare: Smooth Moves."

41. Iwata, "Iwata Asks: WarioWare: Smooth Moves."

42. Iwata, "Iwata Asks: Wii Motion Plus."

43. See Jones and Thiruvathukal, *Codename Revolution* (esp. 53–77).

44. Iwata, "Iwata Asks: Wii Motion Plus."

45. NEC/TOKIN, "NEC TOKIN's Piezoelectric Devices."

46. NEC/TOKIN, "NEC TOKIN's Piezoelectric Devices."

47. Rather than use a gyroscope, the Kinect eliminated the need for a controller altogether by using a combination of cameras, microphones, and depth sensors to track players' movements. Unlike Nintendo, Microsoft was aiming for total immersion—the erasure of the interface itself.

48. Newman, "In Search of the Videogame Player," 416.

49. It's only recently that hackers have managed to use the built-in gyroscope hardware contained in most smartphones to support tilt emulation.

50. *WarioWare Gold*, for the 3DS, explicitly acknowledges this connection to Nintendo's earlier endeavors as a toy company by including a digital version of the Ten Billion Barrel in its microgame collection.

51. Inoue, *Nintendo Magic: Winning the Videogame Wars*, 131.

52. Inoue, *Nintendo Magic*, 131.

53. Sheff, *Game Over: How Nintendo Zapped an American Industry, Captured Your Dollars, and Enslaved Your Children*, 20.

Chapter 4

1. Gaonkar and Povinelli, "Technologies of Public Forms: Circulation, Transfigura-tion, Recognition," 388.
2. Lee and LiPuma, "Cultures of Circulation: The Imaginations of Modernity," 192.
3. On the importance of articulating this distinction, see McCrea, "We Play in Public: The Nature and Context of Portable Gaming Systems," 392.
4. Rambusch, "It's Not Just Hands: Embodiment Aspects in Gameplay," 73.
5. In conducting these interviews, I endeavored to include a cross-section of perspectives along the axes of gender, age, and degree of experience playing videogames. Obviously, with such a local sample, the information I have col-lected is hardly representative of global GBA play, but it nevertheless invites consideration of how radically play can vary from person to person. Although it results in stylistic inconsistencies, I refer to my interviewees here by the name or nickname that they prefer to be called. Throughout this chapter, I cite each interviewee in parentheses after quoting them.
6. See Levy, *Hackers: Heroes of the Computer Revolution*; Coleman and Dyer-Witheford, "Playing on the Digital Commons: Collectivities, Capital, and Contestation in Videogame Culture," 936.
7. Brand, "Spacewar: Fanatic Life and Symbolic Death among the Computer."
8. See Donovan, *Replay: The History of Video Games*; Herz, *Joystick Nation: How Vid-eogames Gobbled Our Money, Won Our Hearts and Rewired Our Minds*; Burnham, *Supercade: A Visual History of the Videogame Age, 1971–1984*; Harris, *Console Wars: Sega, Nintendo, and the Battle That Defined a Generation*; Kent, *The Ultimate History of Video Games: From Pong to Pokémon and Beyond—the Story behind the Craze That Touched Our Lives and Changed the World*.
9. Okada, "In the Chair: Satoru Okada," 95.
10. Harris, "Game Boy Advance's $25 Million Launch."
11. Parikka and Suominen, "Victorian Snakes? Towards a Cultural History of Mobile Games and the Experience of Movement."
12. Huhtamo, "Pockets of Plenty: An Archaeology of Mobile Media," 28–34.
13. Schivelbusch, *Railway Journey: The Industrialization of Time and Space in the Nine-teenth Century*, 54.
14. Schivelbusch, *Railway Journey*, 66.
15. Schivelbusch, *Railway Journey*, 68.
16. Huhtamo, "Slots of Fun, Slots of Trouble: An Archaeology of Arcade Gaming."
17. See Flichy, *Dynamics of Modern Communication. The Shaping and Impact of New Communication Technologies*.
18. Williams, *Television: Technology and Cultural Form*, 19 (emphasis in original).
19. Hjorth and Richardson, *Gaming in Social, Locative, and Mobile Media*, 35.
20. Hjorth and Richardson, *Gaming in Social, Locative, and Mobile Media*, 35.
21. du Gay, Hall, Janes, Mackay, and Negus, *Doing Cultural Studies: The Story of the Sony Walkman*, 15–16.
22. Ngai, "The Cuteness of the Avant-Garde," 819.
23. Chow, "Listening Otherwise, Music Miniaturized: A Different Type of Question about Revolution," 114–115.
24. Bull, "The Seduction of Sound in Consumer Culture," 90.
25. Kogawa, "Beyond Electronic Individualism."

26. Ito, Okabe, and Matsuda, "Introduction," 1–2.
27. Hjorth and Richardson, *Gaming in Social, Locative, and Mobile Media*, 38.
28. Fujimoto, "The Third-Stage Paradigm: Territory Machines from the Girls' Pager Revolution to Mobile Aesthetics," 80–83.
29. The gray-and-purple cable is compatible with the GBA, SP, and GBP. Due to its small size, the Micro has its own version.
30. Allison, "Portable Monsters and Commodity Cuteness: Pokémon as Japan's New Global Power," 388–389.
31. McCrea, "We Play in Public," 398.
32. There's another niche use of the link cable: to disseminate game patches. Over the course of a game's life, it might use several versions as developers try to address bugs and other issues. Early versions of *Ruby* and *Sapphire*, for instance, were subject to what's known as the "Berry glitch," named for the way that Berries planted in the game ceased to grow 366 days after the game was first started, or 366 days after the internal battery was replaced. The glitch occurred due to the real-time clock's conversion function. While developers eventually fixed the bug, they had to figure out a way to disseminate that patch to players who had already purchased the game. One method was to have the player link to a GBA running *FireRed*, *LeafGreen*, or *Emerald* while holding the Select and B buttons; that would prompt the Berry Program Update to download and patch the glitch. Like a virus, the patch moved from GBA to GBA, infecting each with a solution to the Berry problem. Linking to *Pokémon Colosseum* on the GameCube with a separate link cable simarly patched the game.
33. Again, the Micro has a separate Wireless Adapter peripheral, OXY-004.
34. *Emerald* also supported the wireless adapter, but it had to be purchased separately from the game.
35. Nintendo, "Game Boy Advance or Game Boy Micro Wireless Adapter FAQ."
36. Nintendo, "Tips for Setting Up StreetPass."
37. Witkowski, "Cooperative Play," 91.
38. Jakobsson, "Adversarial Couch Co-Op: Joshing and Griefing in Co-Located Cooperative Gaming."
39. Tobin, *Portable Play in Everyday Life: The Nintendo DS*, 106.
40. See Kaneda, "*Rhythm Heaven*: Video Games, Idols, and Other Experiences of Play."
41. Ito, Okabe, and Anderson, "Portable Objects in Three Global Cities: The Personalization of Urban Places," 73.
42. See Hjorth and Richardson, "The Waiting Game: Complication Notions of (Tele)presence and Gendered Distraction in Casual Mobile Gaming," 29–30, for notes on mobile gaming as being characterized by "sporadic or split attention."
43. Chesher, "Neither Gaze nor Glance, but Glaze: Relating to Console Game Screens."
44. Chan, "Convergence, Connectivity, and the Case of Japanese Mobile Gaming" 23.
45. Kaneda, "*Rhythm Heaven*," 442.
46. Kaneda, "*Rhythm Heaven*," 442.
47. Yasumoto-Nicolson, "Gaming in Japan."
48. Ozaki, "Housing as a Reflection of Culture: Privatised Living and Privacy in England and Japan," 223.

49. Bovill and Livingstone, "Bedroom Culture and the Privatization of Media Use," 179.
50. Cunningham, "*Mortal Kombat* and Computer Game Girls," 217.
51. The use of Nintendo products as a way to ignore women is a recurrent theme when it comes to selling the platform. A Walmart ad for the SP featured a straight teenage couple dancing; the girl rests her head contently against her partner's chest while he secretly plays on an SP behind her back, with the word "escape" hovering above the illuminated screen.
52. Schott and Thomas, "The Impact of Nintendo's 'For Men' Advertising Campaign on a Potential Female Market," 51.
53. Harris, "E3 2003: Kojima Loves the Sun."
54. Thunderbird8, forum comment.
55. The Japanese version was released as ボクらの太陽 Django & Sabata (*Bokura no Taiyō: Django & Sabata*).

Chapter 5

1. See GitHub, "Process DMCA Request."
2. See Ernesto, "Nintendo Shuts Down Browser-Based Game Boy Emulator," and Andy, "Nintendo Nukes Hugely Popular iOS Game Boy Emulator."
3. See Ernesto, "Nintendo Sues Console ROM Sites for 'Mass' Copyright Infringement (Update)."
4. United States District Court for the District of Arizona, *Nintendo of America Inc. v. Jacob Mathias, Mathias Designs, and Cristian Mathias.*
5. *TorrentFreak* obtained an unsigned copy of the final judgment, which is available at https://torrentfreak.com/images/romsjudg.pdf.
6. *EmuParadise*, "EmuParadise Is Changing."
7. In September 2017, Nintendo announced that the Wii Shop Channel would close on January 30, 2019. As of March 26, 2018, players could spend their remaining account balance, but they couldn't add Nintendo points using a credit card or Nintendo shop card. See Nintendo, "Wii Shop Channel Discontinuation."
8. Nintendo, E3 2005 Press Conference.
9. Darren Wershler first used the phrase "platformization of nostalgia" to describe Nintendo's concentration of decades of personal and public engagement with their games and game systems into a narrow channel in a blog post on residualmedia.net. This way of thinking about Nintendo's business strategies emerged in part out of a larger research project on modified Wii consoles, which he and I have been working on in the Residual Media Depot along with Abbie Rappaport, Kieran Airee-Lee, and Cody Walker.
10. The authors develop a three-pronged framework for studying this platformization using the theoretical perspectives of: business studies, which typically rely on a transactional perspective and treat platforms as static objects; political economy, which is concerned with power and politics but rarely considers network effects relating to platform infrastructure; and software studies, which attend to the connections between technologies and understand platforms as fluid rather than fixed, but often elide questions of cultural production and commodities. By triangulating these perspectives, they consider the industry-specific shaping of cultural expression with a focus on power relations and issues

11. around the agency of cultural producers. Nieborg and Poell, "The Platformization of Cultural Production: Theorizing the Contingent Cultural Commodity."

11. Nieborg and Poell, "The Platformization of Cultural Production," 4287.

12. Nieborg and Poell, "The Platformization of Cultural Production," 4284.

13. Nathan Altice's *I AM ERROR: The Nintendo Family Computer/Entertainment System Platform* seems to be the exception, not the rule.

14. Guins, *Game After: A Cultural Study of Videogame Afterlife*, 36.

15. Benjamin, "The Work of Art in the Age of Its Technological Reproducibility," 24.

16. Nintendo, "Legal Information (Copyrights, Emulators, ROMs, etc.)."

17. United States Court of Appeals for the Ninth Circuit, *Sony Computer Entertainment v. Connectix Corporation*.

18. *Sony Computer Entertainment v. Connectix Corporation*.

19. *Sony Computer Entertainment v. Connectix Corporation*.

20. Link, "Hand-Held Video Game Platform Emulation," US Patent No. 8,795,090 B2. Nintendo Co. Ltd. is the patent's assignee.

21. *Sony Computer Entertainment v. Connectix Corporation*.

22. Two versions of the e-Reader were released in Japan. The first, known as the Card e-Reader, didn't include linking capabilities. A second version, the Card e-Reader+, with linking capabilities, was released shortly afterward. This was the version that made it to North America.

23. Epoch's Barcode Battler handheld gaming console is the obvious inspiration for and ancestor of the e-Reader. The device sold at retail with a handful of cards, each with its own barcode that, when swiped, gave players different characters, power-ups, or enemies to fight. The barcodes' ubiquity encouraged players to experiment with scanning mundane objects around the home to see what might come up. Although the gameplay was repetitive and uneventful—especially compared to the Game Boy, beside which it was often placed in stores—something about the act of turning the barcodes from household objects into warriors and upgrades captured the interest of Japanese players, even if most of the rest of the world remained unimpressed. Due to a combination of the Barcode Battler's popularity in Japan and Epoch's professional relationship with Nintendo, the two companies collaborated to make the most of the technology. In addition to releasing special-edition *Super Mario* and *Zelda* cards, Nintendo licensed a Barcode Battler II interface that connected to the Famicom and Super Famicom to scan barcodes into certain console games (not unlike how the link cable allows the e-Reader to scan *Animal Crossing*-e cards into the GameCube *Animal Crossing*). Epoch designed a dozen games for the Famicom and Super Famicom to use this interface.

24. Game & Watch titles were also made playable on the e-Reader, though only *Manhole* was released outside Japan.

25. Nintendo, "Virtual Console Games."

26. "How Far Can You Get Your Gamepad from the Wii U."

27. Gitelman, *Always Already New: Media, History, and the Data of Culture*, 7.

28. Consalvo, *Cheating: Gaining Advantage in Videogames*, 21–22.

29. See *Super Mario Advance 2* in the eShop.

30. Parks and Starosielski, *Signal Traffic: Critical Studies of Media Infrastructures*, 13.

31. Nintendo, "Wii Shop Channel Discontinuation."

32. 17 U.S.C. § 109, "Limitations on Exclusive Rights: Effect of Transfer of Particular Copy or Phonorecord."

33. By various in-game and peripheral means, including e-Reader cards and give-aways on Nintendo's website, players could collect up to fifteen fully playable NES games, some of which could be temporarily downloaded to the GBA in Advance Play mode using the Game Boy Advance Game Link Cable. There were limitations to Advance Play. For one thing, the GBA's display resolution skewered the graphics. For another, games larger than 192 KB and games released for the Family Computer Disk System (FDS) couldn't be transferred because their size exceeded the GBA's RAM. Nevertheless, through *Animal Crossing,* players could access a selection of NES titles to run on the platform of their choosing without paying for each one individually.

34. endrift, "Classic NES Series Anti-Emulation Measures."

35. Kawase, "Game Emulator Program," US Patent No. 7,025,677.

36. This wouldn't be the last time that Nintendo pilfered from hobbyists, proving that they're perfectly happy to exploit the work of fans one minute and launch a vicious lawsuit against them the next. NES and SNES games purchased through the Virtual Console contain iNES and SMC headers, bits of information inserted at the beginning of a ROM dump (the extraction of ROM files from their cartridges) to explain details about the cartridge hardware to the emulator. iNES and SMC headers are hobbyist tools, standards developed by the emulation community in the late 1990s. In a brilliant talk at the Game Developers Conference (GDC) in 2006, Frank Cifaldi shows side-by-side images of the opening lines of code of two versions of *Super Mario Bros.*: one timestamped 1996, which he downloaded from the internet, and the other from the Virtual Console. The code was identical. "I would posit," he said to an audience who had already began to chuckle, "that Nintendo downloaded *Super Mario Bros.* from the internet and sold it back to you . . . Nintendo is pirating its own ROMS." Because Nintendo programmer Tomohiro Kawase is rumored to have collaborated on unofficial emulators before coming to work at Nintendo, the presence of the iNES header doesn't provide irrefutable proof that Nintendo downloaded games from where they have long circulated online. But it does indicate that Nintendo was aware of the hobbyist practices and found them useful enough to appropriate for their own systems. See Cifaldi, "'It's Just Emulation'—the Challenge of Selling Old Games."

37. *Boktai* players can also input information on the current weather—if it's night at the moment of playing, the game will prevent the Sun from shining in the virtual environment—based on nothing more than the honor system. The emulator's ReadMe asks players to "please set the weather honestly or it spoils the fun."

38. Although Link is famously left-handed, the Wii's mimetic interface prompted developers to make him right-handed in *The Legend of Zelda: Twilight Princess* and *The Legend of Zelda: Skyward Sword* to account for the fact that the majority of people are right-handed.

39. Special Wii controls exist for games in the *Super Mario, Mario Kart: Super Circuit, Metroid, Mortal Kombat,* and *Harry Potter* series, among others.

40. Inoue, *Nintendo Magic: Winning the Videogame Wars,* 72–73.

41. *NES Remix* (*Famicom Remix* in Japan) is the first installment of a compilation videogame series. The game draws assets and mechanics from sixteen retro NES

games, with a total of 204 playable challenges that reshape or recombine original titles. For instance, one challenge involves playing a stage in *Donkey Kong* as Link rather than Jumpman, despite the Hylian's inability to leap over barrels. Another requires racing through a track in *Excitebike* guided only by a spotlight or speedrunning through a stage in *Super Mario Bros.*

42. Boluk and LeMieux, *Metagaming: Playing Competing, Spectating, Cheating, Trading, Making, and Breaking Videogames*, 15.
43. Boluk and LeMieux, *Metagaming*, 47.
44. Consalvo, *Cheating: Gaining Advantage in Videogames*, 4.
45. Consalvo, *Cheating*, 114.
46. Gach, "Newly Discovered Trick."
47. Players can also load patched ROMs onto a flash cartridge and run it off the 2001 hardware, but there are a few reasons why the community by and large prefers emulation. For one thing, reliable flash cartridges are expensive. For another, these games can become much more challenging than the source games due to the randomization, so save state capabilities come in handy. But most important, these randomized gameplay experiences are designed to be shared within the community. It's much easier to livestream off a personal computer.
48. Iantorno, "Generate Randomized Game."
49. Maiberg, "Nintendo's Offensive, Tragic, and Totally Legal Erasure of ROM Sites."
50. van der Ende et al., *Global Online Piracy Study*.
51. Fils-Aime, "Nintendo of America President on Switch's Big Risk. 'Smash Bros.' Success and Classic Consoles' Future." In 2011, Nintendo CEO Satoru Iwata declared:

> [Mobile gaming] is absolutely not under consideration. If we did this, Nintendo would cease to be Nintendo. It's probably the correct decision in the sense that the moment we started to release games on smartphones, we'd make profits. However, I believe my responsibility is not to short-term profits, but to Nintendo's mid- and long-term competitive strength.

As it happens, the profits that Iwata describes won out over Nintendo's brand, which was subsequently reframed to include casual mobile games and gamers. See Gilbert, "The History behind Nintendo's Flip-Flop on Mobile Gaming."
52. The NES app for the Switch Online is essentially a port of the emulator used in the NES Classic Edition.
53. KapuccinoHeck, "I was finally able to look around the NES Online's strings a bit myself."
54. Nintendo, "Legal Information."
55. *The Film Foundation*, "Film Preservation."

Chapter 6

1. Catanese, "The Evolution of a GBA Artist."
2. Catanese, "The Evolution of a GBA Artist," 127–128.
3. Catanese, "The Evolution of a GBA Artist," 129.
4. Apperley and Parikka, "Platform Studies' Epistemic Threshold," 354.

5. Zielinski, *Deep Time of the Media: Toward an Archaeology of Hearing and Seeing by Technical Means*, 360. In a recent article in *Games and Culture*, Thomas Apperley and Jussi Parikka argue that a limited approach to creative expression often results in a failure to make the most of what the platform studies model has to offer. Zielinski's media anarchaeology is one of the ways that they suggest theories and practices of media archaeology can enrich the field to deepen our understanding of the platform. See Apperley and Parikka, "Platform Studies' Epistemic Threshold."

6. Camper, "Homebrew and the Social Construction of Gaming: Community, Creativity, and Legal Context of Amateur Game Boy Advance Development."

7. Camper, "Homebrew," 133.

8. Camper, "Homebrew," 134.

9. See Jenkins, Ito, and boyd, *Participatory Culture in a Networked Era: A Conversation on Youth, Learning, Commerce, and Politics*.

10. Vijn, *Tonc*.

11. Vijn, *Tonc*.

12. Douglas, *Listening In: Radio and the American Imagination*, 72 (emphasis in original).

13. Douglas, *Inventing American Broadcasting, 1899–1922*, 205.

14. Camper, "Homebrew," 24.

15. Cited in Camper, "Homebrew," 29.

16. Mode 7 was one of the most notable selling points of the SNES. The ability to project a 2D plane into the horizon radically changed the racing game genre because players could now see the track extend in front of them.

17. Camper, "Homebrew," 68–69.

18. gbadev.org, "About."

19. gbadev.org, "5 Million Visitors & 8 Years Online."

20. gbadev.org, "5 Million Visitors."

21. Barbrook, "The High-Tech Gift Economy."

22. Terranova. "Free Labor: Producing Culture for the Digital Economy."

23. Scott, "Repackaging Fan Culture: The Regifting Economy of Ancillary Content Models."

24. Camper, "Homebrew," 43–44.

25. Kline, Dyer-Witheford, and De Peuter, *Digital Play: The Interaction of Technology, Culture, and Marketing*, 112–113.

26. There are other, niche ways for homebrew games to circulate. A hacker named Tim Scheurewegen cracked the e-Reader dot code to print homebrew data onto a piece of paper that could be swiped through the peripheral. But due to the e-Reader's lack of widespread success, this is not the most popular way to circulate homebrew applications.

27. Nintendo, "Legal Information (Copyrights, Emulators, ROMs, etc.)."

28. 17 U.S.C. § 117, "Limitations on Exclusive Rights: Computer Programs."

29. Camper, "Homebrew," 107.

30. Nintendo, "Legal Information."

31. gbadev.org, "2004Mbit."

32. Jenkins, *Textual Poachers: Television Fans and Participatory Culture*, 160.

33. gbadev.org, "5 Million Visitors."

34. FAST6191, *GBA and DS ROM Hacking Guide—2016 Edition*, 3 (emphasis mine).

35. See Nieborg and van der Graaf, "The Mod Industries? The Industrial Logic of Non-Market Game Production," and Sotamaa, "'Have Fun Working with Our Product!' Critical Perspectives on Computer Game Mod Competitions."

36. FAST6191, *GBA and DS ROM Hacking Guide—2016 Edition*, 4.

37. Huhtamo, "Game Patch: The Son of Scratch."

38. Kirtz, "Beyond the Blackbox: Repurposing ROM Hacking for Feminist Hacking/Making Practices."

39. Music trackers are a type of sequencer in which music is represented as discrete notes in chronological positions on a vertical timeline (as opposed to waves on a horizontal timeline).

40. FAST6191, *GBA and DS ROM Hacking Guide—2016 Edition*, 13.

41. It's difficult to pin down an exact date for the patch file's release, much less a definitive final version of the patch itself, due to a process known as *versioning*. Over the course of the development cycle, a game is released in intermediate versions to obtain player feedback. Although Blazer announced a completed patch on August 8, 2012, earlier work-in-progress versions had circulated years prior, and the game has been updated as recently as 2017.

42. Blazer (Crimson Red), "The Last Promise."

43. r/fireemblem. "People's Actual Thoughts on the Last Promise?"

44. lizzledpink and glitteringworlds, "Restoration Queen."

45. Analogs to this project exist across fandoms. For instance, *Minish Cap Zelda* is a player sprite hack that changes Link into a playable Zelda. *Harvest Moon: Friends of Mineral Town, True Love Edition* swaps Clair (the girl) and Pete (the boy) into each other's games to queer the relationships. Its creator explains that the project resonates on a personal level: "If I really wanted a game where I can be myself, where I am allowed to make the choices I wanted to make, I would have to take it upon myself to make that happen. Falling in love is my favorite part of any *Harvest Moon* game, and for the first time, everything feels right." kataiki, "FOMT-TL."

46. Jordan, "From Rule-Breaking to ROM-Hacking: Theorizing the Computer Game-as-Commodity," 709.

47. Jenkins, "Interactive Audiences? The 'Collective Intelligence' of Media Fans," 167.

48. Due in part to bad timing and poor marketing, *Radiant Dawn* failed to meet the expectations of Nintendo's sales department. *Fire Emblem: Awakening* was to be the series' coda, but its immediate success in both Japan and the West resuscitated the series, and it has gone on to become one of Nintendo's most profitable IP.

49. "The Last Promise Is Out!"

50. Fan translations of *The Binding Blade* often circulate under the title *Fire Emblem: The Sword of Seals*, an alternative translation of the Japanese *Fūin no Tsurugi*. *The Binding Blade* later became the preferred translation and is used by Nintendo on the *Fire Emblem Heroes* website.

51. Consalvo, *Atari to Zelda: Japan's Videogames in Global Contexts*, esp. 41–64.

52. Jair, "Text Hacking/Translation Tutorial."

53. Hong and Chen, "Becoming an Ideal Co-Creator: Web Materiality and Intensive Laboring Practices in Game Modding," 291.

54. Omni, "Fire Emblem: Maiden of Darkness."

55. Blazer only ever called the hack "The Last Promise." By adding "Fire Emblem" to the title, Retro Gamer US rhetorically positions *The Last Promise* as a more canonical entry in the series.

56. Kelso, "The Game Boy Advance: A Personal Retrospective."

57. Kelso, "The Game Boy Advance."

58. Kelso, "The Game Boy Advance."

59. Kelso, "The Game Boy Advance."

60. Turkle, *Life on the Screen: Identity in the Age of the Internet*, 34.

61. Olivier, interview with author, February 20, 2019.

62. An optional ten-step brightness controller requires soldering three wires.

63. Olivier, interview with author.

64. Marvin, *When Old Technologies Were New: Thinking about Electric Communication in the Late Nineteenth Century*, 14.

65. Federal Court of Canada, *Nintendo of America Inc. v. King*.

66. Federal Court of Canada, *Nintendo of America Inc. v. King*, paragraph 121.

67. Grand, *Game Console Hacking: Have Fun while Voiding Your Warranty*, xxvii.

68. Foucault, *The Order of Things: An Archaeology of the Human Sciences*. As an example of a cultural technique, Bernhard Siegert discusses the door, which is "both a material object and a symbolic thing" used to create a distinction between what's inside and what's outside. See Siegert, "Cultural Techniques: Or the End of the Intellectual Postwar Era in German Media Theory," 13.

69. Siegert, "Cultural Techniques," xxvii.

70. Freeplay Tech frames the Freeplay Zero (formerly known as the Game Pie Advance) as "a full-blown computer . . . made to fit inside a retro gaming console cabinet." Thus far, their projects use GBA shells exclusively. See Game Pie Advance/Freeplay Zero.

71. "Freeplay Zero/Freeplay CM3."

72. dbak85, "GBA-xl, a Custom 3D Printed Gameboy Advance."

73. Hewer and Brownlie, "On Market Forces and Adjustments: Acknowledging Consumer Creativity Through the Aesthetics of 'Debadging'," 429.

74. Hewer and Brownlie, "On Market Forces," 434.

75. Simon, "Geek Chic: Machine Aesthetics, Digital Gaming, and the Cultural Politics of the Case Mod," 186.

76. Consider, for instance, the tired trope of men who name their cars after women. By participating in the degradation of women, the "geeks"—as Simon labels PC case modders—can align themselves with the masculinist hot-rodders, thereby accruing social capital.

77. Wajcman, *TechnoFeminism*, 44.

78. Wajcman, *Feminism Confronts Technology*, 19.

79. Chun, *Control and Freedom*, 12.

80. Kirtz, "Beyond the Blackbox."

81. Of course, this is not to say that women do not mod or hack, but rather that these infrastructures make modding and hacking difficult and somewhat transgressive acts for women. In "Beyond the Blackbox," Kirtz offers an analysis of feminist ROM hacks.

82. See Hertz and Parikka, "Zombie Media: Circuit Bending Media Archaeology into an Art Method."

83. Zielinski, *Deep Time of the Media: Toward an Archaeology of Hearing and Seeing by Technical Means*, 260.

Conclusion

1. Hertz and Parikka, "Zombie Media: Circuit Bending Media Archaeology into an Art Method," 425.
2. Parks, "Falling Apart: Electronics Salvaging and the Global Media Economy."
3. Parks, "Falling Apart," 36–37.
4. Gabrys, *Digital Rubbish: A Natural History of Electronics*, 4.
5. Parks and Starosielski, *Signal Traffic: Critical Studies of Media Infrastructures*, 5.
6. Nguyen, "Queer Cyborgs and New Mutants," 300.
7. Dyer-Witheford, "Nintendo Capitalism: Enclosures and Insurgencies, Virtual and Terrestrial," 982.
8. Dyer-Witheford, "Nintendo Capitalism," 987.
9. Sarkar, "Nintendo Says Foxconn Taking 'Full Responsibility for Hiring Underage Workers at Supply Factory.'"
10. Shigeru Miyamoto, "Interview."
11. Katayama, *Japanese Business into the 21st Century*, 168.
12. Katayama, *Japanese Business into the 21st Century*.
13. Hertz and Parikka, "Zombie Media," 426.
14. One of Nintendo's early slogans for the GBA in North America was "Life, advanced." It was quickly superseded by the "Who Are You?" campaign.
15. Olivier, interview with author.

Bibliography

Game Cartridges/Discs/Cards, Virtual Console Downloads, and ROMs

Advance Wars. Wii U Virtual Console (eShop Download). Intelligent Systems. NA: Nintendo, April 2014.

Animal Crossing. GameCube (GameCube Game Disc). Nintendo EAD. NA: Nintendo, September 2002.

Animal Crossing-e. Series 1. e-Reader (dot code e-card, set of 60). Nintendo. NA: Nintendo, October 2002.

Boktai: The Sun Is in Your Hand. Game Boy Advance (GBA Game Pak). Konami Computer Entertainment Japan. NA: Konami, June 2003.

Boktai 2: Solar Boy Django. Game Boy Advance (GBA Game Pak). Konami Computer Entertainment Japan. NA: Konami, October 2004.

Boktai 3: Sabata's Counterattack (新 • ボクらの太陽 逆襲のサバタ, *Shin Bokura no Taiyō: Gyakushū no Sabata*). Game Boy Advance (GBA Game Pak). Konami Computer Entertainment Japan. NA: Konami, July 2005.

Brain Age: Train Your Brain in Minutes a Day! Nintendo DS. (DS Game Card). Nintendo SPD, inspired by Dr. Kawashima. Canada: Shinya Takahashi, April 2006.

Castlevania: Circle of the Moon. Game Boy Advance (GBA Game Pak). Konami Computer Entertainment Kobe. NA: Konami, June 2001.

Castlevania: Harmony of Dissonance. Game Boy Advance (GBA Game Pak). Konami Computer Entertainment Tokyo. NA: Konami, September 2002.

Demo Mode 7: Waterfall. GBA ROM. Debray Matthieu. February 2, 2004. Visual Boy Advance. http://www.gbadev.org/demos.php?showinfo=597.

Donkey Kong Jr.-e. e-Reader (dot-code e-card, set of 5). Nintendo. NA: Nintendo, September 2002.

Doom. Game Boy Advance (GBA Game Pak). id Software (ported by David A. Palmer Productions). NA: Activision, October 2001.

Drill Dozer. Game Boy Advance (GBA Game Pak). Game Freak. NA: Nintendo, February 2006.

Excitebike-e. e-Reader (dot-code e-card, set of 5). Nintendo. NA: Nintendo, September 2002.

F8 Creature Campaign Reverse Recruitment. ROM patch file. Katie. Version 3.2, April 28, 2016. Visual Boy Advance. https://www.dropbox.com/s/1jvmomml3leh8nf/FE8%20CC%20RR%20v3.2.ups?dl=0.

Final Fantasy IV Advance. Game Boy Advance (GBA Game Pak). Squaresoft (ported by Tose). NA: Nintendo, December 2005.

Final Fantasy V Advance. Game Boy Advance (GBA Game Pak). Square (ported by Tose). NA: Nintendo, November 2006.

Final Fantasy VI Advance. Game Boy Advance (GBA Game Pak). Square (ported by Tose). NA: Nintendo, February 2007.

Fire Emblem (ファイアーエムブレム 烈火の剣, *Fire Emblem: The Blazing Blade*). Game Boy Advance (GBA Game Pak). Intelligent Systems (localized by Nintendo Treehouse). NA: Nintendo, November 2003.

Fire Emblem: Awakening. Nintendo DS (DS Game Card). Intelligent Systems (localized by 8-4). NA: Nintendo, February 2013.

Fire Emblem: The Binding Blade (ファイアーエムブレム封印の剣, alternately translated as *The Sword of Seals*) Game Boy Advance (GBA Game Pak). Intelligent Systems. JP: Nintendo, March 2002.

Fire Emblem Heroes. Android, iOS (downloadable application). Intelligent Systems and Nintendo EPD. International: Nintendo, February 2017.

Fire Emblem: Path of Radiance. GameCube (GameCube Game Disc). Intelligent Systems. NA: Nintendo, October 2005.

Fire Emblem: Radiant Dawn. Wii (Wii Optical Disc). Intelligent Systems (localized by Nintendo Treehouse). NA: Nintendo, November 2007.

Fire Emblem: The Sacred Stones. Game Boy Advance (GBA Game Pak). Intelligent Systems (localized by Nintendo Treehouse). NA: Nintendo, May 2005.

Fractal. GBA ROM. Jimmy Mårdell (Yarin). February 2, 2002. Visual Boy Advance. http://www.gbadev.org/demos.php?showinfo=346.

Harvest Moon: Friends of Mineral Town, True Love Edition. ROM patch files (boys, girls). kataiki. Version 4.0. September 7, 2014. Visual Boy Advance. https://kataiki.tumblr.com/FOMT-TL#_=_.

Ice Climber-e. e-Reader (dot-code e-card, set of 5). Nintendo. NA: Nintendo, November 2002.

Kirby: Nightmare in Dream Land. Game Boy Advance (GBA Game Pak). HAL Laboratory. NA: Nintendo, December 2002.

Kirby Tilt 'n' Tumble. Game Boy Advance (GBA Game Pak). Nintendo R&D2. NA: Nintendo, April 2001.

Koro Koro Puzzle Happy Panechu! (コロコロパズル ハッピィパネッチュ!). Game Boy Advance (GBA Game Pak). Mobile 21 and Nintendo R&D2. JP: Nintendo, March 2002.

The Last Promise. Fire Emblem ROM patch file. Blazer. Last modified August 8, 2017. Visual Boy Advance. https://www.romhacking.net/hacks/962.

The Legend of Zelda. Nintendo Entertainment System (NES Game Pak). Nintendo EAD. NA: Nintendo, July 1987.

The Legend of Zelda: A Link to the Past and Four Swords. Game Boy Advance (GBA Game Pak). Nintendo and Capcom. NA: Nintendo, December 2002.

The Legend of Zelda: Link's Awakening. Game Boy (Game Boy Game Pak). Nintendo EAD. NA: Nintendo, August 1993.

The Legend of Zelda: Four Swords Adventures. GameCube (GameCube Game Disc). Nintendo EAD. NA: Nintendo, June 2004.

The Legend of Zelda: Majora's Mask. Nintendo 64 (N64 Game Pak). Nintendo EAD. NA: Nintendo, October 2000.

The Legend of Zelda: Ocarina of Time. Nintendo 64 (N64 Game Pak). Nintendo EAD. NA: Nintendo, November 1998.

The Legend of Zelda: Oracle of Ages. Game Boy Color (GBC Game Pak). Capcom and Flagship. NA: Nintendo, May 2001.

The Legend of Zelda: Oracle of Seasons. Game Boy Color (GBC Game Pak). Capcom and Flagship. NA: Nintendo, May 2001.

The Legend of Zelda: Phantom Hourglass. Nintendo DS (DS Game Card). Nintendo EAD. NA: Nintendo, October 2007.

The Legend of Zelda: Skyward Sword. Wii (Wii Optical Disc). Nintendo EAD. NA: Nintendo, November 2011.

The Legend of Zelda: The Minish Cap. Game Boy Advance (GBA Game Pak). Capcom and Flagship. NA: Nintendo, January 2005.

The Legend of Zelda: The Wind Waker. GameCube (GameCube Game Disc). Nintendo EAD. NA: Nintendo, March 2003.

The Legend of Zelda: Twilight Princess. Wii (Wii Optical Disc). Nintendo EAD. NA: Nintendo, November 2006.

Luigi's Mansion. GameCube. (GameCube Game Disc). Nintendo EAD. NA: Nintendo, November 2001.

Luigi's Mansion. Nintendo 3DS. (3DS Game Card). Nintendo EAD. NA: Nintendo, October 2018.

Lunar Knights. Nintendo DS (DS Game Card). Kojima Productions. NA: Konami, February 2007.

Manhole-e. e-Reader (dot-code e-card). Nintendo R&D1. NA: Nintendo, 2002, packaged with e-Reader.

Mario & Luigi: Superstar Saga. Wii U Virtual Console (eShop download). AlphaDream. NA: Nintendo, April 2014.

Mario Bros.-e. e-Reader (dot-code e-card, set of 5). Nintendo. NA: Nintendo, November 2002.

Mario Kart: Super Circuit. Game Boy Advance (GBA Game Pak). Intelligent Systems. NA: Nintendo, August 2001.

Mario vs. Donkey Kong. Game Boy Advance (GBA Game Pak). Nintendo Software Technology. NA: Nintendo, May 2004.

Metroid Fusion. Game Boy Advance (GBA Game Pak). Nintendo R&D1. NA: Nintendo, November 2002.

Metroid Fusion. Wii U Virtual Console (eShop download). Nintendo R&D1. NA: Nintendo, April 2014.

Metroid: Zero Mission. Game Boy Advance (GBA Game Pak). Nintendo R&D1. NA: Nintendo, February 2004.

Mode 7 Demo. GBA ROM. Andrew May. November 2, 2001. Visual Boy Advance. http://www.gbadev.org/demos.php?showinfo=390.

NES Remix. Wii U and 3DS Virtual Console (eShop download). Nintendo EAD Tokyo and indiezero. NA: Nintendo, December 2013.

Ninja Five-O. Game Boy Advance (GBA Game Pak). Hudson Soft. NA: Konami, April 2003.

Pinball-e. e-Reader (dot-code e-card, set of 5). Nintendo. NA: Nintendo, September 2002.

Pokémon Battle-e. Series 1. e-Reader (dot code e-card, set of 54). Nintendo. NA: Nintendo, October 2003.

Pokémon Colosseum. GameCube (GameCube Game Disc). Genius Sonority. NA: The Pokémon Company and Nintendo, March 2004.

Pokémon Emerald. Game Boy Advance. (GBA Game Pak). Game Freak. NA: The Pokémon Company and Nintendo, September 2005.

Pokémon Fire Red/LeafGreen. Game Boy Advance. (GBA Game Pak). Game Freak. NA: The Pokémon Company and Nintendo, September 2004.

Pokémon Ruby/Sapphire. Game Boy Advance (GBA Game Pak). Game Freak. NA: The Pokémon Company and Nintendo, March 2003.

Racing Gears Advance. Game Boy Advance (GBA Game Pak). Orbital Media. NA: Orbital Media, February 2005.

Restoration Queen. ROM patch file. lizzledpink and glitteringworlds. Version 1.0. June 13, 2014. Visual Boy Advance. https://lizzledpink.tumblr.com/post/88714990211.

Rizumu Tengoku or *Rhythm Heaven* (リズム天国). Game Boy Advance (GBA Game Pak). Nintendo SPD and J.P. Room Recordings. JP: Nintendo, August 2006.

Rock Band. Wii (Wii Optical Disc). Pi Studios. NA: Nintendo, June 2008.

RPG Raycast Technology Demo. GBA ROM. Erik Rounds. June 2, 2003. Visual Boy Advance. http://www.gbadev.org/demos.php?showinfo=543.

Super Mario 64. Nintendo 64 (N64 Game Pak). Nintendo EAD. NA: Nintendo, September 1996.

Super Mario Advance. Game Boy Advance (GBA Game Pak). Nintendo R&D2. JP: Nintendo, March 2001; NA: Nintendo, June 2001.

Super Mario Advance 4: Super Mario Bros. 3. Game Boy Advance (GBA Game Pak). Nintendo R&D2. NA: Nintendo, October 2003.

Super Mario All-Stars. Super Nintendo Entertainment System (SNES Game Pak). Nintendo EAD. NA: Nintendo, August 1993.

Super Mario Bros. Nintendo Entertainment System (NES Game Pak). Nintendo EAD. NA: Nintendo, October 1985.

Super Mario Bros. 2. Nintendo Entertainment System (NES Game Pak). NA: Nintendo, October 1988.

Super Mario Bros. 2 or *Super Mario Bros.: The Lost Levels* (スーパーマリオブラザーズ 2). Family Computer Disk System (FC Quick Disk). Nintendo EAD. JP: Nintendo, May 1986.

Super Mario USA (スーパーマリオ). Family Computer (FC Game Pak). Nintendo. JP: Nintendo, September 1992.

Super Mario World: Super Mario Advance 2. Game Boy Advance (GBA Game Pak). Nintendo EAD. NA: Nintendo, February 2002.

Super Mario World: Super Mario Advance 2. Wii U Virtual Console (eShop download). Nintendo EAD. NA: Nintendo, December 2014.

Tetris. Game Boy (Game Boy Game Pak). Bullet-Proof Software and Nintendo. NA: Nintendo, July 1989.

Tetris Worlds. Game Boy Advance (GBA Game Pak). 3d6 Games. NA: THQ, September 2001.

Universal FE Randomizer, version 0.5.2. Executable file. Lushen124. Version 0.5.2.
    September 9, 2018. https://github.com/lushen124/Universal-FE-Randomizer.
WarioWare Gold. Nintendo 3DS (3DS Game Card). Intelligent Systems and Nintendo
    EPD. NA: Nintendo, August 2018.
WarioWare, Inc.: Mega Microgames! Game Boy Advance (GBA Game Pak). Nintendo
    R&D1. NA: Nintendo, May 2003.
WarioWare, Inc.: Mega Party Game$! GameCube (GameCube Game Disc). Nintendo
    R&D1 and Intelligent Systems. NA: Nintendo, April 2004.
WarioWare: Smooth Moves. Wii (Wii Optical Disc). Intelligent Systems and Nintendo
    SPD Group 1. NA: Nintendo, January 2007.
WarioWare: Snapped! Nintendo DSi (DSiWare download). Nintendo SPD Group 1 and
    Intelligent Systems. NA: Nintendo, April 2009.
WarioWare: Twisted! Game Boy Advance (GBA Game Pak). Nintendo SPD Group 1 and
    Intelligent Systems. NA: Nintendo, May 2005.
WarioWare: Touched! Nintendo DS (DS Game Card). Nintendo SPD Group 1 and Intel-
    ligent Systems. NA: Nintendo, February 2005.
Yoshi Topsy-Turvy. Game Boy Advance (GBA Game Pak). Artoon. NA: Nintendo, June
    2005.
Yume Kōjō: Doki Doki Panikku or *Dream Factory: Heart-Pounding Panic* (夢工場 ドキド
    キパニック). Family Computer Disk System (FC QuickDisk). Nintendo EAD.
    NA: Nintendo, July 1987.

Books, Articles, and Online Sources

Acland, Charles R. "Introduction." In *Residual Media*, edited by Charles R. Acland,
    xiii–xxvii. Minneapolis: University of Minnesota Press, 2007.
Adorno, Theodor W., and Max Horkheimer. *Dialectic of Enlightenment: Cultural Memory
    in the Present*. Edited by Gunzelin Schmid Noerr and translated by Edmund Jeph-
    cott. Stanford, CA: Stanford University Press, 2002.
Allison, Anne. "Portable Monsters and Commodity Cuteness: Pokémon as Japan's
    New Global Power." *Postcolonial Studies* 6, no. 3 (2003): 381–395. https://doi.org/
    10.1080/1368879032000162220.
Althusser, Louis. *Lenin and Philosophy and Other Essays*. Translated by Ben Brewster.
    New York: Monthly Review Press, 2001.
Altice, Nathan. *I AM ERROR: The Nintendo Family Computer/Entertainment System Plat-
    form*. Cambridge, MA: MIT Press, 2015.
Andy. "Nintendo Nukes Hugely Popular iOS Game Boy Emulator." *TorrentFreak*. Posted
    May 14, 2014. https://torrentfreak.com/nintendo-nukes-hugely-popular-ios
    -game-boy-emulator-140514.
Apperley, Thomas, and Jussi Parikka. "Platform Studies' Epistemic Threshold."
    Games and Culture 13, no.4 (2018): 349–369. https://doi.org/10.1177/155541201
    5616509.
ARM Limited. *ARM7TDMI Technical Reference Manual Revision r4p1*. 2004. http://
    infocenter.arm.com/help/topic/com.arm.doc.ddi0210c/DDI0210B.pdf.
Arsenault, Dominic. *Super Power, Spoony Bards, and Silverware: The Super Nintendo
    Entertainment System*. Cambridge, MA: MIT Press, 2017.
Barbrook, Richard. "The High-Tech Gift Economy." In *Readme! Filtered by Nettime:
    ASCII Culture and the Revenge of Knowledge*, edited by Josephine Bosma, 133–139.
    Brooklyn, NY: Autonomedia, 1999.

Baudrillard, Jean. *Simulacra and Simulation*. Translated by Sheila Faria Glaser. Ann Arbor: University of Michigan Press, 1994.

Benjamin, Walter. "The Work of Art in the Age of Its Technological Reproducibility." In *The Work of Art in the Age of Its Technological Reproducibility, and Other Writings on Media*, translated by Michael W. Jennings, Brigid Doherty, and Thomas Y. Levin, 19–55. Cambridge, MA: Harvard University Press, 2003.

Blazer (Crimson Red). "The Last Promise." *Serenes Forest*. Posted January 18, 2010, updated June 9, 2012. https://serenesforest.net/forums/index.php?/topic/18554 -the-last-promise.

Bogost, Ian, and Nick Montfort. "Platform Studies: Frequently Questioned Answers." Presented at the Digital Arts and Culture Conference, University of California, Irvine, December 2009. https://escholarship.org/uc/item/01rok9br.

Boluk, Stephanie, and Patrick LeMieux. *Metagaming: Playing Competing, Spectating, Cheating, Trading, Making, and Breaking Videogames*. Minneapolis: University of Minnesota Press, 2017.

Bovill, Moira, and Sonia Livingstone. "Bedroom Culture and the Privatization of Media Use." In *Children and Their Changing Media Environment: A European Comparative Study*, edited by Sonia Livingstone and Moira Bovill, 179–200. Mahwah, NJ: Lawrence Erlbaum Associates, 2001.

Boym, Svetlana. *The Future of Nostalgia*. New York: Basic Books, 2001.

Brand, Stewart. "Spacewar: Fanatic Life and Symbolic Death among the Computer." *Rolling Stone*. December 7, 1972. http://www.wheels.org/spacewar/stone/ rolling_stone.html.

Bull, Michael. "The Seduction of Sound in Consumer Culture." *Journal of Consumer Culture* 2, no. 1 (2002): 81–101. https://doi.org/10.1177/146954050200200104.

Burnham, Van. *Supercade: A Visual History of the Videogame Age, 1971–1984*. Cambridge, MA: MIT Press, 2001.

Camper, Brett Bennett. "Homebrew and the Social Construction of Gaming: Community, Creativity, and Legal Context of Amateur Game Boy Advance Development." MA thesis, Massachusetts Institute of Technology (MIT), 2005.

Catanese, Paul. "The Evolution of a GBA Artist." In *Videogames and Art*, edited by Andy Clarke and Grethe Mitchell, 127–129. Bristol, UK: Intellect, 2007.

Chan, Dean. "Convergence, Connectivity, and the Case of Japanese Mobile Gaming." *Games and Culture* 3, no. 1 (2008): 13–25. https://doi.org/10.1177/155541200 7309524.

Chesher, Chris. "Neither Gaze nor Glance, but Glaze: Relating to Console Game Screens." *Scan Journal* 1, no. 1 (2004). http://scan.net.au/scan/journal/display .php?journal_id=19.

Chess, Shira. *Ready Player Two: Women Gamers and Designed Identity*. Minneapolis: University of Minnesota Press, 2017.

Chien, Jia-Ren Chang, and Cheng-Chi Tai. "The Design of a Portable ECG Measurement Instrument Based on a GBA Embedded System." In *2006 IEEE International Conference on Industrial Technology*, 1782–1787. Mumbai: IEEE, 2006. https://doi .org/10.1109/ICIT.2006.372490.

Chow, Rey. "Listening Otherwise, Music Miniaturized: A Different Type of Question about Revolution." *Discourse* 13, no. 1 (1990): 129–148. http://www.jstor.org/ stable/41389173.

Chun, Wendy Hui Kyong. *Control and Freedom*. Cambridge, MA: MIT Press, 2006.

Cifaldi, Frank. "'It's Just Emulation'—the Challenge of Selling Old Games." Presented at the Game Developers Conference, San Francisco, March 2016.

Clark, Andy. *Being There: Putting Brain, Body, and World Together Again*. Cambridge, MA: MIT Press, 1997.

Clark, Andy, and David Chalmers. "The Extended Mind." *Analysis* 58, no. 1 (1998): 12–13. http://www.jstor.org/stable/3328150.

Coleman, Sarah, and Nick Dyer-Witheford. "Playing on the Digital Commons: Collectivities, Capital, and Contestation in Videogame Culture." *Media, Culture, & Society* 29, no. 6 (2007): 934–953. https://doi.org/10.1177/0163443707081700.

Collins, Karen. *Game Sound: An Introduction to the History, Theory, and Practice of Video Game Music and Sound Design*. Cambridge, MA: MIT Press, 2008.

Consalvo, Mia. *Atari to Zelda: Japan's Videogames in Global Contexts*. Cambridge, MA: MIT Press, 2016.

Consalvo, Mia. *Cheating: Gaining Advantage in Videogames*. Cambridge, MA: MIT Press, 2007.

Crigger, Lara. "Searching for Gunpei Yokoi." *The Escapist*. December 25, 2007. https://v1.escapistmagazine.com/articles/view/video-games/issues/issue_129/2744-Searching-for-Gunpei-Yokoi.

Cunningham, Helen. "*Mortal Kombat* and Computer Game Girls." In *Electronic Media and Technoculture*, edited by John Thornton Caldwell, 213–226. Brunswick, NJ: Rutgers University Press, 2000.

dbak85. "GBA-xl, a Custom 3D Printed Gameboy Advance." *Sudomod*. Posted August 27, 2017. https://sudomod.com/forum/viewtopic.php?t=3916.

Deleuze, Gilles, and Félix Guattari. *A Thousand Plateaus: Capitalism and Schizophrenia*. Translated by Brian Massumi. Minneapolis: University of Minnesota Press, 1987.

DeSpira, Cat. "Pac-Man: The Untold Story of How We Really Played the Game." Posted February 12, 2019. https://retrobitch.wordpress.com/2019/02/12/pac-man-the-untold-story-of-how-we-really-played-the-game.

deWinter, Jennifer. *Shigeru Miyamoto: Super Mario Bros., Donkey Kong, The Legend of Zelda*. New York: Bloomsbury, 2015.

Donovan, Tristan. *Replay: The History of Video Games*. East Sussex, UK: Yellow Ant, 2010.

Douglas, Susan. *Inventing American Broadcasting, 1899–1922*. Baltimore: Johns Hopkins University Press, 1989.

Douglas, Susan. *Listening In: Radio and the American Imagination*. Minneapolis: University of Minnesota Press, 1999.

du Gay, Paul, Stuart Hall, Linda Janes, Hugh Mackay, and Keith Negus. *Doing Cultural Studies: The Story of the Sony Walkman*. London: SAGE, 1997.

Dyer-Witheford, Nick. "Nintendo Capitalism: Enclosures and Insurgencies, Virtual and Terrestrial." *Canadian Journal of Development Studies (Revue Canadienne d'études du développement)* 22, no. 4 (2001): 965–996. https://doi.org/10.1080/02255189.2001.9669951.

Electronic Gaming Monthly. "Nintendo's 32-Bit Color Portable 'Project Atlantis' to Be Ready in Fall." *EGM* 83 (June 1996): 18.

EmuParadise. "EmuParadise Is Changing." August 8, 2018. https://www.emuparadise.me/emuparadise-changing.php.

endrift. "Classic NES Series Anti-Emulation Measures." mGBA website. Posted December 28, 2014. https://mgba.io/2014/12/28/classic-nes.

Eng, Paul. "Game Boy Advance Breaks Sales Records." *ABC News*. June 21, 2001. https://abcnews.go.com/Technology/story?id=98471&.

Ernesto. "Nintendo Shuts Down Browser-Based Game Boy Emulator." *TorrentFreak*. Posted July 12, 2015. https://torrentfreak.com/nintendo-shuts-down-javascript-gameboy-emulator-150712.

Ernesto. "Nintendo Sues Console ROM Sites for 'Mass' Copyright Infringement (Update)." *TorrentFreak*. Posted July 20, 2018. https://torrentfreak.com/nintendo-sues-console-rom-sites-for-mass-copyright-infringement-180720.

Ernst, Wolfgang. *Digital Memory and the Archive*. Translated by Jussi Parikka. Minneapolis: University of Minnesota Press, 2013.

FAST6191. *GBA and DS ROM Hacking Guide—2016 Edition*. January 13, 2016. https://filetrip.net/nds-downloads/utilities/download-gba-and-ds-rom-hacking-guide-2014-preview-1-f32908.html.

Fernández-Vara, Clara, José Pablo Zagal, and Michael Mateas. "Evolution of Spatial Configurations in Videogames." In *Worlds in Play: International Perspectives on Digital Games Research*, edited by Suzanne de Castell and Jennifer Jenson, 159–168. New York: Peter Lang Publishing, 2007.

Film Foundation. "Film Preservation." Accessed January 8, 2020. https://web.archive.org/web/20130312021638/http:/www.film-foundation.org/common/11004/aboutAboutUs.cfm?clientID=11004&sid=2&ssid=5.

Fils-Aime, Reggie. Nintendo E3 Press Conference. May 17, 2005. https://www.youtube.com/watch?v=89GB6bC9_N4.

Fils-Aime, Reggie. "Nintendo of America President on Switch's Big Risk, 'Smash Bros.' Success and Classic Consoles' Future." Interview by Patrick Shanley. *The Hollywood Reporter*. December 11, 2018. https://web.archive.org/web/20190329022510/https://www.hollywoodreporter.com/heat-vision/nintendo-president-smash-bros-classic-console-future-switch-1167948.

Flichy, Patrice. *Dynamics of Modern Communication. The Shaping and Impact of New Communication Technologies*. Translated by Liz Libbrecht. London: Sage, 1995.

Foucault, Michel. *The Order of Things: An Archaeology of the Human Sciences*. New York: Vintage Books, 1994.

"Freeplay Zero/Freeplay CM3." Updated June 20, 2017. https://www.kickstarter.com/projects/1227007236/freeplay-zero-freeplay-cm3-by-freeplaytech.

Fujimoto, Kenichi. "The Third-Stage Paradigm: Territory Machines from the Girls' Pager Revolution to Mobile Aesthetics." In *Personal, Portable, Pedestrian: Mobile Phones in Japanese Life*, edited by Mizuko Ito, Daisuke Okabe, and Misa Matsuda, 77–101. Cambridge, MA: MIT Press, 2005.

Gabrys, Jennifer. *Digital Rubbish: A Natural History of Electronics*. Ann Arbor: University of Michigan Press, 2011.

Gach, Ethan. "Newly Discovered Trick Transforms a *Metroid* Speedrunning Scene." *Kotaku*. April 9, 2018. https://kotaku.com/newly-discovered-trick-transforms-a-metroid-speedrunnin-1825127476.

Gallagher, Shaun. "Body Schema and Intentionality." In *The Body and the Self*, edited by José Luis Bermúdez, Anthony Marcel, and Naomi Eilan, 225–245. Cambridge, MA: MIT Press, 1995.

Gallagher, Shaun. *How the Body Shapes the Mind*. Oxford, UK: Clarendon Press, 2005.

Game Pie Advance/Freeplay Zero. Accessed February 21, 2020. gamepieadvance.com.

Gaonkar, Dilip Parameshwar, and Elizabeth A. Povinelli. "Technologies of Public Forms: Circulation, Transfiguration, Recognition." *Public Culture* 15, no. 3 (2003): 385–397. https://doi.org/10.1215/08992363-15-3-385.

gbadev.org. "About." n.d. http://gbadev.org/about.php.

gbadev.org. "2004Mbit Compo." Updated March 27, 2006. http://2004mbit.gbadev .org.

gbadev.org. "5 Million Visitors & 8 Years Online." July 11, 2006. http://www.gbadev .org/index.php?showinfo=1366.

Gee, James Paul. "Video Games and Embodiment." *Games and Culture* 3, no. 3–4 (2008): 253–263. https://doi.org/10.1177/1555412008317309.

Giddings, Seth, and Helen W. Kennedy. "'Incremental Speed Increases Excitement': Bodies, Space, Movement, and Televisual Change." *Television & New Media* 11, no. 3 (2010): 163–179. https://doi.org/10.1177/1527476409357592.

Gilbert, Ben. "The History behind Nintendo's Flip-Flop on Mobile Gaming." *Endgadget*. March 17, 2015. https://www.engadget.com/2015/03/17/nintendo-mobile-iwata.

Gitelman, Lisa. *Always Already New: Media, History, and the Data of Culture*. Cambridge, MA: MIT Press, 2006.

GitHub "Process DMCA Request." July 19, 2018. https://github.com/github/dmca/ commit/fca0a199638d85b3563318c63c7db01376a7dd53.

Goddard, Giles. "The Making of *Super Mario 64*—Giles Goddard Interview (NGC)." Interview by Mark Green. *Pixelatron*. September 13, 2010. http://pixelatron .com/blog/the-making-of-super-mario-64-full-giles-goddard-interview-ngc.

Grand, Joe. *Game Console Hacking: Have Fun while Voiding Your Warranty*. Rockland, MA: Syngress, 2004.

Gregersen, Andreas, and Torben Grodal. "Embodiment and Interface." In *The Video Game Theory Reader 2*, edited by Bernard Perron and Mark J. P. Wolf, 65–83. New York: Routledge, 2009.

Grodal, Torben. *Embodied Visions: Evolution, Emotion, Culture, and Film*. Oxford: Oxford University Press, 2009.

Grodal, Torben. "Stories for Eye, Ear, and Muscles: Video Games, Media, and Embodied Experiences." In *The Video Game Theory Reader*, edited by Mark J. P. Wolf and Bernard Perron, 129–155. New York: Routledge, 2003.

Guins, Raiford. *Game After: A Cultural Study of Videogame Afterlife*. Cambridge, MA: MIT Press, 2014.

Harris, Blake J. *Console Wars: Sega, Nintendo, and the Battle That Defined a Generation*. New York: Harper Collins, 2014.

Harris, Craig. "E3 2003: Kojima Loves the Sun." *IGN*. May 15, 2003. https://ca.ign .com/articles/2003/05/16/e3-2003-kojima-loves-the-sun.

Harris, Craig. "Game Boy Advance's $25 Million Launch." *IGN*. April 13, 2001. https:// ca.ign.com/articles/2001/04/13/game-boy-advances-25-million-launch.

Harris, Craig. "*WarioWare Twisted* Reviewed on GBA." *IGN*. May 11, 2005. https:// ca.ign.com/articles/2005/05/12/warioware-twisted.

Hayles, N. Katherine. *My Mother Was a Computer: Digital Subjects and Literary Texts*. Chicago: University of Chicago Press, 2005.

Henning, Michelle. "New Lamps for Old: Photography, Obsolescence, and Social Change." In *Residual Media*, edited by Charles R. Acland, 48–68. Minneapolis: University of Minnesota Press, 2007.

Henrik, Jan. "Wait what?" Twitter post. September 20, 2017, 11:36 p.m. https://twitter.com/JanHenrikH/status/910754596422868992.

Hertz, Garnet, and Jussi Parikka. "Zombie Media: Circuit Bending Media Archaeology into an Art Method." *Leonardo* 45, no. 5 (2012): 424–430. https://doi.org/10.1162/LEON_a_00438.

Herz, Jessie Cameron. *Joystick Nation: How Videogames Gobbled Our Money, Won Our Hearts and Rewired Our Minds*. London: Abacus, 1997.

Hewer, Paul, and Douglas Brownlie. "On Market Forces and Adjustments: Acknowledging Consumer Creativity Through the Aesthetics of 'Debadging.'" *Journal of Marketing Management* 26, no. 5–6 (2010): 428–440. https://doi.org/10.1080/02672570903458730.

Hjorth, Larissa, and Ingrid Richardson. *Gaming in Social, Locative, and Mobile Media*. New York: Palgrave Macmillan, 2014.

Hjorth, Larissa, and Ingrid Richardson. "The Waiting Game: Complication Notions of (Tele)presence and Gendered Distraction in Casual Mobile Gaming." *Australian Journal of Communication* 36 (2009): 23–35.

Hong, Renyi, and Vivian Hsueh-Hua Chen. "Becoming an Ideal Co-Creator: Web Materiality and Intensive Laboring Practices in Game Modding." *New Media & Society* 16, no. 2 (2014): 290–305. https://doi.org/10.1177/1461444813480095.

"How Far Can You Get Your Gamepad from the Wii U." *IGN*. Thread started November 24, 2013, accessed July 10, 2018. https://web.archive.org/web/20190329020640/https://www.ign.com/boards/threads/how-far-can-you-get-your-gamepad-from-the-wii-u.453546115.

Huhtamo, Erkki. "Game Patch: The Son of Scratch?" *Switch: New Media Journal* 5 (1999). http://switch.sjsu.edu/archive/nextswitch/switch_engine/front/front.php%3Fartc=119.html.

Huhtamo, Erkki. "Pockets of Plenty: An Archaeology of Mobile Media." In *The Mobile Audience: Media Art and Mobile Technologies*, edited by Martin Rieser, 23–37. Amsterdam: Rodopi, 2011.

Huhtamo, Erkki. "Slots of Fun, Slots of Trouble: An Archaeology of Arcade Gaming." In *Handbook of Computer Game Studies*, edited by Joost Raessens and Jeffrey Goldstein, 3–21. Cambridge, MA: MIT Press, 2005.

Iantorno, Michael. "Generate Randomized Game: The Ambivalences of Online ROM-Patching Applications." Presented at the Symposium Histoire du Jeu, Montreal, November 2019. https://michaeliantorno.com/generate-randomized-game.

Inoue, Osamu. *Nintendo Magic: Winning the Videogame Wars*. Translated by Paul Tuttle Starr. New York: Vertical, 2010.

Ito, Mizuko, Daisuke Okabe, and Ken Anderson. "Portable Objects in Three Global Cities: The Personalization of Urban Places." In *The Reconstruction of Space and Time: Mobile Communication Practices*, edited by Rich Ling and Scott W. Campbell, 67–87. New Brunswick, NJ: Transaction Publishers, 2010.

Ito, Mizuko, Daisuke Okabe, and Misa Matsuda. "Introduction." In *Personal, Portable, Pedestrian: Mobile Phones in Japanese Life*, eds. Mizuko Ito, Daisuke Okabe, and Misa Matsuda, 1–16. Cambridge, MA: MIT Press, 2005.

Itoi, Shigesato. "Iwata Asks: *Super Mario Bros.* 25th Anniversary Volume 1." http://iwataasks.nintendo.com/interviews/#/wii/mario25th.

Iwata, Satoru. "Interview with Nobuo Kawakami and 4Gamer." *4Gamer*. December 27, 2014. https://www.4gamer.net/games/999/G999905/20141226033.

Iwata, Satoru. "Iwata Asks: The History of Handheld: *The Legend of Zelda* Games." http://iwataasks.nintendo.com/interviews/#/ds/zelda/1/2.

Iwata, Satoru. "Iwata Asks: *The Legend of Zelda: Ocarina of Time 3D*." http://iwataasks.nintendo.com/interviews/#/3ds/zelda-ocarina-of-time.

Iwata, Satoru. "Iwata Asks: Nintendo DS Volume 4: Asking Iwata." http://iwataasks.nintendo.com/interviews/#/ds/dsi/3/0.

Iwata, Satoru. "Iwata Asks: Nintendo 3DS Volume 1: And That's How the Nintendo 3DS Was Made." http://iwataasks.nintendo.com/interviews/#/3ds/how-nintendo-3ds-made/0/3.

Iwata, Satoru. "Iwata Asks: Nintendo 3DS Volume 5: Asking Mr. Miyamoto Right before Release." http://iwataasks.nintendo.com/interviews/#/3ds/how-nintendo-3ds-made/4/0.

Iwata Satoru. "Iwata Asks: Rhythm Heaven." http://iwataasks.nintendo.com/interviews/#/ds/rhythm-heaven.

Iwata, Satoru. "Iwata Asks: Super Mario Developers." http://iwataasks.nintendo.com/interviews/#/wii/mario25th/2/3.

Iwata, Satoru. "Iwata Asks: WarioWare: Smooth Moves." http://iwataasks.nintendo.com/interviews/#/wii/warioware_smooth_moves.

Iwata, Satoru. "Iwata Asks: Wii Motion Plus." http://iwataasks.nintendo.com/interviews/#/wii/wiimotionplus.

Jacobson, Lisa. *Raising Consumers: Children and the American Mass Market in the Early Twentieth Century*. New York: Columbia University Press, 2004.

Jakobsson, Mikael. "Adversarial Couch Co-Op: Joshing and Griefing in Co-Located Cooperative Gaming." Presented at DiGRA 2014: <Active Verb> the <Noun> of Game <Plural Noun>, Salt Lake City, UT, August 3–6, 2014. https://e-channel.med.utah.edu/wp-content/uploads/2018/07/DiGRA2014_Proceedings_final.pdf.

Jair. "Text Hacking/Translation Tutorial." *romhacking.net*. Updated November 11, 2017. https://www.romhacking.net/documents/68.

Jenkins, Henry. "Interactive Audiences? The 'Collective Intelligence' of Media Fans." In *The New Media Book*, edited by Dan Harries, 157–170. London: British Film Institute, 2002.

Jenkins, Henry. *Textual Poachers: Television Fans and Participatory Culture*. Updated Twentieth Anniversary Edition. New York: Routledge, 2013.

Jenkins, Henry, Mizuko Ito, and danah boyd. *Participatory Culture in a Networked Era: A Conversation on Youth, Learning, Commerce, and Politics*. Cambridge, UK: Polity Press, 2016.

Jones, Steven E., and George K. Thiruvathukal. *Codename Revolution: The Nintendo Wii Platform*. Cambridge, MA: MIT Press, 2012.

Jordan, Will. "From Rule-Breaking to ROM-Hacking: Theorizing the Computer Game-as-Commodity." Presented at DiGRA 2007: Situated Play, University of Tokyo, Tokyo, September 2007. http://www.digra.org/wp-content/uploads/digital-library/07311.20061.pdf.

Juul, Jesper. *A Casual Revolution: Reinventing Video Games and Their Players*. Cambridge, MA: MIT Press, 2010.

Kaneda, Miki. "*Rhythm Heaven*: Video Games, Idols, and Other Experiences of Play." In *The Oxford Handbook of Mobile Music Studies Volume 2*, edited by Sumanth Gopinath and Jason Stanyek, 427–449. Oxford: Oxford University Press, 2014.

KapuccinoHeck. "I was finally able to look around the NES Online's strings a bit myself and noticed the sheer amount of SNES games planned." Twitter post. January 12, 2019, 9:51 p.m. https://twitter.com/KapuccinoHeck/status/10842 81638962561024.

Katayama, Osamu. *Japanese Business into the 21st Century*. Translated by Richard Walker. London: Athlone Press, 1996.

Kelso, Charles. "The Game Boy Advance: A Personal Retrospective." *Cube*. January 8, 2016. https://medium.com/the-cube/the-game-boy-advance-a-personal -retrospective-1e9e9bd4e236.

Kent, Steven L. *The Ultimate History of Video Games: From Pong to Pokémon and Beyond—the Story behind the Craze That Touched Our Lives and Changed the World*. New York: Three Rivers Press, 2001.

Kirschenbaum, Matthew G. *Mechanisms: New Media and the Forensic Imagination*. Cambridge, MA: MIT Press, 2008.

Kirtz, Jaime Lee. "Beyond the Blackbox: Repurposing ROM Hacking for Feminist Hacking/Making Practices." *Ada: A Journal of Gender, New Media & Technology* 13 (2018). https://adanewmedia.org/2018/05/issue13-kirtz.

Kline, Stephen, Nick Dyer-Witheford, and Greig de Peuter. *Digital Play: The Interaction of Technology, Culture, and Marketing*. Montreal, Quebec, and Kingston, Ontario: McGill-Queen's University Press, 2003.

Kogawa, Tetsuo. "Beyond Electronic Individualism." *Canadian Journal of Political and Social Theory (Reveue canadienne de théorie politique et sociale)* 8, no. 3 (1984): 15–20.

Kohler, Chris. "The Secret History of *Super Mario Bros. 2*." *Wired*. April 1, 2011. https://www.wired.com/2011/04/super-mario-bros-2.

Konzack, Lars. "Computer Game Criticism: A Method for Computer Game Analysis." In *Proceedings of Computer Games and Digital Cultures Conference*, edited by Frans Mäyrä, 89–100. Tampere, Finland: Tampere University Press, 2002.

Korth, Martin. *GBATEK*. Accessed January 7, 2020. problemkaputt.de/gbatek.htm #gbatechnicaldata.

Kutaragi, Ken. Sony E3 2003 Press Conference. May 13, 2003.

"The Last Promise Is Out!" *romhacking.net*. August 18, 2012. http://www.romhacking .net/?page=news&newssearch=1&project=/hacks/962.

Lee, Benjamin, and Edward LiPuma. "Cultures of Circulation: The Imaginations of Modernity." *Public Culture* 14, no. 1 (2002): 191–213.

Levy, Steven. *Hackers: Heroes of the Computer Revolution*. New York: Delta, 1994.

Lindblom, Jessica. *Embodied Social Cognition*. Heidelberg, Germany: Springer International, 2015.

Lizzledpink, and glitteringworlds. "Restoration Queen." Tumblr post. June 13, 2014, 7:46 p.m. https://lizzledpink.tumblr.com/post/88714990211.

Lynch, Diedre Shauna. *Loving Literature: A Cultural History*. Chicago, University of Chicago Press, 2015.

MacDonald, Mark, Che Chou, and EGM staff. "Game Boy Advances." *EGM* 14, no. 7 (2001), 86.

Maiberg, Emanuel. "Nintendo's Offensive, Tragic, and Totally Legal Erasure of ROM Sites." *Motherboard*. August 10, 2018. https://motherboard.vice.com/en_us/ article/bjbped/nintendos-offensive-tragic-and-totally-legal-erasure-of-rom -sites.

Main, Peter. "Gerard Klauer Mattison Press Conference Presentation." New York, November 1999. IGN's transcript of the presentation, uploaded on November 4, 1999, can be found at https://ca.ign.com/articles/1999/11/05/the-main-man-on-nintendo.

Main, Peter. Teleconference Call. August 24, 2000. Audio found at https://cubemedia.ign.com/media/news/audio/interviews/petermain.mp3.

Maravita, Angelo, and Atsushi Iriki. "Tools for the Body (Schema)." *Trends in Cognitive Sciences* 8, no. 2 (2004): 79–86. https://doi.org/10.1016/j.tics.2003.12.008.

Marvin, Carolyn. *When Old Technologies Were New: Thinking about Electric Communication in the Late Nineteenth Century*. Oxford: Oxford University Press, 1988.

McCrea, Christian. "We Play in Public: The Nature and Context of Portable Gaming Systems." *Convergence: The International Journal of Research into New Media Technologies* 17, no. 4 (2011): 389–403. https://doi.org/10.1177/1354856511414987.

Merleau-Ponty, Maurice. *Phenomenology of Perception*. Translated by Colin Smith. London: Routledge and Kegan Paul, 1962.

Mills, Mara. "Hearing Aids and the History of Electronics Miniaturization." In *The Sound Studies Reader*, edited by Jonathan Sterne, 73–78. New York: Routledge, 2012.

Miyamoto, Shigeru. "Interview." *Nintendo Online Magazine*. August 1, 1998. https://web.archive.org/web/20150202021306/https://www.zeldadungeon.net/wiki/Interview:Nintendo_online_magazine_august_1st_1998.

Miyamoto, Shigeru. "Miyamoto, la Wii U et le secret de la Triforce." Interview by William Audureau. *Gamekult*. July 9, 2004. https://www.gamekult.com/actualite/miyamoto-la-wii-u-et-le-secret-de-la-triforce-105550.html.

Montfort, Nick. "Continuous Paper: The Early Materiality and Workings of Electronic Literature." Presented at MLA, Philadelphia, December 28, 2004. Text uploaded January 2005. https://nickm.com/writing/essays/continuous_paper_mla.html.

Montfort, Nick, and Ian Bogost. *Racing the Beam: The Atari Video Computer System*. Cambridge, MA: MIT Press, 2009.

Moore, Gordon E. "Cramming More Components onto Integrated Circuits." *Electronics* 38, no. 8 (1965): 114–117. https://doi.org/10.1109/N-SSC.2006.4785860.

Morris, Sue. "First-Person Shooters—a Game Apparatus." In *ScreenPlay: Cinema/Videogames/Interfaces*, edited by Geoff King and Tanya Krzywinska, 81–97. London: Wallflower, 2002.

Nakamura, Lisa. "'Words with Friends': Socially Networked Reading on 'Goodreads.'" *PMLA* 128, no. 1 (2013): 238–243. www.jstor.org/stable/23489284.

NEC/TOKIN. "NEC TOKIN's Piezoelectric Devices." (The original website can be accessed at archive.org through a capture from April 10, 2005. https://web.archive.org/web/20050410093215/http://www.nec-tokin.com/english/product/piezodevice2/ceramicgyro.html.)

Newman, James. "In Search of the Videogame Player: The Lives of Mario." *New Media & Society* 4, no. 3 (2002): 405–422. https://doi.org/10.1177/1461444802004003005.

Next Generation. "Nintendo's New Color Handheld." No. 18 (June 1996): 20.

Ngai, Sianne. *Our Aesthetic Categories: Zany, Cute, Interesting*. Cambridge, MA: Harvard University Press, 2012.

Ngai, Sianne. "The Cuteness of the Avant-Garde." *Critical Inquiry* 31, no. 4 (Summer 2005): 811–847. https://doi.org/10.1086/444516.

Nguyen, Mimi. "Queer Cyborgs and New Mutants." In *Asian America.net*, edited by Rachel Lee and Sau-ling Wong, 281–305. New York: Routledge, 2003.

Nieborg, David B., and Thomas Poell. "The Platformization of Cultural Production: Theorizing the Contingent Cultural Commodity." *New Media and Society* 20, no. 11 (2018): 4275–4292. https://doi.org/10.1177/1461444818769694.

Nieborg, David B., and Shenja van der Graaf. "The Mod Industries? The Industrial Logic of Non-Market Game Production." *European Journal of Cultural Studies* 11, no. 2 (2008): 177–195. https://doi.org/10.1177/1367549407088331.

Nintendo. "72nd Annual General Meeting of Shareholders Q&A." June 28, 2012. https://www.nintendo.co.jp/ir/en/stock/meeting/120628qa/index.html.

Nintendo. "Changing the Color Palette on Game Boy Advance Systems." https://www.nintendo.com/consumer/systems/gameboyadvance/colorchange.jsp.

Nintendo. "Consolidated Sales Transition by Region (as of March 31, 2018)," https://www.nintendo.co.jp/ir/en/finance/historical_data/index.html.

Nintendo. "Corporate Management Policy Briefing 2006 Q & A. June 7, 2007." https://www.nintendo.co.jp/kessan/060607qa_e/03.html.

Nintendo. E3 2005 Press Conference. May 17, 2005. https://www.youtube.com/watch?v=anRyoJeHeCY.

Nintendo. "Game Boy Advance Developer Team Interview." Translated by Tim Horst. *IGN*. September 13, 2000. https://ca.ign.com/articles/2000/09/14/game-boy-advance-developer-team-interview.

Nintendo. "Game Boy Advance or Game Boy Micro Wireless Adapter FAQ." https://www.nintendo.com/consumer/systems/gameboyadvance/agb_wireless_faq.jsp.

Nintendo. "Game Boy Micro." https://www.nintendo.co.uk/Corporate/Nintendo-History/Game-Boy-Micro/Game-Boy-Micro-627145.html.

Nintendo. NES Classic Edition. https://www.nintendo.com/nes-classic.

Nintendo. "Legal Information (Copyrights, Emulators, ROMs, etc.)." https://www.nintendo.com/corp/legal.jsp.

Nintendo. "Technical Data: Game Boy, Game Boy Pocket, Game Boy Color." https://www.nintendo.co.uk/Support/Game-Boy-Pocket-Color/Product-information/Technical-data/Technical-data-619585.html.

Nintendo. "Technical Data: GameCube." https://www.nintendo.co.uk/Support/Nintendo-GameCube/Product-Information/Technical-data/Technical-data-619165.html.

Nintendo. "Tips for Setting Up StreetPass." https://en-americas-support.nintendo.com/app/answers/detail/a_id/681/~/tips-for-setting-up-streetpass.

Nintendo. "Virtual Console Games." https://www.nintendo.com/games/virtual-console-games.

Nintendo. "Wii Shop Channel Discontinuation." Updated March 26, 2018. https://en-americas-support.nintendo.com/app/answers/detail/a_id/27560/~/wii-shop-channel-discontinuation.

Nintendo of America. *AGB Programming Manual*, version 1.1. April 2, 2001. Accessible via https://archive.org/details/NintendoGbaManualV1.1.

Nintendo of America. *Nintendo Power Advance* 1. 2001.

Nintendo of America. *Nintendo Power: Subscriber Bonus*. 2001.

Norman, Donald A. *Emotional Design: Why We Love (or Hate) Everyday Things*. New York: Basic Books, 2005.

Nostalgia Nerd. "Was the GBA Just a Super Nintendo?" June 30, 2016. http://www
.nostalgianerd.com/gba-super-nintendo.

Okada, Satoru. "In the Chair: Satoru Okada." Interview by Florent Gorges and Darran
Jones. *Retro Gamer*, no. 163 (December 2016): 93–97.

Okada, Satoru. "Okada on the Game Boy Advance." Interview by *Nintendo Online
Magazine*, translated by Tim Horst. *IGN*. September 13, 2000. https://ca.ign
.com/articles/2000/09/14/okada-on-the-game-boy-advance.

Omni. "Fire Emblem: Maiden of Darkness." *FEUniverse*. November 29, 2015. https://
feuniverse.us/t/fire-emblem-maiden-of-darkness-check-the-op-for-updates
-i-do-them-everytime-i-achieve-now/1317.

OSDL. *A Guide to Homebrew Development for the Nintendo DS*. Accessed May 25, 2018.
http://osdl.sourceforge.net/main/documentation/misc/nintendo-DS/homebrew
-guide/HomebrewForDS.html.

Ozaki, Ritsuko. "Housing as a Reflection of Culture: Privatised Living and Privacy in
England and Japan." *Housing Studies* 17, no. 2 (2002): 209–227. https://doi
.org/10.1080/02673030220123199.

Pan of Anthrox, GABY, Marat Fayzullin, Pascal Felber, Paul Robson, Martin Korth,
kOOPa, and Bowser. *Game Boy CPU Manual*, version 1.01. http://marc.rawer.de/
Gameboy/Docs/GBCPUman.pdf.

Parikka, Jussi. *What Is Media Archaeology?* Cambridge, UK: Polity Press, 2012.

Parikka, Jussi, and Jaakko Suominen. "Victorian Snakes? Towards a Cultural History
of Mobile Games and the Experience of Movement." *Game Studies* 6, no. 1 (2006).
http://gamestudies.org/0601/articles/parikka_suominen.

Parks, Lisa. "Falling Apart: Electronics Salvaging and the Global Media Economy." In
Residual Media, edited by Charles R. Acland, 32–47. Minneapolis: University of
Minnesota Press, 2007.

Parks, Lisa, and Nicole Starosielski. *Signal Traffic: Critical Studies of Media Infrastructures*. Champaign: University of Illinois Press, 2015.

Peckham, Matt. "Next Link May Not Be a Girl, But He's Androgynous by Design." *Time*.
June 15, 2016. https://time.com/4369537/female-link-zelda.

Rambusch, Jana. "It's Not Just Hands: Embodiment Aspects in Gameplay." In *Video
Games and the Mind: Essays on Cognition, Affect and Emotion*, edited by Bernard
Perron and Felix Schröter, 71–86. Jefferson, NC: McFarland & Company, 2009.

r/fireemblem. "People's Actual Thoughts on the Last Promise?" *Reddit* thread. Posted
December 15, 2017. https://www.reddit.com/r/fireemblem/comments/7k3uii/
peoples_actual_thoughts_on_the_last_promise.

Roth, Wolff-Michael. "From Action to Discourse: The Bridging Function of Gestures."
Cognitive Systems Research 3 (2002): 535–554. https://doi.org/10.1016/S1389
-0417(02)00056-6.

Ryan, Jeff. *Super Mario: How Nintendo Conquered America*. New York: Penguin, 2011.

Sarkar, Samit. "Nintendo Says Foxconn Taking 'Full Responsibility' for Hiring
Underage Workers at Supply Factory." *Polygon*. October 24, 2012. https://www
.polygon.com/2012/10/24/3547542/nintendo-foxconn-investigation-confirms
-underage-workers.

Schivelbusch, Wolfgang. *Railway Journey: The Industrialization of Time and Space in the
Nineteenth Century*. Oakland: University of California Press, 1977.

Schott, Gareth, and Siobhan Thomas. "The Impact of Nintendo's 'For Men' Advertising Campaign on a Potential Female Market." *Eludamos: Journal for Computer*

Game Culture 2, no. 1 (2008): 41–52. http://www.eludamos.org/index.php/eludamos/article/view/vol2no1-6.

Schultz, Peter. "Rhythm Sense: Modality and Enactive Perception in Rhythm Heaven." In *Music Video Games: Performance, Politics, and Play,* edited by Michael Austin, 251–274. New York: Bloomsbury, 2016.

Scott, Suzanne. "Repackaging Fan Culture: The Regifting Economy of Ancillary Content Models." *Transformative Works and Culture* 3 (2009). https://doi.org/10.3983/twc.2009.0150.

Shaw, Adrienne. *Gaming at the Edge: Sexuality and Gender at the Margins of Gamer Culture.* Minneapolis: University of Minnesota Press, 2014.

Shaw, Adrienne. "On Not Becoming Gamers: Moving beyond the Constructed Audience." *Ada: A Journal of Gender, New Media & Technology* 2 (2013). https://adanewmedia.org/2013/06/issue2-shaw.

Sheff, David. *Game Over: How Nintendo Zapped an American Industry, Captured Your Dollars, and Enslaved Your Children.* New York: Random House, 1993.

Siegert, Bernhard. "Cultural Techniques: Or the End of the Intellectual Postwar Era in German Media Theory." *Theory, Culture, & Society* 30, no. 6 (2013). https://doi.org/10.1177/0263276413488963.

Simon, Bart. "Geek Chic: Machine Aesthetics, Digital Gaming, and the Cultural Politics of the Case Mod." *Games and Culture* 2, no. 3 (2007). https://doi.org/10.1177/1555412007304423.

Simon, Bart. "Wii Are Out of Control: Bodies, Game Screens, and the Production of Gestural Excess." *Loading* 3, no. 4 (2009). http://journals.sfu.ca/loading/index.php/loading/article/view/65.

Slack, Jennifer Daryl, and J. Macgregor Wise. *Culture and Technology: A Primer.* New York: Peter Lang, 2005.

Sotamaa, Olli. "'Have Fun Working with Our Product!' Critical Perspectives on Computer Game Mod Competitions." Presented at DiGRA 2005: Changing Views—Worlds in Play, Vancouver, Canada, June 16–20, 2005. http://www.digra.org/digital-library/publications/have-fun-working-with-our-product-critical-perspectives-on-computer-game-mod-competitions/.

Sterne, Jonathan. "The mp3 as Cultural Artifact." *New Media & Society* 8, no. 5 (2006). https://doi.org/10.1177/1461444806067737.

Sugino, Kenichi. "Interview with Game Boy Micro Developer Kenichi Sugino." Interview by Famitsu. Translated by CTU Kyoto. July 5, 2005. http://famitsu.blogspot.com/2005/07/interview-with-game-boy-micro.html.

Sugino, Kenichi. "Interview: The Man behind the GBA SP." Interviewed by Fennec Fox. *GamePro.* June 4, 2003. https://archive.li/A3hTU.

Suzuki, Toshiaki, Takashi Tezuka, and Hiroyuki Kimura. "Super Mario Advance." Interview by Nintendo. Translated by embyr_75. https://www.nintendo.co.jp/nom/0103/031/index.html.

Swalwell, Melanie. "Movement and Kinaesthetic Responsiveness: A Neglected Pleasure." In *The Pleasures of Computer Gaming: Essays on Cultural History, Theory and Aesthetics*, edited by Melanie Swalwell and Jason Wilson, 72–93. Jefferson, NC: McFarland & Company, 2008.

Terranova, Tiziana. "Free Labor: Producing Culture for the Digital Economy." *Social Text* 18, no. 2 (2000): 33–58. https://muse.jhu.edu.

Thunderbird8. "Overheat? Boktai: The Sun Is in Your Hand." *GameFAQs*. February 25, 2009. https://web.archive.org/web/20190309024521/https://gamefaqs .gamespot.com/gba/589655-boktai-the-sun-is-in-your-hand/answers/39969 -overheat.

Tobin, Joseph. "Introduction." In *Pikachu's Global Adventure: The Rise and Fall of Pokémon*, edited by Joseph Tobin, 3–11. Durham, NC: Duke University Press, 2004.

Tobin, Samuel. *Portable Play in Everyday Life: The Nintendo DS*. New York: Palgrave Macmillan, 2013.

Turkle, Sherry. *Life on the Screen: Identity in the Age of the Internet*. New York: Simon & Schuster, 1995.

Turkle, Sherry. "The Things That Matter." In *Evocative Objects: Things We Think With*, edited by Sherry Turkle, 3–10. Cambridge, MA: MIT Press, 2007.

van der Ende, Martin, Mathijs Hageraats, Joost Poort, João Pedro Quintais, and Anastasia Yagafarova. *Global Online Piracy Study*. Amsterdam: Institute for Information Law, July 2018. https://www.ivir.nl/publicaties/download/Global-Online -Piracy-Study.pdf.

van Tilburg, Carolien. *Curiosity: 30 Designs for Products and Interiors*. Amsterdam: Frame Publishers, 2002.

Vijn, Jasper (Cearn). *Tonc*, version 1.4.2. https://www.coranac.com/tonc.

Wajcman, Judy. *Feminism Confronts Technology*. University Park: Pennsylvania State University Press, 1991.

Wajcman, Judy. *TechnoFeminism*. Cambridge, UK: Polity Press, 2004.

Williams, Raymond. *Marxism and Literature*. Oxford: Oxford University Press, 1977.

Williams, Raymond. *Television: Technology and Cultural Form*. Edited by Ederyn Williams. London: Routledge, 2003.

Winner, Langdon. "Upon Opening the Black Box and Finding It Empty: Social Constructivism and the Philosophy of Technology." *Science Technology and Human Values* 18, no. 3 (1993). https://www.jstor.org/stable/689726.

Witkowski, Emma. "Cooperative Play." In *Debugging Game History: A Critical Lexicon*, edited by Henry Lowood and Raiford Guins, 89–95. Cambridge, MA: MIT Press, 2016.

Yasumoto-Nicolson, Ken. "Gaming in Japan." *What Japan Thinks*. May 24, 2006. http://whatjapanthinks.com/2006/05/24/gaming-in-japan.

Yoshino, Akira. "Development of the Lithium-Ion Battery and Recent Technological Trends." In *Lithium Ion Batteries: Advances and Applications*, edited by Gianfranco Pistoia, 1–20. Amsterdam: Elsevier, 2014.

Zielinski, Siegfried. *Deep Time of the Media: Toward an Archaeology of Hearing and Seeing by Technical Means*. Translated by Gloria Custance. Cambridge, MA: MIT Press, 2006.

Patents

Kawase, Tomohiro. "Game Emulator Program." US Patent No. 7,025,677. Filed January 3, 2003; issued April 11, 2006.

Link, Patrick J. "Hand-Held Video Game Platform Emulation." US Patent No. 8,795,090 B2. Filed April 4, 2013; issued August 5, 2014.

Okada, Satoru. "System for Preventing the Use of an Unauthorized External Memory." US Patent 5,134,391. Filed January 8, 1990; issued July 28, 1992.

Okada, Satoru et al. "Gaming Machine That Is Useable with Different Game Cartridge Types." US Patent 6,810,463 B2. Filed May 23, 2001; issued October 26, 2004.

Okada, Satoru et al. "Memory for Video Game System and Emulator Using the Memory." US Patent 7,445,551 B1. Filed November 28, 2000; issued November 4, 2008.

Rhode, Mitchell M. "Portable Modular Diagnostic Medical Device." US Patent 5,876,351. Filed April 10, 1997; issued March 2, 1999.

Takata, Hidekazu, and Yuji Tanaka. "Security System Method and Apparatus for Preventing Application Program Unauthorized Use." US Patent 7,089,427 B1. Filed November 28, 2000; issued August 8, 2006.

Legal Documents

17 U.S.C. § 109. "Limitations on Exclusive Rights: Effect of Transfer of Particular Copy or Phonorecord."

17 U.S.C. § 117. "Limitations on Exclusive Rights: Computer Programs."

Federal Court of Canada. *Nintendo of America Inc. v. King.* 2017 FC 246. 2017.

United States Court of Appeals. *Atari Games Corporation and Tengen Inc. v. Nintendo of America Inc.* 897 F.2d 1572. 1990.

United States Court of Appeals. *Sega Enterprises Ltd. v. Accolade, Inc.* 997 F.2d 1510. 1992.

United States Court of Appeals. *Sony Computer Entertainment v. Connectix Corporation.* 203 F.3d 596. 2000.

United States District Court for the District of Arizona. *Nintendo of America Inc. v. Jacob Mathias, Mathias Designs, and Cristian Mathias.* 2:2018cv02282. 2018.

Index

Technological determinism, 25
Television
  display technology, 19, 86, 99–101
  and domestic space, 95, 98, 128
Tetris, 35
3D games
  development techniques for, 16–17,
    46–47
  graphics simulation, 46, 182–183
  hardware technology for, 46, 72–73,
    232n23
  shift to, 15–16
3DS, 83–85, 127, 153
3DS Ambassador Program, 83–85, 153
Three-pillar strategy, 75, 77
Tile-based graphics, 49–50
Trade-in program, 220
TradeMark Security System (TMSS),
  55
Translation hacking, 196–197, 198
Triton Labs. *See* Afterburner
Twitch Plays Pokémon, 170

User
  as cultural producer, 29, 145, 146
    (*see also* Homebrew; ROM hacking;
    Translation hacking)
  experience, 19, 94–95, 98, 101–102,
    107, 120, 121, 158, 195, 209, 216
  feedback, 69, 71–72
  idealized vs. actual, 21, 28, 94
  identity, 3, 20, 23, 181, 207 (*see also*
    "Who Are You?" campaign)
  interventions, 5, 70–71, 164, 169–170,
    176–177, 212 (*see also* Modding)
  vs. modder, 202

Vertical flicker scaling, 163
Videogame crash, 54
Videogames
  and embodiment, 28, 76–77, 91–92,
    94–96, 102–103, 111–112, 125,
    164–166
  and gender, 21–22
  generational metaphor, 85–86
  history of, 85–86, 118
Virtual Boy, 72–73, 221

Virtual Console, 144, 153–154, 155,
  156–157, 171, 240n36
Visual Boy Advance GX, 164

WarioWare: Twisted!, 107–113, 164
Wear on handhelds, 93–94
"Who Are You?" campaign, 3, 20–24,
  103, 134, 227n33
Wii
  console, 94, 164
  MotionPlus, 14, 109
  Remote (Wiimote), 102, 164–165
Wii Shop Channel, 144, 157
Wii U, 153, 218
  asymmetric design, 4, 64
  Virtual Console, 153–154
Williams, Raymond, 6, 120
Wireless adapter. *See* Game Boy
  Advance Wireless Adapter

Yamauchi, Hiroshi, 66, 74–75
Yokoi, Gunpei, 9–11, 14–15, 32–33,
  112–113, 118
Yume Kōjō, 57–59

Zielinski, Siegfried, 26, 177, 212
Zombie media, 7, 212
Z-targeting, 16–17